The United Nations Decade for Human Rights Education and the Inclusion of National Minorities

The United Nations Decade for Human Rights Education and the Inclusion of National Minorities

Claudia Mahler
Anja Mihr
Reetta Toivanen
(eds.)

PETER LANG
Frankfurt am Main · Berlin · Bern · Bruxelles · New York · Oxford · Wien

Bibliographic Information published by the Deutsche Nationalbibliothek
The Deutsche Nationalbibliothek lists this publication in the Deutsche Nationalbibliografie; detailed bibliographic data is available in the internet at <http://www.d-nb.de>.

ISBN 978-3-631-56807-1

www.peterlang.de

Table of Content

III Teaching Human Rights in Different Political and Cultural Contexts

IV Minorities and Human Rights Education

Introduction

Raising human rights awareness, disseminating the idea of human rights and human rights education has been on the United Nations (UN) agenda since it was founded in 1945. The adoption of the Universal Declaration of Human Rights in 1948 can be seen as a starting point for the establishment of human rights law and human rights education. However, for a long time teaching human rights was not a primary field of activity in the UN. In 1994, the United Nations General Assembly adopted a Decade for Human Rights Education (HRE) (1995-2004). With this resolution UN member states not only assured the adoption of the relevant human rights documents, but also to start educating their populations about the rights which every human being has simply through their humanity. Also in Europe, especially under the auspices of the Council of Europe with its (now) 47 member states, new institutional and legal frameworks have increasingly been designed and mobilised both at the international and national levels to foster human rights teaching.

This book intends to give an insight into the analysis of human rights education efforts, programmes, school curricula development and country cases during the period of the UN Decade from 1994-2004. It is based on the research project "Teaching Human Rights in Europe," kindly funded by the *VolkswagenStiftung* in Germany from 2003-2007. The research project was interdisciplinary and conducted by three senior researchers in the field of human rights: Claudia Mahler, a jurist at the Centre for Human Rights at Potsdam University, Anja Mihr, a political scientist at the University of Magdeburg and later Humboldt University in Berlin who now works at the European Inter-University Centre for Human Rights and Democratisation in Venice, and Reetta Toivanen, a social-anthropologist at Humboldt University who now is senior researcher at the Centre of Excellence in Global Governance Research at the University of Helsinki.

Beyond the general approach of analysing what human rights education programmes mean in theory and in practice, the majority of the articles in this book focus on human rights education on and with national minorities. Mapping out the societal situation of minorities gives important information on the state of play with human rights and human rights education in general. For the editors it was therefore especially interesting to focus on the consequences of human rights education on the life of the vulnerable - members of ethnic and national minorities. The contributions in this book are based on the concluding symposium of the research project held in October 2006 at Humboldt University in Berlin, Germany. During the symposium the contents and results of the research project were discussed with other scholars and interested audience. This book is, however, not a collection of presentations but papers written after the symposium reflecting on the discussion in Berlin. The authors of this volume are colleagues who have supported the research project "Teaching Human Rights in Europe" in substantial ways.

The first chapter on human rights in the area of globalisation includes contributions by the representative of the United Nations Office of the High-Commissioner for Human Rights in Geneva, Elena Ippoliti. She summarizes the UN Decade for Human Rights Education and its basic outcomes from the UN perspective and introduces the successive UN World Programme for Human Rights Education which started in 2005. In the second chapter, the editors of this compilation, Claudia Mahler, Anja Mihr and Reetta Toivanen elucidate on the results of their European research on the UN Decade and national minorities. They conclude that the UN Decade and education for national minorities were only as effective as the UN member states allowed it to be; without the commitment of the governments and civil society actors no changes could have been accomplished. Paul Martin analyses the new challenges of human rights research in the academic field. He asks for more engagement of scholars with an interest in human rights to analyse and evaluate human rights developments globally in order to investigate better the impact and the shortcomings of the human rights movements over the past few decades.

The second part of the book is committed to human rights education versus education for democratic citizenship and seeks to show the major and important differences between human rights and political education. Its contributors share their strong analysis and give a number of examples from the field of human rights education in central Asia, USA, Armenia, Spain and elsewhere. Audrey Osler describes the different standards in this educational field and shows that both educational fields ought to go hand in hand in order to have most impact. Carolyn Kissane focuses on some case studies in central Asian countries and addresses the role human rights education can play there in increasing opportunities to influence and change societies. Sia Spiliopoulou Åkermark differentiates between the intentions of many educators and teachers in the field of human rights have and the actual outcome when the idea of teaching human rights turns into practice. Her argument similar to that of Osler, is that human rights education and citizenship education have to go hand in hand in order to achieve the best results. In her contribution Anja Mihr gives examples from Armenia and Spain and deals with the question of how human rights education can be easily misinterpreted by governments to use it for political education. She warns that the combination of both civic education and human rights education can lead to a confusing idea of what human rights are about among educators in this field.

The third part of the book tackles human rights education in different political and cultural contexts. Sulev Valdmaa illustrates how civic education has contributed to changes in the educational system in Estonia and analyses the local reactions to the international 'democratization' pressure. Similarly, Theresa Khorozyan shows in her contribution using the example of Armenia that undertaking school book reforms does not automatically lead to major changes in the political culture. Both are pleading for better teacher training and substantive changes in the curricula in order to change the behaviour of people regarding human rights. Reetta Toivanen tackles the question of sustainability of human rights and minority education. She analyses different efforts undertaken particularly in Germany and Estonia, to implement human rights values into the educational sectors and pays attention to the factors which hinder the sustainability of human rights education.

The last part of the book deals explicitly with minority issues which was one of the main focus areas of the research project of the editors. Theodore S. Orlin demonstrates some of the difficulties in defining minority rights – and their implementation. He shows how the definitional uncertainty is used as the explanation for the shortcomings in minority education programmes. Jana Luptakova and Inken Stern illustrate these problems with the case study on education programmes for Roma in Slovakia. They describe the achievements and future challenges for Roma in Slovakia and elsewhere. Claudia Mahler addresses the question whether human rights education is an adequate means for supporting minorities. She illustrates her conclusion with examples from the country case studies. She concludes that it can be a very fruitful tool to empower minorities if the relevant institutions coordinate their efforts and resources.

Without the wonderful help, support and advice of so many colleagues and of our student assistants and interns during the research period, the project would have achieve only part of the results we have now in our hands. We would like to give our gratitude to all who supported us in our efforts to conduct the fascinating but laborious interdisciplinary team project. We would like to thank by name Eckart Klein, Karl-Peter Fritzsche, Wolfgang Kaschuba, Norman Weiß, Inken Stern, Rebecca Siegert, Anna Boucher, Claudia Lohrenscheit, Jördis Winkler, Anna Galova, Jennifer Reynolds, Heli Mäkipää, Sophie Seyfert, Carolin Philipp, Eddie Bruce, Anna Poghosyan, Anna Osepyan, Artur Mkrityan, Tigran Zargayan , Antonio Frutos , Elena Voussou, Jesus Casquete, Esteban Beltran, Simone Holzwart, Jan-Friedrich Klein, Daniela Manke, Maria Vogel, Lynda Anyango Mbingham, Fiona Wright, Antonis Pitsios, Kaido Soom, Külli Hansson, Stefan Ehricke, Marcus Beiner and Michael McIntosh. Many more colleagues contributed to our work in the countries of research we would all like to thank and express our deepest appreciation. The greatest gratitude goes to our families who supported us; even during the long absences from home on field trips far away or just nearby in our offices.

The editors in February 2008

Claudia Mahler, Potsdam/Berlin, Germany
Anja Mihr, Venice, Italy
Reetta Toivanen, Helsinki, Finland

I Human Rights and the Challenge of Globalisation

Human Rights Education: Global Initiatives at the United Nations

Elena Ippoliti

Introduction

Over the past few decades, the international community has increasingly expressed consensus on the fundamental contribution of human rights education to the realization of human rights. Human rights education provisions have been included in United Nations documents, and specific initiatives have been adopted at the United Nations to encourage the elaboration and implementation of national human rights education programmes, including the United Nations Decade for Human Rights Education (1995-2004) and the World Programme for Human Rights Education (2005-ongoing). This article provides some information concerning the above-mentioned processes and highlights concrete opportunities for related action by academic institutions in cooperation with the United Nations, particularly the Office of the United Nations High Commissioner for Human Rights (OHCHR).

Human Rights Education: A Programmatic Priority at the United Nations

The creation of the United Nations Organisation, in 1945, provided a forum for its Member States to develop and adopt international documents related to human rights. They contain internationally agreed human rights standards placing an obligation on states to act in accordance with those standards or prohibiting states from engaging in human rights violations. In most of those documents, states have also committed, through specific provisions, to engage in human rights education, training and public information activities as a means of contributing to the respect of human rights. Those documents include, among many others[1]:

- Universal Declaration of Human Rights, 1948 (article 26)
- International Convention on the Elimination of All Forms of Racial Discrimination, 1965 (article 7)
- International Covenant on Economic, Social and Cultural Rights, 1966 (article 13)
- Convention on the Elimination of All Forms of Discrimination against Women, 1979 (article 10)
- Convention on the Rights of the Child, 1989 (article 29)

---

[1] For a compilation of human rights education provisions in international and regional documents, see "The Right to Human Rights Education", HR/PUB/DECADE/1999/2, Office of the United Nations High Commissioner for Human Rights 1999.

- Declaration and Programme of Action of the World Conference on Human Rights - Vienna, 1993 (Part I, paragraphs 33-34 and Part II, paragraphs 78-82)
- Declaration and Programme of Action of the World Conference against Racism, Racial Discrimination, Xenophobia and Related Intolerance - Durban, 2001 (Declaration, paragraphs 95-97 and Programme of Action, paragraphs 129-139)
- World Summit Outcome – New York, 2005 (paragraph 131).

In accordance with those instruments and documents, which provide elements for a definition of human rights education as agreed upon by the international community, human rights education can be defined as "education, training and information aiming at building a universal culture of human rights through the sharing of knowledge, imparting of skills and moulding of attitudes directed to:
(a) The strengthening of respect for human rights and fundamental freedoms;
(b) The full development of the human personality and the sense of its dignity;
(c) The promotion of understanding, tolerance, gender equality and friendship among all nations, indigenous peoples and racial, national, ethnic, religious and linguistic groups;
(d) The enabling of all persons to participate effectively in a free and democratic society governed by the rule of law;
(e) The building and maintenance of peace;
(f) The promotion of people-centred sustainable development and social justice."[2]

In order to achieve these goals, human rights education must necessarily encompass various dimensions:

- Knowledge and skills — learning about human rights and mechanisms for their protection, as well as acquiring skills to apply them in daily life;
- Values, attitudes and behaviour — developing values and reinforcing attitudes and behaviour which uphold human rights;
- Action — taking action to defend and promote human rights.

In terms of methodology[3], any educational activity should start from an analysis of the learning needs of the target audience – it would be useless to adopt the same approach (both in terms of content focus and methodologies) with audiences so heterogeneous as schoolchildren, police trainees or development officers. Educational activities should be practical - relating human rights to learners' real-life experience and enabling them to build on human rights principles found in their own cultural context. Through such activities, learners are empowered to identify and address their human rights needs and to seek solutions consistent with human rights standards. Human rights education should make use of interactive pedagogical techniques, in order to secure the active involvement of the audience; such techniques would include for instance working groups, brainstorming, role plays, panel discussions, field trips and so on. In order to maximize resources and impact, it is also important that human rights

---

[2] See UN Doc. A/59/525/Rev.1, "Plan of Action for the first phase (2005-2007) of the World Programme for Human Rights Education", paragraph 3.

[3] On human rights education and training methodology see "Human Rights Training", HR/P/PT/6, Office of the United Nations High Commissioner for Human Rights 2000.

education focuses on sustainable and strategic courses of action, such as the training of trainers and the inclusion of human rights in educational curricula and policies.

United Nations Initiatives to Encourage Human Rights Education at the National Level

United Nations Member States have adopted specific international frameworks for national action in the area of human rights education, such as the United Nations Decade for Human Rights Education (1995-2004) and the World Programme for Human Rights education (2005-ongoing).

In encouraging the proclamation of a the UN Decade for Human Rights Education, all Member States gathered at the 1993 Vienna World Conference on Human Rights considered "human rights education, training and public information essential for the promotion and achievement of stable and harmonious relations among communities and for fostering mutual understanding, tolerance and peace" (Vienna Declaration and Programme of Action, Part II.D, paragraph 78). Accordingly, in December 1994 the United Nations General Assembly proclaimed 1995-2004 the United Nations Decade for Human Rights Education, upon the initiative of the Costa Rican government. The Decade aimed at encouraging the elaboration and implementation of comprehensive, effective and sustainable national plans for human rights education, as well as the strengthening of partnerships at all levels.

Periodic evaluations[4] of progress have highlighted both achievements and challenges with regard to activities undertaken within the Decade. On the positive side, the Decade has "put human rights education on the agenda", helped to increase awareness of the need for human rights education and provided a framework for international cooperation in this area. At the beginning of the Decade, human rights education had a low profile on the national and international agendas; at its end, national, regional and international human rights education networks were in place, the issue was regularly addressed by United Nations organs as a strategic priority and cooperation in this area had increased at all levels. The Decade facilitated the human rights education work of those already engaged in relevant activities and encouraged others to develop them. In some countries, it provided a platform for dialogue and cooperation among governments, national human rights institutions and NGOs.[5]

In the case of the Philippines, for instance, action has been prompted by national authorities at the highest level through the adoption of related legislation and even a Presidential Decree, proclaiming 1998-2007 the Philippine Decade for Human Rights Education. A coalition of concerned actors, led by the National Human Rights Commission, has developed a National Plan for Human Rights Education including

[4] See, for instance, the report on the mid-term global evaluation of the progress made towards the achievement of the objectives of the Decade, 2000 (UN Doc. A/55/360), and the report on achievements and shortcomings of the Decade and on future United Nations initiatives in this area, 2004 (UN Doc. E/CN.4/2004/93).

[5] Specific examples of activities undertaken within the Decade are available through OHCHR's website (www.ohchr.org) under "Human rights by issues" → "Human rights education and training" → "Decade for Human Rights Education".

objectives, target audiences (organised and unorganised elements of society), strategies (trainers' training, organisation of networks, integration of human rights in all educational curricula, utilization of village-level officials to reach out to the community level, promotional campaigns including artistic and cultural activities, development of monitoring and evaluation systems) and programmes, including the creation of a human rights training, documentation and research centre (the Human Rights Academy). In the implementation of the Plan, the Commission entered into a number of formal agreements with other national partners for human rights education to define in detail specific areas of responsibility. Those partners included Amnesty International/Philippine Section, the Department of Interior and Local Government, the Liga NG MGA Barangay (an organisation of village chiefs), the Department of Justice, the Department of National Defence, the Department of Education, Culture and Sports, and the Commission on Higher Education.

The World Programme for Human Rights Education (2005-ongoing)

As the Decade was approaching its end, the United Nations Commission on Human Rights requested the OHCHR to develop and submit a study[6] on the follow-up to the Decade, in cooperation with all relevant actors. The input received by the Office, through consultations with member states, intergovernmental and non-governmental organisations, highlighted the importance of continuing a global framework for human rights education in order to – *inter alia* - provide a sense of common collective vision, goals and action and an opportunity to increase partnership at all levels, as well as to provide support for programmes created during the Decade, an incentive to continue them and to start new ones building on those experiences. Proposals focused around the proclamation of a second decade, to be properly structured also through the organisation of regular periodic events to create momentum and continuity, with a plan of action formulated in realistic terms and an indication of at least minimum action for each country.

In the following months, the Costa Rican government led related negotiations which prompted, on 10 December 2004, the proclamation by the UN General Assembly of a new World Programme for Human Rights Education (2005-ongoing). Instead of a limited timeframe like a second decade, the consensus of the international community gathered around the concept of an open-ended Programme structured around an ongoing series of phases, the first one covering the period 2005-2009[7] and focusing on the primary and secondary school systems.

Developed by a broad group of education and human rights practitioners from all continents, the Plan of Action[8] for the first phase, adopted by the United Nations

[6] The study has been published as UN Doc. E/CN.4/2003/101.

[7] At the proclamation of the World Programme (General Assembly resolution 59/113 A), the first phase was to cover three years, i.e. 2005-2007. Subsequently, by resolution A/HRC/RES/6/24, the United Nations Human Rights Council extended the first phase to the end of 2009 "in order to allow all relevant actors to accomplish the implementation of the Plan of Action" (paragraph 3).

[8] The Plan of Action is contained in UN Doc. A/59/525/Rev.1. It was adopted by the United Nations General Assembly in July 2005 by resolution 59/113 B.

General Assembly in July 2005, proposed a concrete strategy and practical ideas for implementing human rights education nationally. It builds on worldwide research and experience, and identifies good practices with regard to five key interdependent components necessary for the successful integration of human rights education in the school system:

1. *Educational policies.* Understood as statements of commitment on the part of a Government, educational policies should explicitly promote a rights-based approach to education and infuse human rights throughout the education system. Policies should be developed in a participatory manner in cooperation with all stakeholders and fulfill a country's international treaty obligations to provide and promote quality education.

Good practices in this area may include reviewing and revising educational laws, adopting specific legislation, ensuring coherence in related plans of action, reviewing and revising curricula and developing a comprehensive training policy for educational personnel.

2. *Policy implementation.* A policies implementation strategy would include measures such as the allocation of adequate resources and the setting-up of coordination mechanisms that ensures coherence, monitoring and accountability.

Good practices in this area may include providing adequate human and financial resources, setting up coordination mechanisms developing a concrete implementation strategy (see below, Stages 1-4), conducting research on impact and establishing resource centres.

3. *The learning environment.* Human rights education can only take place in an environment where human rights are practiced and lived in the daily life of the whole school community. A rights-based environment respects and promotes the human rights of all school actors and is characterized by mutual understanding, respect and responsibility.

Good practices in this area may include adopting explicit and shared rules such as charters of school actors' rights and responsibilities, adopting non-discrimination policies protecting all school actors, recognizing and valuing positive contributions, providing opportunities for students' self-expression and participation in decision making and ensuring interaction between the school and the community.

4. *Teaching and learning processes and tools.* Introducing or improving human rights education requires using an approach to teaching and learning that reflects human rights values. For example, curriculum content and objectives should be rights-based, methodologies should be democratic and participatory and all materials and textbooks should be consistent with human rights values.

Good practices in this area may include reviewing and revising curricula, at all levels, reviewing and revising textbooks at all levels, using and developing complementary materials, adopting learner-centred and empowering teaching methods, developing support projects (networking/exchanges, information technologies, resource centres) and developing assessment and evaluation tools.

5. *Education and professional development of school personnel.* For the school to serve as a model of human rights learning and practice, all teachers and staff need to be able to both transmit and model human rights values. As rights-holders them-

selves, school personnel need to work and learn in a context of respect for their dignity and rights.
Good practices in this area may include addressing, in educational programmes for school personnel, not only human rights content but also teaching methodologies, social skills and leadership styles, using learner-centred training methodologies, tailoring to contextual need and target group, using and developing appropriate training resources and supporting networking. According to the adopted Plan of Action, each country should establish realistic goals and means for action in accordance with national context, priorities and capacity. The Plan of Action proposes four stages for the national process of planning, implementation and evaluation of human rights education in the school system (i.e., the "national implementation strategy").
Stage 1: Analyse the current situation of human rights education in the school system.
This first stage calls for a national study on human rights education in the school system. With wide dissemination and discussion, this report can serve as a basis for developing a national implementation strategy for human rights education at "Stage 2".
Stage 2: Set priorities and develop a national implementation strategy.
The strategy developed at this stage addresses the five above-mentioned key components and focuses on issues that can have a sustainable impact. It sets realistic objectives and priorities and anticipates at least some implementation during 2005-2007.
Stage 3: Implement and monitor activities.
At this stage, the national implementation strategy is widely disseminated and put into practice. Its progress is monitored using fixed milestones. Outcomes will vary according to national priorities, but might include legislation, new or revised learning materials and methodologies, training courses or non-discriminatory policies protecting all members of the school community.
Stage 4: Evaluate.
Using evaluation as a means of both accountability and learning for the future, this stage calls for an assessment of what the implementation strategy has accomplished. It results in a report on the national implementation strategy for human rights education in schools, with recommendations for future action based on lessons learned.

As ministries of education (or equivalent institutions) have the main responsibility for primary and secondary education, the implementation strategy proposed in the Plan of Action addresses their functions, such as educational policy development, programme planning, research, teacher training, development and dissemination of materials. However, others need to be involved in the implementation of the Plan of Action, including teacher training institutions, teachers' associations, national human rights institutions, nongovernmental organisations, parents' and students' associations, and so on. The Plan of Action also highlights additional stakeholders which should be involved to ensure effective implementation.[9]

[9] More and updated information on the World Programme is available through OHCHR's website (www.ohchr.org) under "Human rights by issues" → "Human rights education and training" → "World Programme for Human Rights Education".

The Contribution of Academic Institutions

The UN World Programme provides several opportunities for action by academic institutions. For instance, in the framework of the Programme's first phase, those institutions could consider, in cooperation with education authorities, carrying out a national study on the situation of human rights education in the school system mentioned above under "Stage 1"; in some countries, ministries of education have specifically requested university faculties to undertake this activity, given the research capacities available in these institutions. In addition, in order to further the World Programme's objectives, universities could also establish and/or develop a human rights resource and training centre as well human rights education programmes for students and professors; the focus within the first phase of the World Programme could be on including human rights in the curricula of education faculties, which in many countries are responsible for the pre-service training of teachers. Academic institutions may also conduct research on important issues which require dedicated time, such as documentation of good practices and evaluation of the impact of human rights education activities on the realization of human rights in the schools and in the community.

Academic institutions have a role to play in drawing the attention of relevant authorities and civil society to international initiatives such as the World Programme, and cooperating with them in the elaboration, implementation and evaluation of effective human rights education strategies and activities. To support this work, OHCHR has developed various programmes and resources which are at the disposal of all interested actors and would also benefit from their involvement[10]. They include, for instance:

- OHCHR's on-line Database on Human Rights Education and Training on related institutions, programmes and materials (address: http://hre.ohchr.org);
- OHCHR's Resource Collection on Human Rights Education and Training, a thematic and publicly-accessible collection of the OHCHR Library;
- The ACT (Assisting Communities Together) Project, which makes small grants available to national and local non-governmental organizations for the implementation of community-based human rights education and training projects;
- A selected number of human rights training and education materials; and
- Various resources and tools on the Universal Declaration of Human Rights (UDHR).

Conclusion

By launching global initiatives in the area of human rights education, the international community has expressed a consensus that education plays a vital role in fostering

[10] More information on these programmes and resources is available through OHCHR's website (www.ohchr.org) under "Human rights by issues" → "Human rights education and training".

respect, participation, equality and non-discrimination – human rights standards to which all individuals are entitled – in our societies.

It is too early to assess progress made in the context of the first phase of the World Programme. Governments have reported having appointed focal points within their Ministries of Education and some activities are under implementation; an account of these initiatives is regularly updated and made available on OHCHR's website. However, the experience of the previous Decade demonstrates that such United Nations programmes can constitute useful mobilization and advocacy tools for relevant actors – whether they are governmental agencies, non-governmental organisations, professional associations, national human rights institutions, the academic world and so on. The Decade has been a catalyst in eliciting some response from Governments in terms of human rights education programming, and has provided a common platform for cooperation among different actors within and among countries.

Still, it is important to bear in mind that international programmes can only support – and not substitute – a committed, vigorous and concerted national action. In the end, the success of global initiatives, including the World Programme, depends mainly on the willingness of national and local stakeholders to take action and to use them in order to pursue human rights education in their societies.

The UN Decade for Human Rights Education 1995-2004 and its Contribution to the Furtherance of the Rights of National Minorities in Europe

Claudia Mahler/ Anja Mihr/ Reetta Toivanen

Introduction

The aim of this chapter is to discuss the results of the interdisciplinary research assignment which was undertaken from November 2003 to May 2007. The research question focused on which ways human rights education played a role in fostering of minorities' societal and legal status during the United Nations Decade for Human Rights Education from 1995-2004.

The study was conducted by the three authors focusing on six different countries in Europe, including three post-socialist countries. During the project, different research methods were used: comparative legal analysis, applying theories of institution building and conducting interviews. In order to gain a more profound understanding of the different societies, the researchers organised and participated in joint academic and civil society workshops, meetings, and conferences with minority representatives and experts dealing with human rights and human rights education. The methods can, in short, being described as a combination of interdisciplinary and team research technique.[1] The methods, results of the research and the conclusions will be briefly summarized in this article.[2]

Interdisciplinarity as a Method?

The research which forms the basis of this article had an interdisciplinary approach combining methods of international law, political sciences and anthropology. Our assessment was that in uniting the efforts of these disciplines we could contribute in new ways to the understanding of how human rights education influences majority-minority relations in the European context. Our research methods were interdisciplinary to such an extent that everybody in the team had to adopt new research methods:

[1] See for example Apostel, Léo / Berger, Georg. (eds.), Interdisciplinarity: problems of teaching and research in universities; this report is based on the results of a Seminar on Interdisciplinarity in Universities, Nice, 7.-12.9.1970, OECD Publications, Paris: OECD, 1972; Klein, Julie T., Interdisciplinarity, History, Theory & Practice, Detroit,1990.

[2] Three other chapters in this volume will explore some of the common findings of the project in further detail. Anja Mihr examines in her chapter "State and Non-State Actors in Human Rights Education" the political participation and role of different actors in integrating national minorities into the general human rights education schemes during the UN-Decade and Reetta Toivanen looks at in her chapter "International support vs. national adaptation? On the sustainability of human rights education" what sustainability actually means in the area of human rights education and how sustainable human rights education has been during the past decade. Claudia Mahler discusses in her chapter "Is human rights education an accurate means of supporting minority rights?" the ways in which human rights education can be considered as a means to support minority rights.

international lawyers had to learn how to interview political actors and minority representatives, political scientists had to include more legal and cultural dimensions of the political settings to their analysis and anthropologists had to grasp the importance of national constitutions and international treaties as well as the political institutions to their micro level analysis. At the beginning of the research project we produced a "guideline", literally to keep the group focused on the commonly agreed goals of the research. The guideline included the most important questions and topics which had to be addressed during the assignment in order to be able to answer the analytical questions of the project. With the help of this guideline we generated a questionnaire for our first research trips. All researchers focused on the same major questions in the six European countries which were chosen as our target countries: Armenia, Estonia, Finland, Germany, Slovakia and Spain. Fieldtrips were considered as crucial for our research work.[3]

Access to weak minority groups like the Yezidi and Roma/Gitano communities was difficult and we needed strong personal networks in the countries like Slovakia, Armenia, Estonia and Spain to gain access to the Yezidi villages in Armenia or Roma settlements in Slovakia. In 2004, we started with the first round of research trips and before the end of the project we had spent between 4 and 12 weeks in each of the countries. The most important goal for the duration of our first research trips was to identify the key actors in the field of human rights education and to decide which national minorities could and should be studied. In the following years we visited the countries on a regular basis and interviewed target group representatives and activists who were involved in human rights education, either in general or particularly for minorities. The 'snowball effect' worked effectively since at every visit new activists and institutions were mentioned to us. For instance, representatives of non-governmental organisations (NGO) who had worked successfully with state authorities or international foundations also wanted us to interview their colleagues, who were involved in human rights education or were or had been important representatives for minority issues. Since the research was conducted retrospectively on a time period from 1995-2004 it was important to find as many as possible of the "former" and long-term actors who had dealt with human rights education or minority issues. This way we were able to figure out how the networks between NGOs, state institutions and international agencies worked. We also visited schools and observed classes in which human rights were taught. As researchers we interviewed national minority representatives, leaders and young people and asked whether the state programmes to foster their human rights matched with the needs and claims of the minorities.

What we saw and heard during our field trips, often declared to be "off the record", were important for our analysis. The needs and problems of many of these groups would not have become evident if we had only analysed the reports and statements produced by the different interest groups. The vast amount of official documents, programmes and textbooks produced in these six countries during the UN Decade was impressive, and our assessment was that they could only be interpreted with the background of personal experience and visits in the field. The fieldtrips re-

[3] In countries like Armenia and Slovakia where we do not speak the local language we had interpreters who also understood our research questions in order to be able to translate adequately.

vealed many problem areas faced by members of minorities which could not be communicated to the NGOs or representatives of governments. For example, we could observe that the contacts between human rights NGOs and minority groups were in most cases, almost or entirely non-existent. This observation raised a new set of questions about the problems faced by national minorities in Europe.

To analyse the collected materials and observations we have used international regime analysis[4], theories of institution building[5], comparative legal methods[6], comparative social analysis and ethnological fieldwork with qualitative interviews and participant observation.[7] The methodological approaches are not discussed here in depth or portrayed in detail due to the fact that we combined the different approaches in new ways and that the composition of the methodological combinations was subjected to modification during the course of our work.[8] The selection of the methods was constantly critiqued and debated within the project team, and often only certain aspects of a given method remained, serving as a viable compromise on which all members of our research team could agree upon.

The International Objectives for Human Rights Education in Europe

The United Nations' Decade for Human Rights Education which began in 1995 and lasted until the end of 2004 served as the time frame for our analysis. This Decade had been welcomed not only by all UN member states, but also by all the six countries on which we focused our study.

Prior to the UN Decade for Human Rights Education, there had been several meetings at the UN level to discuss how the knowledge and awareness of the Univer-

---

4 Krasner, Stephen (ed.), International Regimes, Ithaca, London, 1995, p. 1-22; Schmidt, Rainer: Die politische Theorie der Rationalisierung Max Weber, in: Brodocz, André/ Schaal, Gary S. (eds.): Politische Theorien der Gegenwart I, Opladen 2001, p. 372-398.

5 Dahl, Robert A., Who Governs? Democracy and Power in an American City, New Haven, 1961; Bachrach, Peter / Baratz Morton S.: Power and Poverty. Theory and Practice, NewYork, 1970; Lukes, Steven, Power. A Radical View, London, 1974; Kraus, Peter A.,: Nationalismus und Demokratie. Politik im spanischen Staat der Autonomen Gemeinschaften, Wiesbaden, 1996.

6 Donnelly, Jack, Universal Human Rights in Theory and Practice, Ithaca, 2003, p. 127-134, Tomuschat, Christian, Human Rights: Between idealism and realism, Oxford, 2003; Zweigert, Konrad / Kötz, Hein, Indroduction to comparative law, 3rd ed., Oxford,1996; Hailbronner, Kay, Ziel und Methoden völkerrechtlich relevanter Rechtsvergleich', ZaöRV 36, 1976, p. 190-226; Bernhardt, Rudolf, Eigenheiten und Ziele der Rechtsvergleichung im öffentlichen Recht, ZaöRV 24, 1964, p. 431-452; Kropholler, Jan, Comparative Law, Functions and Method', EPIL 10, 1987, p. 52-58; Markesinis, Basil, Rechtsvergleichung in Theorie und Praxis: ein Beitrag zur rechtswissenschaftlichen Methodenlehre, München, 2004; Baer, Susanne, Verfassungsvergleichung und reflexive Methode: Interkulturelle und intersubjektive Kompetenz, ZaöRV 64 , 2004, p. 735-758.

7 Erickson, Kenneth Cleland / Stull, Donald, Doing Team Ethnography – Warnings and Advice, Qualitative Research Methods, 42, Thousand Oaks et a, Sage, 1998; Kaschuba, Wolfgang, Einführung in die Europäische Ethnologie, München, 1999.

8 See Mahler, Claudia / Mihr, Anja / Toivanen, Reetta, Teaching Human Rights in Europe and its Future Role for Minority Movements, in: Brosig, Malte (ed.), Human Rights in Europe – A Fragmented Regime, Frankfurt a.M, , 2006, p. 169-183.

sal Declaration on Human Rights could be fostered. In these meetings, the dominant view was that strengthening the protection of human rights implied more than just teaching and learning human rights. In 1998, fifty years after the Universal Declaration for Human Rights the fact remained that human rights violations occurred on a daily basis all over the world.[9] Different studies showed that human rights knowledge was scarce even in well-established democratic states.[10] The UN World Plan of Action on Education for Human Rights and Democracy which had been adopted by the International Congress on Education for Human Rights and Democracy convened by the United Nations Educational, Scientific and Cultural Organisation (UNESCO) in Montreal in 1993[11] stressed that education for human rights and democracy is itself a human right and a prerequisite for the realization of human rights, democracy and social justice.

In 1993, the participants of the UN Vienna World Conference on Human Rights agreed that people should be further empowered to defend their own and others' human rights.[12] Special attention was accordingly to be paid to persons belonging to minorities. The Vienna Declaration says very clearly:

"Considering the importance of the promotion and protection of the rights of persons belonging to minorities and the contribution of such promotion and protection to the political and social stability of the States in which such persons live. The World Conference on Human Rights reaffirms the obligation of States to ensure that persons belonging to minorities may exercise fully and effectively all human rights and fundamental freedoms without any discrimination and in full equality before the law in accordance with the Declaration on the Rights of Persons Belonging to National or Ethnic, Religious and Linguistic Minorities. The persons belonging to minorities have the right to enjoy their own culture, to profess and practise their own religion and to use their own language in private and in public, freely and without interference or any form of discrimination".[13]

Additionally, in 1993 the UN Commission on Human Rights linked human rights education very closely with enhancing democratic developments in member states.[14]

Nils Rosemann writes that the "knowledge of fundamental rights and mechanisms for their protection will permit the strengthening and consolidation of democrat-

---

[9] Lohrenscheit, Claudia, Dialogue and Dignity-Linking Human Rights Education with Paulo Freire´s "Education for Liberation", in Journal of Social Science Education (1-2006) http://jsse.org/2006-1/lohrenscheit_freire.htm visited July 2007.

[10] See for example for Germany: Sommer, Gert / Stellmacher, Jost / Brähler, Elmar, Menschenrechte in Deutschland: Wissen, Einstellungen und Handlungsbereitschaft', in: Frech, Siegried / Haspel, Michael (eds.), Menschenrechte, Schwalbach/Ts, 2005, p. 211-230.

[11] World Plan of Action on Education for Human Rights and Democracy, adopted by the International Congress on Education for Human Rights and Democracy convened by the United Nations Educational, Scientific and Cultural Organization (UNESCO) in Montreal, 8-11 March 1993, UN-Doc. UNESCO: SHS-93/CONF.402/4 (http://www.unesco.org/webworld/peace_library/UNESCO/HRIGHTS/342-353.HTM, visited in March 2007).

[12] UN Document: Vienna Declaration and Plan of Action, A/CONF.157/23, 12 July 1993 (http://www.unhchr.ch/huridocda/huridoca.nsf/(Symbol)/A.CONF.157.23.En (last visited 29 June, 2007).

[13] Ibid. para 19.

[14] UN Document: Commission on Human Rights resolution 1993/56 of 9 March 1993; UN Document: UN Resolution adopted by the General Assembly A/RES/48/127 20 December 1993.

ic process" leveled the way for a UN Decade for Human Rights Education.[15] Following the suggestion of the UN World Conference in 1993, the UN General Assembly in resolution 49/184[16] of 23rd December 1994, proclaimed the 10-year period beginning on 1st January 1995 as the UN Decade for Human Rights Education. Simultaneously, the UN General Assembly welcomed the Plan of Action for the Decade enclosed in the report of the UN Secretary-General.[17] The idea behind this was that the UN, together with other organisations such as UNESCO would be able to rationalize, coordinate and enhance efforts for human rights education. In 1993 the General Assembly had created the position of the United Nations High Commissioner for Human Rights with the purpose of strengthening the coordination between different UN activities in the field of human rights and also in the field of promotion and education on human rights.[18]

One of the aims of the United Nations Decade was "to translate human rights norms into domestic day-to-day reality".[19] The Plan of Action of the UN Decade for Human Rights Education aimed to bring the objectives of the Decade to as wide an audience as possible through both formal and non-formal education and to encourage the building of a permanent capacity for human rights education.[20] It was stressed that the human rights education activities should give special attention to vulnerable groups such as women, children, minorities, indigenous peoples as well as to those persons who are in the position to carry out human rights education such as teachers, police and governmental officials.[21]

During the UN Decade the UN Office of the High Commissioner for Human Rights (OHCHR) expected the member states, other international organisations such as the Council of Europe (CoE), the Organisation for Security and Cooperation (OSCE) and NGOs to support projects and programs to promote in an adequate way the human rights of minorities and national minorities in particular.[22]

---

15 Rosemann, Nils, Human Rights Education – Towards the End of the UN Decade, Nordic Journal of Human Rights, Vol. 21, No. 4, 2003, p. 461-469 (http://www.hrea.org/erc/Library/rosemann03.pdf, visited in March 2007).

UN Resolution adopted by the General Assembly A/RES/49/184 6 March 1995 (http://www.unhchr.ch/huridocda/huridoca.nsf (A.RES.49.184.En?OpenDocument, visited in March 2007).

17 UN Document: Plan of Action of the Decade for Human Rights Education, Appendix to the UN-Doc. A/51/506/Add.1, 12. December 1996 (http://www.ohchr.org/english/issues/education/training/decade.htm, visited in March 2007).

18 UN Document: General Assembly Resolution High Commissioner for the promotion and protection of all human rights 48/141, 20 December, 1993, http://www.un.org/documents/ga/res/48/a48r141.htm, last visited 11 June, 2007.

19 Pace, John The Significance of the UN Decade for Human Rights Education: Its Background and Future (http://www.hurights.or.jp/asia-pacific/no_02/05significance.htm, 6.12.2005).

20 Op. cit. fn. 17.

21 Ibid. para. 23f.

22 Robinson, Mary, 'Foreword', The United Nations Decade for Human Rights Education 1995-2004, Lessons for Life, Geneva:,United Nations Publication, 1998, HR/PUB/DECADE/1998/1.

National Minorities: Weak and Strong

As the focus of our research was on Europe, it was necessary that we also analysed the regional European human rights system. The Council of Europe is considered to be the most effective regional system of human rights protection and we had a look at its role in promoting human rights education on and for minorities. The European Convention on Human Rights (1953) does not address the problems of minorities in a separate clause. It only includes a non-discrimination clause in conjunction with the article 14.[23] The State parties to the convention have until today not been able to agree on a special protocol on minority rights even though there have been several high ranking proposals in this direction.[24] Instead of an additional protocol on the rights of minorities, the Council of Europe adopted the Charter on Regional and Minority Languages in 1992[25] and the Framework Convention on National Minorities in 1995.[26] Even though both documents lack a decisive definition of what is meant by a national minority, it is generally agreed that a national minority must have settled at least around four generations in the territory in which it resides and distinguish themselves through cultural, historical, and linguistic differences from the majority population. In addition, minority groups must take a non-dominant position in that country.[27]

In our case study, national minorities are such groups as Sorbs and Friesian minorities in Germany, Yezidi in Armenia, Basques in Spain, Hungarians in Slovakia, "old-Russians" in Finland[28] or Setu in Estonia. The Roma and Sinti minorities

---

[23] Convention for the Protection of Human Rights and Fundamental Freedoms (ECHR), as amended by Protocol No. 11, adopted 4 November 1950 by the Council of Europe, entered into force 3 September 1953 (http://conventions.coe.int/Treaty/en/Treaties/Html/005.htm, visited in March 2007). The protocol No. 12 guarantees additional and extended protection of discrimination beyond the current guarantees of article 14. The protocol's purpose is to offer a general prohibition of discrimination in form of an independent, free-standing guarantee (http://conventions.coe.int/treaty/en/Treaties/Html/177.htm, visited in March 2007).

[24] See several proposals for an additional protocol to the ECHR i.e. the Proposal by the Venice Commission for an European Convention for the Protection of Minorities, CDL(1991)007, Austrian proposal for an additional protocol to the ECHR (26.11.1991), Bozen Proposal of the Federal Union of European Nationalities (28.5.1992). For a discussion on these, see Toivanen, Reetta, Minderheitenrechte als Identitätsressource, Hamburg, 2001.

[25] European Charter for Regional or Minority Languages, adopted 5 November 1992 by the Council of Europe, entered into force 1 March 1998 (http://conventions.coe.int/Treaty/en/Treaties/Html/148.htm, visited in March 2007).

[26] Framework Convention for the Protection of National Minorities, adopted 1 February 1995 by the Council of Europe, entered into force 1 February 1998 (http://conventions.coe.int/Treaty/en/Treaties/Html/157.htm , visited in March 2007).

[27] Here: Capotorti, Francesco, Study on the Rights of Persons Belonging to Ethnic, Religious, and Linguistic Minorities ,1979, UN Doc. E/CN.4/Sub.2/384/Rev.1 (Geneva: United Nations, 1991); Klein, Eckart, Die Frage der Minderheitendefinition, in: Mohr, Manfred (ed.): Friedenssichernde Aspekte des Minderheitenschutzes in der Ära des Völkerbundes und der Vereinten Nationen in Europa, Berlin,1996, p. 211-213; Toivanen, Reetta :Paradox der Minderheitenrechte in Europa, SWS-Rundschau 2/ 2005, p. 185-207, at p. 191.

[28] Finland makes an interesting differentiation between Russians who have immigrated to Finland prior the end of Second World War and those who have come since the beginning of the 1990s. The old and new Russians differ in their legal position and the new are not (yet) considered to be a part

who are in most European countries a de facto national minority, can be found in five of our research countries, the exception being Armenia. In Finland, Germany, Slovakia and Spain they have achieved the official status of a national minority. In Estonia, the Roma still have major problems in achieving the recognition of their existence.[29]

National minorities can be found in almost all European states.[30] Their real sizes and their officially recognized numbers differ from country to country.[31] The primary purpose behind recognizing minorities and their protection is that governments should take responsibility in fostering and supporting the cultural and political rights, e.g. the right to use and teach their language and the right to follow their customs and engage in political parties or other civil society groups. This is the idea of official recognition. The UN Fact Sheet stresses:

> *"Special rights are not privileges but they are granted to make it possible for minorities to preserve their identity, characteristics and traditions. Special rights are just as important in achieving equality of treatment as non-discrimination. Only when minorities are able to use their own languages, benefit from services they have themselves organised, as well as take part in the political and economic life of States can they begin to achieve the status which majorities take for granted. Differences in the treatment of such groups, or individuals belonging to them, are justified if it is exercised to promote effective equality and the welfare of the community as a whole. This form of affirmative action may have to be sustained over a prolonged period in order to enable minority groups to benefit from society on an equal footing with the majority."*[32]

In order to have a basis for comparative analysis, we chose six countries with similar legal standards in respect to minority protection. Each one of these countries is a member state of the Council of Europe and has ratified the Framework Convention on National Minorities of 1995 and the Charter for Regional and Minority Languages of 1992. Even though for example, Spain has never defined which groups are recognized under the convention they do not extend the definition to other minorities beyond the Roma/Gitanos population.[33] Although the Basques fall under the international definition of a minority, they claim themselves to be a "nation", a term which is interpreted and used in international documents with a great many variations.

---

of the national minority. See Lepola, Outi / Suurpää, Leena, Vallan syrjässä? Tutkimus etnisten suhteiden neuvottelukunnan toiminnasta (Työministeriö) ,2003.

[29] Toivanen, Reetta, Unwissen, Vorurteile und andere Gewohnheiten – Notizen aus einer Feldforschung mit Roma in Estland, in: Toivanen,Reetta / Knecht, Michi (eds.) Europäische Roma – Roma in Europa, Berliner Blätter Heft 39/2006, p. 143-153.

[30] Weiß, Norman, Sind Minderheitenrechte Menschenrechte?, in: Mahler, Claudia / Weiß, Norman (eds.): Menschenrechtsschutz im Spiegel von Wissenschaft und Praxis, Menschenrechtszentrum der Universität Potsdam, Bd. 20, Berlin, 2004, p. 292-320.

[31] Mahler, Claudia / Toivanen, Reetta, Nationale und ethnische Minderheiten im Prozess der Erweiterung der Europäischen Union, Europa Ethnica 61, No. 1-2, 2004, p. 16-20.

[32] UN Document, OHCHR: Fact Sheet No. 18 (rev. 1) "Minority Rights", Geneva 1998. See also Scheinin, Martin, Minority rights or added protection, in: Bergsmo, Morten (ed.), Human Rights and Criminal Justice for the downtrodden: essays in honour of Asbjørn Eide, Leiden/Boston, 2003, p. 486-504.

[33] Eg. First report submitted by Spain pursuant to Article 25 paragraph 1 of the Framework Convention for the protection of National Minorities, 19 December 2000, ACFC/SR. The whole report deals only with Roma (http://www.coe.int/t/e/human_rights/minorities/2._framework_convention_(monitoring)/2._monitoring_mechanism/3._state_reports_and_unmik_kosovo_report/1._first_cycle/PDF_1st_SR_Spain.pdf, visited September 2007)

However, governmental authorities in Spain emphasise the notion of "historical nations" like the Basques and the Catalans, which according to governmental definitions are not minorities. Neither the Framework Convention nor the UN Declaration on the Rights of Persons Belonging to National or Ethnic, Religious and Linguistic Minorities[34] have been able to establish a common binding international definition as to what is exactly understood under the expression 'national minority'.[35] It shows the differences in terms of definition when and how national minorities are promoted and equally treated. Likewise, this fact of "no-definition" leaves room for national interpretations which may weaken the protection of this vulnerable group.[36]

In order to be able to compare our research results, we chose in each of the six focus countries two or three different minority groups which allowed for a constructive comparison pointing out the often ambivalent relationship of states towards different minorities: one group being socially, economically and/or legally stronger and the other weaker. It is important to understand that the "weaker" or "stronger" status is always a result of historical developments. A group which has a paternal state outside of the state borders such as Hungarians in Slovakia or a group which has been recognized as an equal partner during the nation building phase such as the Swedish speakers in Finland can be considered strong in terms of possibilities to influence their own socio-economic and political living situation. The Roma (in Spain referred to as *Gitanos)* – a label for highly heterogeneous groups of people – can be considered to be a weak minority across Europe.[37] They face similar economic and social problems wherever they live. The high unemployment rates among Roma adults, high numbers of school abstainers among Roma children and poor living and housing conditions in eastern and western Europe are some examples of the social situation of the Roma in Europe.[38] The Roma are underrepresented in most countries in local and/or national parliaments and often over-proportionally rely upon some form of social welfare. Although their social and political situation has slightly improved over the past decade, the major economic problems, poverty and discrimination in the labour market have remained.[39]

---

[34] Declaration on the Rights of Persons Belonging to National or Ethnic, Religious and Linguistic Minorities, adopted by General Assembly resolution 47/135 of 18 December 1992, UN-Doc. A/RES/47/135.

[35] See for further discussion Hofmann, Rainer, 'Der Schutz von Minderheiten in Europa', in: Weidenfeld, Werner (ed.), Europa-Handbuch, Gütersloh, 1999, p. 823-846, p. 824ff.

[36] Ibid.

[37] Friedman, Eben, Minority Rights in Europe: Roms in Slovakia and the Czech Republic, in: Brosig, Malte (ed.), Human rights in Europe: a fragmented regime? (Frankfurt a.M., Wien [u.a.]: Lang, 2006), p. 153-168.

[38] See here also European Commission, Directorate-General for Employment and Social Affairs (ed.), The Situation of Roma in an Enlarged European Union, Fundamental rights and anti-discrimination, Luxembourg, 2005.

[39] Åkerlund, Tuula, The Case of the Roma in Finland, in: Horn, Frank (ed.), Minorities and Their Right of Political Participation, Juridica Lapponica No. 16, Rovaniemi: Lapland's University Press, 1996; International Centre for Migration Policy Development, Migrants, Minorities and Employment: Exclusion, Discrimination and Anti-Discrimination in 15 Member States of the European Union; EUMC Comparative Study, October 2003 (http://eumc.europa.eu/eumc/material/pub/comparativestudy/CS-Employment-en.pdf, visited 12 March 2007).

Strong minority groups like the Sorbs in Germany, Hungarians in Slovakia, Russians in Armenia or Basques in Spain face problems of a different kind: their members may enjoy high education standards, their native language is at least in principle respected and often even taught at state-owned schools, their unemployment rate does not differ from the average and they are in many cases represented in local or state parliaments. These groups face problems of structural discrimination, lack of national recognition and the exclusion of their history and culture in the national history of the state, as can be witnessed for example in school books.[40] Groups like the Basque and Sorbs demand more political independence in their historical territory while Russians in Armenia demand more language autonomy and cultural recognition.[41] Hence, their demands are above the basic needs of those whom we refer to as weak minorities like the Yezidies or Roma/*Gitanos* who face poverty and discrimination on a daily basis.

Human Rights Education in the Rapidly Changing Europe

In the mid 1990s there was growing societal pressure for enhancing human rights awareness worldwide and so the 1994 declaration of the United Nations' Decade for Human Rights Education was welcomed as one factor among many others.[42] The aim was not only to increase worldwide knowledge of human rights but to also change behaviour in order to enhance respect for human rights as a common value. The rapidly growing civil society community and NGOs worldwide particularly in western and Eastern Europe were the key players in fostering human rights. Some have called this phenomenon "cultural globalization" meaning that civil society can also be seen as a result of the globalization of ideas as well as a vehicle in promoting these ideas.[43] The cultural globalization can function as a regulatory movement with the aim of controlling the potential negative side-effects of global political and market changes which may cause further suffering especially of vulnerable groups such as minorities.[44]

---

[40] We wish to thank the competent personnel of the Georg-Eckert-Institute for schoolbook research in Braunschweig for their kind assistance in finding school books for review.

[41] Mihr, Anja / Mkritchyan, Artur / Mahler, Claudia / Toivanen, Reetta (eds.), Armenia: a human rights perspective for peace and democracy: human rights, human rights education and minorities, Potsdam, 2005.

[42] Especially the regional initiatives by the Council of Europe see Mahler, Claudia, Menschenrechtsbildungsprogramme im Bereich des Europarates, in: Mihr, Anja / Mahler, Claudia (eds.), Menschenrechtsbildung; Wiesbaden, 2004, p. 105-116: and Organization for Cooperation and Security in Europe Toivanen, Reetta, Organisation für Sicherheit und Zusammenarbeit in Europa: Menschenrechtsbildung als Mittel zum Frieden, in: Mihr, Anja/Mahler, Claudia (eds.), Menschenrechtsbildung, Wiesbaden, 2004, p. 93-103, i.e. citizenship education programs by the Council of Europe or Copenhagen Document in 1990 and the Lund Recommendation by the OSCE 1999.

[43] Suarez, David / Ramirez, Francisco, Human Rights and Citizenship: The Emergence of Human Rights Education', CDDRL Working Papers, No. 12, 19 August 2004 (http://iis-db.stanford.edu/pubs/20682/ramirez_suarez_6.25.2004.pdf, visited 12 March 2007), p. 2.

[44] Guy, Will (ed.), Roma migration in Europe: case studies, Münster, 2004; Okely, Judith, The Traveller-Gypsies, Cambridge Univ. Press, 1998; Tomasevski, Katarina, Education Denied – Costs and Remedies, London: Zed Books, 2003.

Minorities at Stake in Europe

On the European continent political changes occurred at the end of the 1980s and beginning of the 1990s as the socialist regimes collapsed and the beginning of transition periods transformed the political geography of the region. In this process, divergent human rights movements, civil society participants, individual and non-governmental initiatives played a crucial role in introducing and enhancing human rights and human rights awareness in the former socialist countries according to the so-called western standards.[45] In many of these countries, minority groups re-emerged and claimed participation rights, property and cultural identity. There was a certain risk that even those rightful claims could lead to societal unrest, since many of the transition countries were not yet politically and socially prepared to integrate those groups which had been marginalized for decades. Some of the large minority populations in former socialist countries were defined as potentially unstable and as entities carrying security risks.[46] In order to prevent the risks, new political procedures and institutions were established. The OSCE established for example an institution of the High Commissioner for National Minorities in 1992 which was designed to take diplomatic steps (an early warning procedure) in order to settle potential future disputes.[47] The OSCE meetings in Copenhagen and Moscow on the so called "Human Dimension", which includes human rights, paid attention to the question of how to deal with minority populations in Eastern European countries.[48] In 1993, the European Union agreed on the Copenhagen Criteria[49] which made it an accession requirement for the new member states such as Estonia and Slovakia to implement international human rights standards and respect for minorities.[50]

These changes and the process of implementation of international standards were crucial for the development of human rights education in the post-socialist countries of Armenia, Estonia and Slovakia. New legal provisions were drafted, declarations were adopted and programmes proclaimed by intergovernmental organisations in Europe to enhance the political and societal integration of minorities.[51] Internationally it was recognized that new and profound measures to change legislation

---

[45] See the report, OSCE, Supplementary human dimension meeting "Human Rights Education and Training", Final Report, Vienna, 25-26 March 2004 ODIHR.GAL/33/04, 4 May 2004.

[46] See Open Society, Justice Initiative, Activities Report 2003, New York: Open Society Institute.

[47] For further information see van der Stoel, Max, Gedanken zur Rolle des Hohen Kommissars der OSZE für nationale Minderheiten als Instrument zur Konfliktverhütung, OSZE-Jahrbuch 5 (1999), p.429-441; homepage of the High Commissioner on National Minorities: http://www.osce.org/hcnm/ (visited in March 2007).

[48] Studnitz, Ernst Jörg von, Minderheitenschutz im KSZE-Prozeß, in: Blumenwitz, Dieter et al. (eds.), Neubestätigung und Weiterentwicklung von Menschenrechten und Volksgruppenrechten in Mitteleuropa; Staats- und völkerrechtliche Abhandlungen der Studiengruppe für Politik und Völkerrecht, 10, Kolen, 1991, p.31-37.

[49] See Europe Glossary, http://europa.eu/scadplus/glossary/accession_criteria_copenhague_en.htm (visited in March 2007).

[50] More in Mahler, Claudia / Toivanen, Reetta op. Cit. Fn. 31.

[51] On the national level of Slovakia, the Office of the Plenipotentiary for Roma Issues was established and it started some projects to support Roma, the Methodological Pedagogical Centre in Presov started with a new section for Roma Education in Slovakia, the National Human Rights Centre was re-established and started human rights education trainings for multiplicators.

and policies in the new Council of Europe states had to be undertaken. The UN Declaration for Minorities, the Council of Europe's Framework Convention for the Protection of National Minorities and the establishment of the OSCE High Commissioner for National Minorities are just a few amongst many measures introduced by the international human rights regime. An interesting consequence was that these developments in the former east motivated western European minorities to raise their voices and ask for more recognition of minority rights as seen in our research countries Finland, Germany and Spain.[52]

Human Rights Education as a Method to Combat Inequality

At the beginning of the 1990s and during the whole UN Decade for Human Rights Education (1995-2004), eastern and western European states were interested in finding common solutions to the old and new problems of discrimination and marginalization of minorities. The overall political, social and economic situation in Eastern Europe was less stable than in Western Europe. However, in terms of national minorities, the social, economic and educational conditions have been – embedded in their particular national contexts – similar throughout Europe. Worth noticing is that the educational circumstances among the "weak" and among the "strong" minority groups have actually been quite similar in both eastern and western Europe. For example, a higher percentage of children from such minority groups as the Roma/*Gitanos* in Slovakia, Spain and Finland or Yezidi in Armenia failed to finish primary or secondary school than the majority population.[53] In contrast, children belonging to socio-economically better situated national minority groups such as the Sorbs, Finland's Swedes or the Basques usually received the national average standard education – partly even in their own mother tongues.[54]

The main difference between the proclamation of the UN Decade and the national implementation of it was caused by the diverse understandings of what human rights education is and what it aims at. In both western and eastern European countries state officials were convinced that they had complied with the international requirements for human rights education when they had introduced some political education or education for democratic citizenship (EDC). EDC has largely been understood by governments as means to educate young people to become good and loyal

[52] See here Toivanen op. Cit. fn. 42.

[53] Luciak, Mikael, Migrants, Minorities and Education, Documenting Discrimination and Integration in 15 Member States of the European Union, EUMC comparative study (Luxembourg: Office for Official Publications of the European Communities, 2004; http://eumc.europa.eu/eumc/material/pub/comparativestudy/CS-Education-en.pdf, visited in March 2007).

[54] Hornberg, Sabine, Entwicklungslinien, Problemstellungen und Perspektiven der Schulsituation von Sinti und Roma in Europa, in: Hornberg, Sabine (ed.), Die Schulsituation von Sinti und Roma in Europa; Reihe historisch-vergleichende Sozialisations- und Bildungsforschung, 4, Frankfurt a.M, 2000, p. 9-15.

citizens.[55] Analyzing the national curricula in the target countries has provided strong evidence that political and democratic education was not interpreted as a means to increase human rights awareness in a holistic way. Neither did it mean to seriously include the human rights aspects of national minorities into the formal sector or to educate non-minorities about minorities' human rights, history, culture or particular needs. Consequently, it seems most likely that the ignorance of the majority of people towards national minorities has remained the same with or without EDC. At the same time, members of national minorities themselves, like the Roma or Yezidi, did not have an equal opportunity to learn their own history or about minority rights and the possibilities of participating in society. Education for democratic citizenship and political education in most cases, according to the data, clearly privileged the majority in all the countries of our analysis.

Tolerance education, anti-racism education and many more projects and initiatives which were aimed at reducing hostility and prejudice in societies did not achieve what was meant by human rights education as proclaimed by the UN-Decade for Human Rights Education in 1994 which was to raise human rights awareness among all societal groups, regardless of their ethnic or historical background. The Decade had also aimed at making clear that all people have equal human rights but sometimes different needs, and therefore equal opportunities are needed on the one hand and help in claiming for a change of societal structures on the other. National minorities not only need recognition and respect by the rest of society in order to have an equal opportunity of a dignified life; they also need access to political and societal bodies, educational support and job opportunities.

In summary, it seems fair to state that most of the European governments and their authorities did not pay enough attention to the contents of the Plan of Action for Human Rights Education. In some of the countries there were efforts undertaken to reform national school curricula in terms of human rights.[56] But the actions were clearly insufficient, did not necessarily comply with the demands of the UN Decade and failed in general to address the specific aspects and demands of national minorities.

In all the countries of our analysis some aspects of national minorities were addressed during the national school book reforms.[57] The reforms were either initiated by international organisations like the Council of Europe or associations of national minorities and human rights NGOs who lobbied ministries and school reform com-

---

[55] See here the critique by Katarina Tomasevski in her reports at http://www.ohchr.org/english/issues/education/rapporteur/annual.htm, visited on February 1, 2007, See also the contribution of Audrey Osler in this book.

[56] Finland included human rights as a mainstream basic value in the core curricula. It was however impossible to say what was or is taught in school as regard to human rights. The teachers are also left without proper training in this basic value of human rights as only two Finnish universities include human rights in their teacher education. The conclusion could be made that only teachers who are interested in human rights issues include them in their teaching. (Personal interviews in Finland with representatives of minorities, authorities at the Board of Education, teachers and researchers, in August and September 2005).

[57] The analysis of school materials took place in Georg-Eckert-Institute for schoolbook research in Braunschweig and of course more randomly during the field trips when we visited schools. Only for Slovakia we do not have the data for comparison.

mittees to introduce aspects of minorities and human rights into school books. Common for human rights education activities in all countries with minorities was that very seldom any particular reference to the UN Decade for Human Rights Education was given. In Germany, the major lobby organisation for human rights education, the German UNESCO Commission, stressed the importance of including diversity in the teaching materials in order to have the school books reflect the situation of the pupils.[58] In 2003 and 2004, Amnesty International Spain together with the "Asociación Pro Derechos Humanos de Espana" lobbied the Ministry of Education in Madrid to include elements of human rights education into the formal educational sector. Under the title "Debate educativo: Reforma Ley de Educación" Amnesty International started a nationwide campaign which also referred to the UN-Decade. In January 2005 an Amnesty delegation met representatives of the Ministry of Education and later received feedback confirming that the revised education curricula would include more references to human rights.[59] Minorities and their rights, however, were not explicitly mentioned.

Consequences: Evidence, Compliance, Sustainability and Accomplishments

During the course of our three and half year research, we had the opportunity to analyse many different policies towards minorities and concerning human rights education in particular. Some of the policies could be described as systematic approaches towards minority inclusion whereas others were quite hopeless efforts to "do something" against minority marginalisation. The material we collected for further analyses comprised of school textbooks, interviews, human rights course materials, legislative proposals and legal documents, political party and election programmes, and proposals by NGO and intergovernmental organisations. This material was collected with the help of our colleagues, students and interns in the countries of our research. In the following chapter we will focus on the main outcomes of our research and draw conclusions which can in the best case open paths for further research in this field. Even though we did find evidence of compliance with the UN Decade, it must be said that a sustainable approach to human rights education for and with national minorities was hardly found anywhere.

Evidence: Human Rights Education and National Minorities

Most of the human rights education initiatives, programmes, and evidence of activities found during our research were designed for educators in youth work, basically working with persons under the age of 25. Most of the projects were initiated by small NGOs. These in turn were dependent on external (national and international) donors. Both the initiatives and the NGOs were in most cases short-lived.

[58] They only paid attention to immigrants and refugees – national minorities were not a theme (personal communication with the former president of the Committee in December 19, 2005)
[59] Amnesty International Spain, Internal Document, Madrid office, Letter from the Ministra de Educación y Ciencia, Sansegundo from 26 January 2005.

Teaching material targeted at people above the age of 25 belongs in the category of adult education or "life long learning". In all of our focus countries these projects and programmes rarely addressed the specific needs of minority populations in general or national minorities in particular. If minorities were mentioned, then the emphasis was on combating racism and discrimination against immigrants or other ethnic minorities in that country. In the best (or worse) cases, even the long established groups of Roma were included in the group of refugees or immigrants.[60] The fact that members of national minorities who are considered historic groups having lived for several generations in a country or determined territory was not at al an issue found in the data material.

Only those minority groups who have been able to send representatives to official and governmental bodies, such as ministries of education, were – if at all – in a position to emphasize that human rights education and education of minorities should be a part of a national school curriculum. In the Basque country the school book reforms in the 1990s, independent from the UN Decade for Human Rights Education, included more aspects of the Basque history in a geographical context. Attention was also paid to nationalistic understandings of the Basque Country. In many of the school books students learn about "Euskal Herria" a united Basque nation and country which includes parts of southern France and the neighbouring province of Navarra in Spain.[61] The school book reforms were carried out primarily by the regional government of the autonomous Basque country and its' Ministry of Education.[62] The Basque authorities have been criticized by the Central government in Spain for being too nationalistic. School books in Armenia were reformed in 2001 under the auspices of the Council of Europe, the World Bank and the UN-office in Yerevan.[63] As a result of that reform, the Yezidi minority in Armenia are now mentioned in one chapter of the textbook for 8th grade students.[64] In Germany the teachers can freely choose which school books they use but the books must be accredited by the state.[65] The lists are long and it is too difficult to find out which books are actually used. The Forum Human Rights[66], an umbrella organisation of German human rights NGOs, prepared a recommended list of school books which included education on human rights but

---

[60] In Germany "The Regional Centre for Education, Integration and Democracy" groups for example refugees and Roma and Sinti in the same category, see e.g. http://www.raa-berlin.de. In Finland the constitution mentions the Saami as an especially vulnerable group together with "Roma and other groups", Finnish Constitution, Chapter 2, Section 17, 731/1999, adopted June 11, 1999, entered into force March 1, 2000. Many of the interviewed Roma also complained that even though they have lived for generations in Europe, they are often grouped together with recent immigrants (personal communications with representatives of Roma in Finland, Slovakia and Germany).

[61] Fourth grade history book at Basque speaking schools: Ebebé Publisher (ed.), Giltza (secondary school book) 2002.

[62] See various other school books for example: Ibaizabal, VN (ed.), Geografia e historia Vol. 1, 1996; Erein (ed.), Ciencias Sociales, geografica e historia Vols.1,2,3,4, 1996; Elkar, VN (dd.), Ciencias Sociales Vol. 1,2,3, 2003.

[63] Armenia became a full member of the Council of Europe on 25 January 2001.

[64] Khazinyan, Garik (ed.), Human Rights, Textbook for 8th grade, Yerevan, 2001, p. 100-101.

[65] "Liste der zugelassenen Schulbücher", the lists are published every year by the German ministries of cultures in the different states.

[66] For further information see http://www.forum-menschenrechte.de, visited January 10, 2007.

not even on this list could be found school books addressing minority rights.[67] In Estonia, there is a Presidential Round Table for Minorities with the task of discussing urgent needs of minority populations. It seems that minority representatives attending the Round Table have not demanded that minority rights should be addressed in the school materials; however the school books do present the Setu minority in their traditional dresses but do not mention Russian speakers or Roma. A representative of a Russian organisation said that this would be seen as a provocation in Estonian public discourse if someone demanded minority rights for the Russians to become a theme for schools.[68] In Slovakia, the Hungarian minority established the first Hungarian University, some Roma schools were established and the special Roma assistant programme was launched. A similar idea of Roma assistants (persons who could be the bridge between the Roma community and schools) were found in many of the studied states. In Finland, the Board of Education, working under the auspices of the Ministry of Education had established a Roma education curricula already in 1992[69] and in some Finnish school books Roma and their special needs are addressed, often together with other traditional minorities such as the Sámi indigenous people.[70] But in Finland we also discovered that nobody was able to provide statistics on which school books were used in schools because the teacher is able to choose freely what material is used in class.[71] With this matter in mind, a NGO initiative, financially supported jointly by the Ministries of Education, Foreign Affairs and Social and Health, established an internet resource site for human rights education.[72] However, these materials are used by those teachers who personally find them important.

In none of our target countries were national minorities a focal point of state activities during the UN Decade for Human Rights Education It was interesting to see that even the activists of the "stronger" minorities did not demand their "human rights" to be respected. Although members and leaders of national minorities are usually aware of the existence of international and national minority rights, they seldom declare them as human rights because they are unable to make the connection between minority rights and human rights. Thus, one major conclusion of the research project is that particularly national minorities need to learn and understand why minority issues need special measures and protection. This is one accurate way to promote human rights of minorities and increase acceptance of minorities in societies.[73]

---

[67] Amsler,Peter/ Lohrenscheit,Claudia/ Möller, Lutz, Standards der Menschenrechtsbildung für die Achtung der Menschenrechte in Schulen, Berlin, Forum Menschenrechte, 2006.

[68] Personal communication with a Russian umbrella organisation in Tallinn May 31, 2004.

[69] Sosiaali- ja Terveysministeriön muistioita 2001, p. 24.

[70] Research at the Georg Eckert Institute für Schulbuchforschung in Braunschweig, in December 2004.

[71] Personal Interviews with teachers, trade union representatives and researchers in Finland during the research visit in August/September 2005.

[72] See: www.ihmisoikeudet.net, visited November 2007.

[73] See also similar conclusion in the study of May, Stephen, Accommodating and Resisting Minority Language Policy: The Case of Wales', International Journal of Bilingual Education and Bilingualism Vol. 3, No. 2 (2000), pp. 101-128.

Complying with International Standards: Political Will versus Ignorance?

Human rights education has never been at the top of the agenda of political decision makers in any of the six countries on which we focused. Before and during the UN Decade for Human Rights Education, human rights issues as well as minority protection were usually brought into the public discourse by NGOs and pressure groups like the Simecka Foundation and the Open Society Institute in Slovakia, the Estonian Union of Nationalities in Estonia, the League of Human Rights in Finland, the Forum Menschenrechte (NGO network) in Germany, the Union Romani and Amnesty International in Spain or the Constitutional Rights Protective Center in Armenia.[74] Other key players were international organisations such as the Council of Europe or the OSCE or their national branches like the national UNESCO Commissions in Germany and Finland who actively contributed to raising awareness by publishing information booklets and books and organising seminars. For example, the Council of Europe introduced the European Year of Citizenship through Education (EYCE) in 2005[75] and the Decade of Roma Inclusion was adopted by participating governments, the Council of Europe and the Soros Foundation for the years 2005 to 2015.[76] Intergovernmental organisations and private foundations supported conferences and gave project grants to NGOs in the field, carrying out human rights education training for lawyers and teachers and other interested parties. These activities were in the best cases initiated, planned and carried out in cooperation with state officials, with local NGOs and minority groups in the relevant countries.

What could be seen as a pattern when comparing the six countries in Europe was the fact that when human rights education or problems faced by minorities were brought up on the political agenda of governments' or states' authorities it was due to the efforts, initiatives and pressure of one or a few people or an NGO in that country. These actors were human rights activists or members of pressure groups who had dealt with minority issues for a long time and hence had personal experience or an interest in human rights education and minority questions.[77] They lobbied decision makers, the ministries of education, school directors, international or national donors, foundations or international organisations like the UNESCO Commissions, EU or the Council of Europe. It seems fair to say that it was precisely these private and NGO sectors who had implemented what the UN Decade had called for. Some were more concerned with stressing human rights in general and ignoring the minority rights as a central issue. They argued that the main purpose for making political decisions and providing human and financial resources for human rights education was the fact that more human rights awareness led to more self-assertion and the democratic political participation of all. Some were more concerned with emphasizing minority rights and ignoring the general framework of human rights. Their main motivation was to integrate minorities into the political decision making processes of each country. This

[74] See contribution of Anja Mihr in this volume.

[75] For further information see http://www.coe.int/T/E/Com/Files/Themes/ECD/ visited September 2007.

[76] For further information see http://www.romadecade.org/ visited September 2007.

[77] Obviously a few of them had fewer ideals in mind but saw a chance for a personal career in the field of human rights education.

agenda got further fuel by those who claimed that if minorities were not allowed to share the power and to participate democratically in their state, they would turn to other, maybe violent means, to fight for their causes and interests.[78] These scenarios were especially tangible in central and eastern Europe at the beginning of the 1990s but they continued to form the basis for the human rights education discourse especially in the OSCE.[79]

Although we found evidence and patterns of implementing international human rights standards, fostering human rights education programmes and increasing the activities of private and NGO actors, there was no clear coordination between the main actors in the field: first, the international organisations (UN, UNESCO, OSCE, Council of Europe and EU), second, state authorities and governments, third, local actors or NGOs, and fourth the minority members themselves. There was no UN or European agency which coordinated the activities of the UN Decade, although the Office of the High Commissioner for Human Rights (OHCHR) in Geneva together with UNESCO in Paris were formally responsible. But due to the lack of resources and capacities, coordinating activities in the field of human rights education of 192 member states was a challenge. It was meant to be left to the regional interstate organisation and to the state governments, their ministries of education and other official bodies whom in 1994 had formally agreed to implement measures to enhance human rights education for all. But as mentioned before, on the state level and in governmental bodies, the understanding of what human rights education is, and how to foster and promote the rights of national minorities differ from country to country and region to region. There were no common understandings and standards, no common ways of implementation and no common guidelines as to whom and which groups, schools, NGOs or others should get support in order to promote human rights education.

We can conclude that if something happened in the field of implementing and enhancing human rights education in a country – particularly in the non-formal education sector – it was because of individual activists or due to some dedicated state officials. As we can see in Spain, for example, due to the fact that NGOs lobbied for several years to change the school curricula, textbooks were changed towards the end of the UN-Decade to include education on human rights. Without private initiatives or personal dedication not much would have happened in any of the countries examined. The same patterns were found when human rights issues were linked to the interests and needs of national minorities like Roma/*Gitanos* in Spain, Finland's Swedes in Finland or the Hungarians in Slovakia. However, it has to be stated that those groups who had lobbyists and activists calling for better inclusion of minority rights subjects like history, culture and minority languages in the school textbooks, interestingly did not refer to the UN Decade for Human Rights Education, even though the Plan of Action called for such a measure.

---

[78] Horowitz, Donald L., Ethnic Groups in Conflict, Berkley, University of California Press, 1985; Taras, Ray, National Identities and Ethnic Minorities in Eastern Europe, Selected Papers from the Fifth World Congress of Central an East European Studies, Warsaw, 1995, London, 1998.

[79] Toivanen op. cit. fn. 42.

Sustainability: Short Term versus Long Term Human Rights Education Programmes

It was certainly not the easiest task to implement the recommendations of the UN Action Plan for Human Rights Education which were; to include human rights in the formal and non-formal education sector, to pay attention to the sensitive and specific needs of national minorities and to change curricula accordingly from what has been understood as "good political education" towards holistic human rights education. It helps to explain why the task was left to activists and pressure groups. At the same time, minority activists as well as other NGOs had to cope with the fact that financial grants were given to them only after a complicated application procedure e.g. from the EU or international foundations like the SOROS Foundation (especially in eastern Europe). Many initiatives and projects were supported for short periods, sometimes less than six months or a year in order to organise human rights training, workshops or lobbying work. This was not enough to actually achieve sustainability which can be defined as conducting follow-up programmes, evaluating human rights education techniques and proceeding with what sometimes takes years to achieve: changing school curricula, train teachers and those who disseminate human rights information and to reach out to a wider public – or to closed communities like the Yezidi or some Roma communities in Europe.

When preparing our trips to the countries, each of us had identified the main actors in the field of human rights education and named those NGOs or governmental offices which seemed relevant for the realisation of human rights education programmes. Publications, web-pages, the UN documents (such as the midterm evaluation of the UN Decade), and especially the personal recommendations by colleagues were very helpful in identifying those people who were or had been active in human rights education in the given country. What became a pattern during our research project was that many of the younger activists left their working place quite quickly after they had started and even whole NGOs disappeared at an astonishing speed. The human rights "education business" was not able to offer attractive employment visions for future and short term contracts were certainly not helpful in trying to establish a coherent stock of human rights educators. Those minority members who got involved in empowerment programmes seldom returned to their minority organisations but received much better job offers with intergovernmental organisations and international NGOs. This was particularly true for the countries in central and eastern Europe where during the transition period the young and well-educated elite with language skills were desperately needed and therefore had various good job offers to choose from. Thus, sustainable work by these people and NGOs was almost impossible.

Accordingly, one of our conclusions is that without long-lasting programmes even the most engaged person, organisation or institution cannot carry out the process of human rights education in a sustainable manner. NGOs are under constant pressure and in a rush. They have to change their programmes and strategies to get new support from donors and international organisations and they constantly write new applications with new target groups, priority areas and even themes. This is why these associations or groups do not have the capacity to maintain human rights education projects for longer time periods, and often instead of offering something sustainable over a period of years, they in the end offer just a weekend seminar – and write applications the rest of the time. When the bigger NGOs have problems of capacity building and management, one can easily imagine the frustration of smaller organisations of national minorities. Several of the interviewed minority representatives had failed even in setting up primary organisational structures such as forming an NGO or registering the NGO, establishing an office, getting an internet access and so forth.

International organisations, like the UN/ UNDP, the Council of Europe, the EU or the OSCE played an important role in realizing and promoting human rights education in the six countries of our research. Although these organisations faced budget cuts and a revision of priorities and therefore shortcomings in human and technical support, they provided different kinds of support according to their mandate. This again led to the fact that some representatives of national minorities particularly in the former socialist countries have been exposed to organisational representatives of the UN or EU over the past decade. They learned that these organisations can function in differing supportive ways. The OSCE, the Council of Europe, the EU and the UN impacted national politics but had to leave the final decision of what programmes, projects and how to reform for example state curricula in schools, to the national decision making bodies, the governments and ministries. In this respect national politics sometimes differ from what was once declared by the UN Decade for Human Rights Education in 1994 and the Plan for Action sent out by the UN Secretary General in 1995.

Accomplishments and Implementation

The accomplishments during the UN-Decade in terms of human rights education and national minorities varied widely in the countries of research. As mentioned previously they ranged from individual initiatives and actions, sometimes taking a couple of days or weeks, to longer term activities of one to two years led by NGOs in close cooperation with international governmental organisations and state authorities.[80]

NGOs cooperate with the governmental sector and the governmental sector seems to pursue a policy according to which the more short term projects, the broader awareness raising campaign instead of financing a few long lasting programmes which would cost the same amount of money. While doing the research, however, the quick turnover of leaders and those responsible in this field turns out to be a challenge. Long term research depends on constant variables and actors who can give reliable information. If the leadership of the NGO sector changes often, it is difficult to receive reliable information.

This leads to another aspect which can be found in all of our research countries. It is the missing communication and lack of networks particularly between the actors among minority group leaders. This absence of exchange and cooperation, not only at the non-governmental level but also between state actors and non-state actors,

[80] Roma leader training carried out by the Simecka Foundation, Obcan Democracia and the Open Society Institute in Slovakia; Training from Amnesty International, Red Cross, and Youth Alliance in Finland on Human Rights Education and inclusion of human rights in some of the teacher training courses;

is common. Such cooperation is crucial in order to achieve wide changes in the field of human rights education and national minority issues. If NGOs do not get governmental officials involved or are not able to convince them of the importance of their project, little or no change will be achieved in terms of changing school curricula or education work for weak minorities like the Roma for example. The same happens if the target groups are not included in the planning and drafting of programmes addressing the human rights of minority populations. This non-involvement of people who were to be the target of educational activities was very typical; one of the paramount cases being the theatre project of the Estonian Ministry of Education for Roma people. No Roma activist was consulted during the whole planning phase, not even the educational committee for Roma at the ministry.[81]

Implementation problems clearly remain the major problem at all levels. Due to the lack of human and financial resources, the lack of political will or simple awareness of the main struggles resulted in a lack of governmental monitoring capacities in implementing human rights education measures at the national levels and no clear strategy by state actors to link the "paper" and the wordings of the UN declaration for the UN Decade with the "reality" and needs of people and groups in the countries. For example, we did not find any evidence that there was a clear linkage between the commitment by states to endorse human rights education measures and the vulnerable groups, like national minorities in particular, in any of the six countries.[82] We barely found any evidence of parallel activities and achievements either in the field of human rights education programmes or the fostering of national minority rights. It was only due to pressure groups such as the Yezidi community in Armenia that their minority group was taken up as an issue during school book reforms in 2001.

As mentioned at the beginning of this article, all six countries have signed and ratified the most important international treaties on the protection of human rights and minority rights which include the agreement to foster national minority rights and participation. But none of the efforts which included national minorities in the sector of formal or non-formal education were linked clearly to the UN Decade for Human Rights Education during 1995-2004. As we have shown previously, all our research countries are state parties of the UN Decade on Human Rights Education and one would have assumed that we had found many programmes and projects which are focused on promoting themes like equality of minorities and human rights.

This was found not to be the case. State and non-governmental institutions rather worked parallel to each other, although major initiatives were undertaken by non-state actors and NGOs with some short term and (exceptional) longer term support and help by governmental authorities or international organisations.

The general conclusion is that even though all actors involved in our analysis stressed the importance of raising the awareness of minority rights as general human rights, there is however, a tremendous gap in the realisation of raising awareness. Long established groups such as the German Sorbs or the Setu minority in Estonia can enjoy special minority rights and financial support for their language and culture

[81] See here Toivanen op.cit. fn. 29.

[82] By the end of the Decade none of the countries had managed to launch a national action plan on human rights.

maintenance, but still very few members of majorities living with them in the same country or even in the same county or city know much about them and even less about the reasons why this minority should be protected.

Future Research: Two Basic Recommendations

In a democratic society it is certainly fair to share resources of human rights education between many different actors and institutions. However, this activity needs good coordination both at international as well as at the national level. In order to achieve long lasting and sustainable results in human rights education, local and small NGOs who do most of the human rights education work on the ground have to be strengthened and supervised to aim at long term implementation. Education and changing peoples' minds takes years and sometimes decades. States have to be able to guarantee that programmes which have been positively evaluated will be able to continue. A life-long-learning approach must also be guaranteed so that human rights education becomes part of education even after the normal school years.

Strong cooperation between the entrepreneurs in human rights education, the NGOs, governmental agencies and the minority groups is essential if any long-lasting changes in the "human rights culture" of any given country are to be achieved. Engaging all the different actors on a long term basis can make a difference and lead to adequate and suitable human rights education programmes. These programmes and efforts have to be assessed and evaluated on a regular basis in order to enhance their impact and their outcome. The cooperation should be fostered over national borders and there should be quality standards to guarantee that minority populations can also participate in all human rights education projects. Minority rights are one essential part of human rights and should be addressed as such in any educational activity.

Human Rights Advocacy and the Academy

J. Paul Martin

Introduction

Over the last twenty years human rights studies has seen prolific growth in North America, Europe and other parts of the world, not the least in universities where it has taken the form of new research and teaching in the social sciences and the humanities, as well as in its more traditional home of law. The early emphasis on civil and political rights has been expanded to encompass economic and social rights and there is a growing commitment to interdisciplinary research and teaching. In the academy, more than in primary, secondary and adult education, the continuing dominance of legal scholarship has assured primacy to a strict view of rights, namely as universally accepted legal obligations on states, rather than more inclusive definitions encompassing humanitarian and philanthropic concerns. Today, human rights studies is a large and open field driven by many intellectual and real-life forces that attract young and old scholars. One potentially negative outcome of this expansion has been scholarly output that appears very random. Is the overall situation good or bad? Will all the activity inevitably bring an intellectual winnowing as the best research and teaching are separated from those that will not bear the test of time? This paper identifies some of the problem-driven tasks that call for academic attention and argues that the promotion of human rights in the real world can best be achieved through more systematic engagement among scholars, between scholars, policymakers and practitioners, and especially in ways that bridge these groups in rich and poor countries.

Human Rights Studies Yesterday and Today

In just one semester in 2007 Columbia University graduates and undergraduates could have chosen from among more than 50 courses on human rights-related topics offered in its various departments and schools. In spite of heterogeneity in the way the courses were designated as human rights, the number of courses illustrates a high level of faculty commitment and student interest. Similar levels of interest and commitment are to be found in many other universities in both the industrialized and the developing worlds. This interest on the part of the academy reflects the increasing role that human rights and concerns for social justice play in popular discourse and public policy. As a step towards assessing the academy's offerings and their impact on the promotion of human rights around the world, this paper offers a survey of the field, identifying issues and intellectual drivers that could enrich human rights studies in the world's academies. In general, the profile of human rights studies in the world's academies appears as follows. In terms of quantity (articles published), core themes and theoretical premises, human rights research and teaching continue to be dominated by legal scholarship[1] and its dominant focus on civil and political rights and processes. Philosophy, ethics and the social sciences and their concerns of distributive justice and social welfare are a rising second. The impact of the academy on public policy is especially visible in the legal field, where scholars such as Philip Alston, Antonio Cassese, Francis Deng, Louis Henkin, Harold Koh, Mary Robinson and many others, have visibly influenced domestic and international law and institutions.[2] Domestic law strategies used to fight discrimination, for example, have been transposed into international law and institutions, often also as a sort of back door to promote economic and social rights when the justiciability of the latter have been in question.[3] Today, the emphasis of legal research on civil and political rights has been reinforced by the rights' problems raised around the world by the war on terror.

Over the last fifteen years research in the human rights field as a whole, including for example economic, social and cultural rights, has been expanding in the social sciences and the humanities, particularly as a result of international campaigns to promote access to basic rights in education, healthcare and employment. New foci and methodologies explore the wider field of human rights, but they are also less systematized than legal studies and thus hard to categorize on account of their being distributed across many fields and disciplines. Moreover, while interdisciplinary research might be much lauded as central to human rights studies, such research is still constrained by traditional disciplinary divides and funding patterns. In most universities in Europe and the Americas, formal human rights research programmes are still to be found primarily in law schools and in a few independent institutes. In the US, funding for human rights research and education in the major academies has been disappearing, with U.S. foundations like Ford and the John D. and Catherine T. Macarthur preferring to support advocacy and work in the field. Support for human rights research by scholars in developing countries has been almost non-existent. Without a major international association of human rights scholars, dialogue among human rights scholars tends to take place through journals and informally, such as at conferences for other purposes.[3] In addition to debates within the field, such as recently with respect to government policies initiated after 9/11, human rights debates appear in related fields such as in peace studies, conflict resolution, the treatment of refugees and displaced persons, and economic and political development. Human rights studies is thus not a clearly defined field.

The case for more interdisciplinary research in human rights was made in the early 1980s in a report funded by the Ford Foundation and prepared by the Chilean jurist and former head of Amnesty International, Jose Zalaquett. He proposed a pre-

---

[1] See for example The Role of the University in the Human Rights Movement, Harvard Law School, Human Rights Programme, 1999. All but two of the participants were legal scholars.

[2] While it is impossible to assess the impact of their individual work, the contributions of Cassese, Henkin and others are illustrated in: Charney, Jonathan I./ Anton, Donald K./ O'Connell, Mary Ellen, Politics and Function: International Law in the 21st Century, Essays in Honor of Professor Louis Henkin, Cambridge, Mass. Kluwer Law International, 1997. Koh's and other's contributions cane be found in: Claude, Richard Pierre/ Weston, Burns H., Human Rights and World Community, Philadelphia, University of Pennsylvania Press, 2006. In it he discusses the role of "norm entrepreneurs" dating back to Lord William Wilberforce.

[3] One example of a small voluntary network of human rights scholars is the International Human Rights Education Consortium. See www.utica.edu/academic/institutues/ihnrec/.

scient list of priority topics for such research: universalism and cultural diversity, the rights of indigenous populations, economic and social rights, the use of violence and fear for political goals and the roles of NGOs and the media.[4] Already then there was talk about then need for an international human rights consortium to promote interaction among researchers from the north and the global south as well as the relevance of health and welfare, and attention to the needs of women and children due to the global breakdown of family based social security systems and the challenge women were facing to provide food, shelter and healthcare as single heads of household. This presaged a major expansion in women's (and women's human rights) studies around the world which has been interdisciplinary, theoretically innovative and based on major international collaboration, suggesting a model that other human rights field could follow.

Although not in the official rhetoric of the U.S. Government, in the ensuing years, both human rights advocacy and human rights research have began to reflect the need to address not only civil and political rights but also economic and social rights. Under pressure from their own members as well as others organisations like Human Rights Watch and Amnesty International have expanded their agenda from their original mandates to include economic and social rights.[5] This broadening of the human rights and humanitarian agenda has also encouraged students and faculty in different disciplines to engage in human rights research. Interdisciplinary thinking and an inclusive human rights agenda are also encouraged by human rights journals such as *The Human Rights Quarterly, Journal of Human Rights, Human Rights Review, Human Rights and Human Welfare, Health and Human Rights* and more recently by the new *SUR International Human Rights Journal,* based in Sao Paulo, Brazil and *MenschenRechtsMagazin*, Potsdam, Germany. Although they remain within the law framework, other research journals published in the US such as the *Yale Human Rights and Development Law Journal* (online), *Columbia Human Rights Law Review,* and the annual *Harvard Human Rights Journal,* also regularly address economic and social rights. Other university human rights programmes such as those at MIT, Deusto in Bilbao and Åbo Akademi in Finland regularly publish monographs and other volumes on human rights drawing on the different disciplines and adopting the inclusive view of human rights. A similar agenda has been embraced by such human rights publishing houses as The University of Pennsylvania, Greenwood, Kluwer, Kumarian, Praeger, Routledge and Westview presses. Both Oxford and Cambridge University presses regularly publish research addressing the broader field of human rights by authors from all over the world. As most of the authors writing for

---

[4] Today, twenty-three years after the Zalaquett report, we might add to his list abuses caused by civil wars, refugees and displaced persons and the role of non-state actors.

[5] Roth, Kenneth, Defending Economic, Social and Cultural Rights: Practical Issues Faced by an International Human Rights Organization, 26 Human Rights Quarterly, 63, 2004; Rubenstein, Leonard, How International Human Rights Organizations Can Advance Economic, Social and Cultural Rights: A Response to Ken Roth, 26 Human Rights Quarterly 845, 2004; On Amnesty's expanding mandate see Hegarty, Angela/ Leonard, Siobhan (Eds.), A Human Rights Agenda for the 21st Century, London, Cavendish, 1999, p. 234. On Human Rights Watch see Brown,Wendy, Human Rights an Overview in Claude/ Emerson/ Welch, (Eds.), NGOs and Human Rights: Promise and Performance, Philadelphia, University of Pennsylvania Press, 2001, p. 77.

these publications come from universities, the total output adds up to a significant quantity of research in human rights from the world's academies.

The academy's participation in the advocacy struggle itself has not been so prolific, even when it involved colleagues. Individual academics and academies, for example, have been, and remain targets for control if not repression by their civil authorities. Even when these violations of academic freedom are seen as early bellwethers of an overall political climate and receive attention from the major human rights NGOs, individual universities without such restrictions have been slow to respond. Typically any response will take the form of an influential academic rising up to advocate for and perhaps provide a refuge for an endangered colleague. There has been no attempt on the part of the world's academies to develop strategies for responding when governments close down institutions and dismiss or arrest scholars for arbitrary reasons. Concern for endangered fellow academics can also be found within individual professional associations, but even there it typically reflects the commitment and assiduity of individuals rather than a priority for the association itself. More recently groups like Scholars at Risk have been established to help find alternative employment for scholars fearing for their lives. This situation reflects larger questions about how the international academic community should respond when the human rights of colleagues and academic freedom are in danger at other institutions.[6] The place of the academy as bulwark against human rights violations is a topic worthy of conscious intellectual scrutiny over and beyond responding to threatened or imprisoned fellow academics.

Human Rights as an Expanding Field of Intellectual Endeavour

Human rights is an inclusive field of intellectual endeavour in a number of ways. In addition to calling for the resources of many disciplines, its normative standards apply to many dimensions of human life. The basic intellectual tasks cover (a) empirical issues such as basic data collection and reporting (and accuracy here is the core of the credibility of human rights monitoring), (b) the analysis of data with a view to identifying systems and remedies, (c) norm-setting, their implementation and reconciling conflicts among norms and between norms and other social goals, (d) the design and maintenance of policies, and of public and private institutions with human rights and related mandates, and finally (e) the evaluation of the advocacy strategies used to protect and promote rights. Addressing all of these topics clearly calls for the resources of a range of disciplines. The common theme, however, of human rights scholarship is the tension, contrast or disconnect between the ideals spelt out in law and ethics on one hand, and the day-to-day reality faced by the millions of human beings around the world whose rights are being abused on the other. The human rights movement as a whole seeks to reduce this gap. This paper examines the particular role of human rights studies.

As indicated above, human rights scholarship found a comfortable home and identity within the fields of international law and constitutional studies, and at the in-

[6] The university's responses to government control is raised with respect to Iran in Nafisi, Azar. Reading Lolita in Tehran, New York, Random House, 2004.

terface between the two. Recognizing that the promotion of human rights requires more than laws and legal institutions, human rights advocates, already as far back as the anti-slavery campaigns of the 18th century, turned to other, non-legal strategies such as lobbying and the mobilization of public opinion. Today these strategies are especially needed in societies where law and legal institutions are weak and ineffective. Moreover, it has also become apparent that many human rights violations can only be eliminated through systemic change. Hence legal scholars have expanded their fields of research beyond law, and together with activists have turned to political scientists, economists and other social scientists. Dialogues with ethicists and philosophers, for example, were especially productive in the U.S. during the 1970s policy debates about the death penalty. Today's debates on poverty, access to healthcare and education and on economic and social rights as a whole bring together scholars concerned with the variety of issues. One excellent example of interaction among scholars, development activists and policy makers has been the work of Nobel Prize economist Amartya Sen, who, as much as any other single scholar, has convinced the scholars and policy makers of the close relationship between human rights and economic well-being.[7] In most cases when such interaction is successful, the arguments draw on a mix of the deontological, conceptual or theoretical arguments, namely those oriented to identifying and making human rights values and standards reality, and practical arguments, namely cause-effect relationships among the forces that can alleviate poverty in real life.

The major ongoing debates such as those on cultural diversity, development and rights, government policies initiated after 9/11, the north-south divide, global economic systems and corporate social responsibility, have been important intellectual drivers in that they produce numerous scholarly articles. The rights and development debate has proved especially sustained. World Bank policies, for example, have long been a particular target for academic criticism led in the 1980s by scholars such as James Paul of Rutgers University. One focus was the position of the Bank that categorized human rights as a political issue and therefore outside its scope. In the 1980s other scholars focused on the implications for human rights of its social adjustment policies. Today, debates on rights and the global economy have expanded significantly to include the growing power of the World Trade Organisation and the absence of human rights criteria in its mandate and work. Some scholars such as the Kenyan lawyer Yash Ghai, question the capacity of the World Bank to overcome the current international monetary system. In 2004 he said,

"Poverty eradication is not compatible with the agenda of international players, whether bilateral or intergovernmental agencies. The World Bank and the International Monetary Fund are cases in point. They have no interest in fundamental change in Kenya."[8] These are powerful statements. Scholars not only need to ask if they are valid, but also to identify alternatives and then find arguments to persuade the global institutions. Examining complex questions such as these requires sustained study and thus the long-term research

---

[7] Sen's influence is illustrated through his authorship of Chapter I and the incorporation of his ideas elsewhere in the 2000 UNDP Human Development Report which focused on development and human rights. See http://hdr.undp.org/en/reports/global/hdr2000/.

[8] Proceedings of the 20th Anniversary Celebration of the Harvard Law School Human Rights Program. October 2004, Harvard Law School Human Rights Program. p.104.

commitments and intellectual exchanges that are possible for academics, free, as they are, from both the time and other constraints of advocacy groups, and from the political constraints of policymakers.

There is no dearth of opportunities and challenges for the academic community coming from the policy makers. Each year, for example, every U.S. embassy must prepare a report on human rights conditions in its host country. These are compiled and published each year and, as much as the reports of Human Rights Watch and Amnesty International, they are treated as comprehensive and credible by the world media and are used accordingly. No academic reporting enjoys such an extensive influence. Only occasionally are the reports subject to published academic scrutiny. In 1998 the US Congress passed the International Religious Freedom Act. The Act requires global reporting, establishes new offices and defines the actions that a U.S. President should, and even must take to promote religious freedom around the world. This was the outcome of extensive lobbying by some U.S. domestic NGOs and church organisations, with little input from the academic community. Few of the resulting thousands of pages of human rights reporting data have been subject to either conceptual or factual analysis by the scholarly community. At the same time they are accepted as authoritative by the media and policy makers, including of course the U.S. Government and the U.S. Congress, both of which form policies accordingly. One challenge to the academic community is to evaluate the quality of this and other reporting and the ways in which those reports underpin policymaking.

Human rights play a role in the foreign policies of most of the world's governments. The issue, however, must compete with, be reconciled with, and perhaps even subordinated to, other competing policy concerns, notably national security, the war on terror and geopolitics, as well economic and commercial priorities. Within such contexts human rights and humanitarian arguments can easily, and are often also, used as a cover or pretext for other objectives and interests. Evaluating the use of human rights in foreign policy and international affairs is an intellectual challenge and thus a target for the critical thinking that is the mandate of academies around the world. The challenge so far for human rights scholars outside law has been access to policy formation, as their inputs typically come more post-factum in the form of a review of past events rather than, for example, in an edition of *Foreign Affairs.* In practice academics, have probably been most influential in policy making by working with and through the NGO community. More studies on human rights and foreign affairs would also complement the more focused inputs of the advocacy organisations.

Among the international organisations, the UN and its associated agencies merit continual scrutiny with respect to human rights if for no other reason than the fact that the UN was founded precisely to prevent the human rights abuses that were seen to lead to World War II. There are many units within the UN which have human rights in their mandate, but there is one in particular that could immediately benefit from strong links with the world's academies. It is the new Human Rights Council. A long tradition of cooperation between NGOs and scholars facilitated academic contributions to debates at its predecessor institution, the Human Rights Commission, and to the various special procedures it generated. Many of the UN special rapporteurs, for example, are and have been academics, as were many members of the treaty body committees. As the new Council struggles for identity and effectiveness, a key building block is access of its members to timely and accurate information. NGOs can provide some but their inputs come in the context of lobbying and input is often limited to NGOs with the funds to carry out the research and to support lobbyists in New York and Geneva. The academies of the Council member home countries could, for example, be mobilized to generate some information and analysis of the issues. However, even those low-income countries whose universities have UNESCO human rights chairs and thus enjoy a certain legitimacy and visibility, have little in the way of the resources necessary to support the regular, independent and wide-ranging research that would enable them to meet the needs of their country's delegates at the Council. This raises the broader question of inequalities and solidarity across the world's academies. Should not the richer ones be helping the poorer? Indeed might it not be in the interests of the both richer and the poorer institutions to carry out collaborative research on problems of common concern such as poverty alleviation and access to drinking water? Together they could be asking the questions of how, and to what degree, do human rights perspectives contribute to solving these problems, and to sharing their findings with their respective missions at the many UN agencies dealing with human rights.

Items for Academic Scrutiny

Scholars from many disciplines as well as activists and politicians have taken a great and varied interest in the efforts by some states, international agencies and international NGOs to promote democracy and human rights on the part of others. These activities have raised many questions, notably whether such initiatives are truly altruistic or more a cover for other interests, and how such a change is best brought about. The first is a question of goals and the second of strategy or means. Both are potentially contentious topics for human rights practitioners and scholars as human rights principles emphasize the rights of all human beings, not just of citizens, to participate in the decisions which affect their lives. The problem is that in practice the external agents, with their individual allegiances and mandates and their very different access to resources, frequently obscure local aspirations and minimize local capabilities. Thus development as "the process of expanding the real freedoms that people enjoy"[9] a basic goal in many development projects, can often leave a lot to be desired on the ground. Given the millions of dollars invested annually in economic and political development in low-income countries, the academy could contribute significantly through studies that showed which projects contributed best to the goal "of expanding the real freedoms that people enjoy." Once again partnerships between scholars and institutions in donor and recipient countries might result in findings that more accurately reflect the interests and perspectives of both.

In addition to democracy promotion, the language of the promotion of human rights is also often associated with other forms of external social intervention, notably

[9] Sen, Amartya, Development and Freedom, p.3. He sees development as the overall goal which "requires the removal of the major sources of unfreedom: poverty as well as tyranny, poor economic opportunities as well as systematic social deprivation, neglect of public facilities as well as intolerance or overactivity of repressive states." Ibid.

economic liberalization through open markets, economic and political development and rule of law. Unfortunately the obstacles to these projects are not just limited resources. Governments in low-income countries often see their universities as well as their local human rights NGOs as potential opposition, and the promotion of human rights and rule of law as interference in their affairs. Even a mutually agreed-upon programme can have ambiguities. Rule of law programmes, for example improving the criminal justice system, can be attractive to recipient and donor governments for quite different reasons. For the former it can be a means to maintain power and for the latter, to promote human rights and democracy. It is thus important to distinguish between the goals such as promoting human rights, the strategies chosen and the actual outcomes, latent as well as overt. Once again academics (from either recipient, donor or another country, ideally however, in partnership) are better placed to evaluate such programmes than a development agency anxious to receive its next grant.

Another intellectual challenge for scholarly human rights analysis is the relationship between the promotion and protection of human rights and the prevention of violence. This theme has its roots in the belief among the authors of the UN Charter and the Universal Declaration of Human Rights that human rights violations were one of the major causes of the two world wars. Thus one of the purposes of the UN, outlined in the preamble of its Charter is to prevent human rights violations and thus future conflagrations. This ostensibly self-evident belief has yet to be examined systematically by scholars. It is also a recurring daily problem for human rights advocates working in zones of conflict where the questions are whether, and if so, how, human rights tools can effectively prevent violent acts? Such research would address the use, functions and effectiveness of coercion, force and violence by states as well as by non-state actors.

These are but some of the intellectual challenges that could benefit from the concerted attention of scholars. They are more problem- rather than idea-driven. Each of them is an invitation to complement the human rights research and reporting that can be carried out by the major advocacy NGOs and organisations like the UN, the European Union and individual governments. They are complex situations which call for analysis and new insights beyond the capacity of the agencies on the ground.

New Thinking in Human Rights Studies

One successful problem- rather than idea-driven mobilization has come in the field of women's studies where universities around the world have created courses and research programmes, and where there are extensive sub-fields, notably woman and public health. These initiatives have resulted in a substantial intellectual and policy impact within international and domestic organisations. By identifying the ways in which ostensibly neutral or universal rights can impact negatively on a given group, this field of research and practice shows how rights meet the needs of different groups in differing ways. Women's studies has shown human rights scholars that the realization of rights, even of universal human rights, functions within, and are conditioned by, asymmetrical power structures and enact power relations that are not necessarily obvious or desired. The intellectual analysis emanating from women's studies has helped inspire writing and even normative documents examining the rights of women and children in specific contexts, such as with respect to HIV/AIDS, access to education, domestic violence, peace building, trafficking and the protection of the environment. The new approaches underlying this scholarship have implications for other areas of human rights scholarship and advocacy. In the fields of healthcare and public health, these new approaches have expanded the rights dimensions of these two fields that are hardly mentioned in the 1948 UDHR. In each case the issues reflect analyses of the role played by the claimants and the obligations on government. One important recent example of fruitful partnerships between activists, scholars, diplomats and an aggrieved group was the approval by the UN General Assembly in 2006 of the Convention on the Rights of Persons with Disabilities. More than any previous UN document, this Convention incorporates many of the insights argued for in this essay.

Following on the heels of the critiques of human rights coming from the concerns of women are new inputs beginning to come from the humanities, and especially from comparative literature where the emphasis has been to reach beyond the great, mostly European, writers recognized by traditional scholarship to integrate the work of other traditions, including especially those that interpret the experience of populations that have been subjected to human rights abuses. These groups include the colonized, the enslaved, the socially marginalized and ostracized. The net effect of this interest is to focus on the experience of the victim as both victim and as agent of his or her own redress. Another interesting movement within literary scholarship is its examination of the moral awareness of populations with respect to the abuses faced by others.[10] Why do some respond positively and others not? These questions bring us some distance from legal scholarship by raising the question of the role that victims and citizens play in the debates defining the human rights culture writ large. By bringing these other voices to the debate, the humanities can open new windows on human rights violations and on the responses or lack of response of the part of those in a position to alleviate the abuses.[11]

Human rights and the world's religions lay claim to much of the same moral territory, notably concepts of human dignity, equality and social justice. The religions are also powerful humanitarian and political forces with the means to mobilize and call upon their members to make great sacrifices. While there have always been

[10] A recent conference at the University of Connecticut illustrates a potentially new and enriching debate within the humanities. The conference entitled, "Humanitarian Responses of Narratives of Inflicted Suffering" examined among other things the political and social responses to narratives depicting human suffering and rights violations. It encouraged reflection on the language of human rights and the use and effectiveness of that language in public discourse and advocacy. It challenged researchers to be more critical/insightful with respect to the discourse that underpins current politics, including the war in Iraq and the various ongoing humanitarian crises. It did not quite ask: "Should scholars be in a better position to distinguish for their fellow citizens between spin, rhetoric, rationalization, propaganda, and deceit and sound reasoning?" A question it did address was "how does language influence responses to suffering in situations like Darfur, Chechnya, Iraq and Palestine?" The conference examined the legitimacy, strengths and weaknesses of the various messages and messengers and the ethical sensitivity of those to whom it was addressed. No publication has yet followed the conference.

[11] An example in the humanities of a writer facing oppression is Azar Nafisi see note 8 above.

scholars and politicians who have worked on religion and the state, the problems associated with religion in public life have re-asserted themselves globally with the Islamic revival. Scholarship with respect to religious freedom and freedom from religion is only just beginning to re-focus its fields of research, moving from privileging a strict separation to one that admits a blurring of those lines and significant variations from society to society. No longer is it just debating the religious roots of human rights or of maintaining a secular society as essential pre-conditions for democracy and non-discrimination. Faced especially with the growth and complexities of Islam and militant Islam in particular, scholars are examining religions, relations among them and their social impact in greater detail. The new scholarship works from the premise that religions *de facto* influence the daily lives of millions, the decisions of many political leaders, and thus the lives of many others, whether they are believers of not. This perspective looks beyond traditional liberal paradigms of separation of church and state, calling for new ways to understand religions as change agents in the public sphere. Once again, scholars in religion and the social sciences have much to offer those policymakers whose domestic and international activities seek to mitigate tensions among religious groups.

Last, but by no means least, is the relatively limited attention given by scholars to the effectiveness of the now numerous strategies employed by the human rights community to advance its goals.[12] Evaluating the many old, and devising new, strategies has so far remained within the purview of the advocacy groups, their reports and their websites. Writings on human rights NGOs have been largely descriptive.[13] Two important individual topics calling for sustained inquiry and learning from experience concerns relations between international and local NGOs, as well as between local NGOs and governments.

Human Rights Education Programmes

The leaders of human rights NGOs have long known that their work will not prosper without some support on the part of the populace as a whole. They were thus influential in persuading the UN in 1994 to launch the Decade for Human Rights Education that urged every member state to develop a national plan for the promotion of human rights. The NGOs from developing countries who lobbied for this were seeking ways to expand human rights consciousness beyond their immediate colleagues. The education called for includes the sharing and generation of knowledge about human rights, advocacy skills training and, more recently, institutional development and capacity building. This recent growth in human rights education programmes for citizens at large has, however, received little critical appraisal from academies. In low-income countries there are few programmes and most are funded and designed by ex-

[12] Outside the academy the publications of the Geneva-based International Council on Human Rights Policy have begun to sift through and consolidate human rights strategies on different topics. The Minnesota-based New Tactics in Human Rights (http://www.newtactics.org/ main.php) provides a wide range of information (training tools, materials etc.) on human rights strategies.

[13] Among the exceptions are Korey, William, NGOs and the Universal Declaration of Human Rights, NGO's, New York, Palgrave, 1998.

ternal agents. Those funded by UN agencies are administered through national governments and education systems. Their content tends to be factual and conceptual rather than useful outside the classroom in daily life. Online tests recently designed by UNESCO, for example, emphasize book knowledge and legal provisions rather than the information and skills needed to improve human rights on a day-to-day basis.[14] Nevertheless human rights education for citizens is an active field promoted by many public and private organisations. There are inevitably significant differences between those offered in low-income countries (occasional training programmes for NGOs) and in Europe and North America (curricula at virtually all levels). While it could be said that these curricula are all based on the conviction that human rights education is a necessary step towards a national human rights culture writ large, the field is diverse in terms of subject matter and teaching methodologies. Even in the most ideal circumstances, a given course or programme must exclude many more topics more than it can include. The design and content of a human rights education programme therefore impose value choices, such as the way in which it will address the human rights of women or an ethnic or religious minority, given the culture, history and practices of the surrounding society. All human rights education programmes promise and are designed on the basis of presumptive goals and outcomes. Some of these programmes in Western Europe have been evaluated professionally in terms of post-project benefits using established methodologies. Most, however, have not, suggesting one more challenge for the world's academies. Is the money being well spent? We do not know. Yet more human rights education programmes are being planned for tomorrow.[15] The lack of consolidated evaluation is especially unfortunate as it also leads to initiatives in different parts of the world ignoring one another's experiences and to spending time and resources to develop similar materials.[16] Collecting, evaluating and disseminating the worldwide trove of existing human rights teaching materials would be a significant contribution to the promotion of human rights.

Looking Forward

To promote human rights studies, the first step must be *to make the case better that human rights teaching and research can make a real difference in practice* and that investment in research and teaching is at least as beneficial an investment as in direct advocacy. The argument implied throughout this paper is that human rights research and teaching will be strongest intellectually and most effective in real life when they

[14] See: http://194.185.158.105/SCRIPT/Unesco/scripts/student/serve_new_quiz?ACTION =SHOW_QUIZ2&ARG1=2113114924. Among the forty questions: Which rights are non-derogable? In which region was the first legally binding human rights document adopted?

[15] A recent study for the United States Institute of Peace by Cole, Elizabeth A./Barsalou, Judy examined one aspect of post conflict teaching, namely the challenges of teaching history in societies emerging from violent conflict. Unite or Divide, Special Report # 163, June 2006.

[16] Groups in Thailand had already produced classroom materials on child prostitution and child labor in 1986. Teaching of Human Rights in Asia and Pacific, A Study for UNESCO, Vitit Muntarbhorn. Background paper for UNESCO Conference, Valletta, Malta August 31-September 5, 1987.

evolve in close engagement with the human rights movement and with those grappling with abuses and violations on the ground.

The next step is to identify and make the case for the strategies that result in the most beneficial outcomes. Historically, major intellectual breakthroughs have come both from major social change and from encounters between conflicting ideas and practice. For this to happen with respect to human rights in the world's academies, it is necessary to *foster more intellectual interaction among ideas, ideals and practice.* The belief that democratic structures can diminish extremism and violence needs to be tested and refined by scholars and practitioners (activists and policy makers). What are the key intervening variables? Compared to the practitioners, scholars are more likely to have the time and resources to carry out the necessary studies engagement, and sustained engagement also require that these be permanent bridges and not just occasional encounters between scholars and practitioners. A third influential constituency is the media. Given its role in mobilizing public concern and international action, it needs to be represented in the scholars' debates.

Greater engagement is needed is between *these rich/poor partnerships and the major international public organisations whose mandates call for them to address human rights.*[17] The UN, for example, organises many major peace-building operations around the world but little is seen of any evaluation of its individual projects in academic literature. In comparison with the other costs of a given mission, the small amount of funds needed for independent evaluative reports would go a long way to cost-savings in future missions. Such evaluative missions would provide an excellent context for collaboration between scholars and other experts in the north and those in the south, as well as being more likely to produce analyses that are responsive to the uniqueness of local histories, cultures and institutions. They might also create a pool of expertise that the UN could call upon when having to create a new mission.

Underlying these various issues is the belief that the academies, even if they do not have to take a stand on issues or become major social reformers, ought to be places of challenging debate and analysis, where the principles and outcomes of social policies, and in this case the various human rights paradigms, are subject to critical analysis. This is both an intellectual imperative and a social service directed not only to the needy populations but also to the media who often rely more on politicians than academics for their facts and analyses. Unfortunately, perhaps the biggest obstacle is that fact that our modern academies are intellectually fragmented and are not truly market places where broad assortments of faculty members come together regularly to debate other than in such limited fora as dissertation defences or tenure hearings. The controversies around human rights provide both intellectual drivers and

---

[17] Academies in rich and poor countries can collaborate in other ways, such as by providing short-term, in-service training for human rights leaders. The extended presence on campuses in income-poor countries of academics from the industrialized world would not only motivate and inform students with human rights interests, they would also be a stimulus to local faculty who feel, and really often are, intellectually isolated from colleagues in richer countries. Other options are internships and forms of experiential learning as integral parts of graduate or undergraduate student human rights programmes in both rich and poor countries. Again the basic principle is to bring together persons with different ideas, ideals and practices in the expectation that both will be enriched and that the gap between human rights ideals and practices will also be narrowed.

an opportunity for concrete outcomes. Depending on the location of a given institution, there is no shortage of issues; topics such as the methods used to prevent terrorism, economic rights and economic conditions, the death penalty, ethnic cleansing, torture, western bias, violence and democracy, global inequities, continuing brain drain (including human rights scholars) and development aid priorities are all relevant to scholars in both rich and poor countries. In those countries where there is strong state control of universities, these agenda may be limited, but this is where greater effort is needed on the part of the freer institutions.

My personal experience at Columbia University over the last thirty years has convinced me that the greater the engagement between faculty and students, as well as between scholars, practitioners, policy makers and the media, the greater the intellectual vitality. Thus, the growth of human rights studies will depend on creating spaces for such engagement, especially in ways that bridge the gap between the scholars, practitioners and policymakers in rich and in poor countries.

II Human Rights Education vs. Education for Democratic Citizenship, Political Education

Human Rights Education and Education for Democratic Citizenship: Competing or Complimentary Agendas?

Audrey Osler

Introduction

We can never get civil rights in America until our human rights are first restored. We will never be recognised as citizens there until we are first recognized as humans. Malcolm X, 25 August 1964[1]

Malcolm X made this claim at the climax of the civil rights struggle in the United States. Although in 1954 the Supreme Court had ruled in the pivotal *Brown v. Board of Education* that segregated schools were unconstitutional, racial segregation remained an everyday reality for American citizens in the Southern states. In July 1964, just a few weeks before Malcolm X made this statement, the Civil Rights Act was passed, which enforced the constitutional right to vote, and prohibited discrimination in public facilities, in government, and in employment. It became illegal, and therefore punishable, to continue to enforce segregation in schools, housing or in employment. The struggle for formal equality was not immediately realized, as it took some years before the powers to enforce all aspects of the new law were strengthened.

Malcolm X's statement reminds us that citizenship, and education for democratic citizenship, must be premised on recognition of our shared humanity. In those places in the United States where African Americans experienced overt and structural discrimination, recognition of shared humanity required not only legal provisions, but also, over a longer period, a cultural and emotional shift; it required a recognition among individuals in white communities that civil rights implied more than a formal legal equality. This cultural and emotional shift demands the recognition that fellow citizens, regardless of ethnicity, gender, culture, sexuality, religious or political belief, or any other difference, are also human beings, capable of feeling as we do. Our commonality is important. It extends beyond national boundaries and requires us to acknowledge a shared heritage with those we live alongside who do not share our citizenship, and to strangers in distant places. Human rights are universal and all human beings, regardless of their behaviour or even their commitment to human rights, have an equal entitlement to these rights.

The human rights project is itself a cosmopolitan one, requiring us to acknowledge, and where appropriate to defend, the dignity and rights of our fellow human beings who are characterised as members of the same 'human family'. This is made explicit in the opening sentence of the preamble of the Universal Declaration of Human

[1] Malcolm X, 'Racism: the Cancer that is Destroying America', Egyptian Gazette, 25 August 1964.

Rights: '*...recognition of the inherent dignity and of the inalienable rights of all members of the human family is the foundation of justice and peace in the world.*'[2]

During 1964, Malcolm X travelled extensively in Africa and the Middle East and these travels seem to have opened his mind to a new cosmopolitan vision. He began to situate the struggles of African Americans within the broader international struggle for the realisation of human rights for all.

I suggest, in this chapter, that such a cosmopolitan vision requires a new form of citizenship education, based on a cosmopolitan world view. I aim to examine some of the differences and similarities between programmes of human rights education (HRE) and citizenship education. I highlight some of the problems that exist in realising human rights education in schools and look at the strengths and limitations of programmes of education for democratic citizenship (EDC) as a means of realising the right to human rights education.

International and National Commitments to Human Rights Education

At the United Nations World Conference on Human Rights, held in Vienna in June 1993, representatives of 171 States adopted by consensus the *Vienna Declaration and Programme of Action*,[3] a common plan for the strengthening of human rights around the world. Over 800 non-governmental organisations (NGOs) were represented at the conference, two thirds of whom were working at grass roots level to protect human rights. The Vienna Conference thus reaffirmed the universality of human rights, recognised not only by governments, but also by the wider global community.

The *Vienna Declaration and Programme of Action* reminds us that education is at the heart of the human rights project:

States are duty-bound, as stipulated in the Universal Declaration of Human Rights and the International Covenant on Economic, Social and Cultural Rights and in other international human rights instruments, to ensure that education is aimed at strengthening the respect of human rights and fundamental freedoms. The World Conference on Human Rights emphasizes the importance of incorporating the subject of human rights education programmes and calls upon States to do so. Education should promote understanding, tolerance, peace and friendly relations between the nations and all racial or religious groups and encourage the development of United Nations activities in pursuance of these objectives. Therefore, education on human rights ... should be integrated in the education policies at the national as well as international levels.[4]

The then United Nations Secretary-General Boutros Boutros-Ghali, in a message to the World Conference, told delegates that not only had they strengthened and renewed the international community's commitment to the promotion and protection of human rights but had forged 'a new vision for global action for human rights into the next century'.[5] At the centre of this new vision is the duty of governments 'to en-

---

[2] Universal Declaration of Human Rights, adopted and proclaimed by UN General Assembly, resolution 217 A (III) 10 December 1948. http://www.un.org/Overview/rights.html.

[3] Vienna Declaration and Programme of Action, UN World Conference on Human Rights, adopted 25 June 1993, A/CONF.157/23.
http://www.unhchr.ch/huridocda/huridoca.nsf/(Symbol)/A.CONF.157.23.En

[4] Vienna Declaration and Programme of Action, loc. cit., section 1: Para 33, my emphasis.

[5] Office of the High Commissioner for Human Rights, World Conference on Human Rights 14-25 June 1993, Vienna, Austria http://www.unhchr.ch/html/menu5/wchr.htm.

sure that education is aimed at strengthening the respect of human rights and fundamental freedoms'[6] and the expectation that HRE be integrated into national education policies.

Following a proposal at the World Conference, the United Nations Decade for Human Rights Education (1995-2004) was proclaimed by the UN General Assembly on 23 December 1994.[7] During the Decade we saw progress in the global development of HRE, although it remains a long way from being at the heart of educational planning across the globe. Recognising this, on 10 December 2004 the UN General Assembly proclaimed the World Programme for Human Rights Education (2005 - ongoing)[8] to advance the implementation of HRE programmes in all sectors. The first phase of the World Programme (2005-2007) focused specifically on primary and secondary schools, with a specific Plan of Action to support this sector.

Challenges and Progress in Implementing HRE

Although a number of governments have now made substantial commitments to HRE, the task of implementing HRE into the school curriculum is one fraught with challenges. An examination of the situation in South Africa illustrates some of the difficulties that may be encountered in seeking to implement HRE policies, even when there is goodwill and relatively strong political commitment to the project.

Post-apartheid South Africa is widely recognised as having one of the most progressive constitutions in the world, designed to support 'a society based on democratic values, social justice and fundamental human rights'.[9] The advancement of human rights and freedoms is one of the founding provisions of the Republic of South Africa, as spelt out in the constitution, yet incorporating human rights education into the school curriculum has not been a straightforward or simple procedure. Rather than introduce a new curriculum subject labelled HRE or even civics, the education authorities have sought to integrate HRE and awareness of social justice into established curriculum areas. The curriculum statement for grades 1-9 states:

> *The curriculum can play a vital role in creating awareness of the relationship between human rights, a healthy environment, social justice and inclusivity. In some countries this is done through subjects such as civics. The Revised National Curriculum Statement has tried to ensure that all learning Area Statements reflect the principles and practices of social justice, respect for the environment and human rights as defined in the Constitution. In particular, the curriculum attempts to be sensitive to issues of poverty, inequality, race, gender, age, disability, and such challenges as HIV/AIDS.*[10]

---

[6] Vienna Declaration and Programme of Action, loc. cit.
[7] UN General Assembly Resolution, 49/184, 23 December, 1994
[8] UN General Assembly Resolution, 59/113, 10 December 2004. http://daccessdds.un.org/doc/UNDOC/GEN/N04/483/04/PDF/N0448304.pdf?OpenElement.
[9] Republic of South Africa, Constitution of South Africa, Preamble http://www.southafrica.info/ess_info/sa_glance/constitution/constitution.htm.
[10] Quoted in Keet, A./ Carrim, N., Human Rights Education and Curricular Reform in South Africa, Journal of Social Science Education, 2006, 1. On line at: http://www.jsse.org/2006-1/keet_carrim_s-africa.htm.

Despite the central and symbolic place which HRE has been assigned in the South African curriculum, and goodwill among curriculum planners, the challenges of developing appropriate HRE curricula which allow learners to understand and explore the relationship between human rights and the specific social justice issues facing their own communities and the nation as a whole have proved considerable. Keet and Carrim[11] argue that the absence of a coherent implementation strategy and consequent de-contextualised and ahistorical approaches to HRE have meant that learners in South African schools have not been able to access their entitlement. Efforts to infuse HRE into conventional subject disciplines have been further hindered by the complex processes of curricular reform which have been enacted in the post-apartheid era. Thus, an education in human rights, which is every young person's entitlement under the UN Convention on the Rights of the Child (CRC)[12] and which, addresses children's specific social and cultural needs, and is 'sensitive to issues of poverty, inequality, race, gender, age, disability, and such challenges as HIV/AIDS' has not yet been made available to all South African learners as a right. Notwithstanding the often complex challenges of introducing HRE, a number of governments have made significant steps forward in enabling learners to access their right to HRE. Sometimes these commitments have come about, at least in part, as the result of efforts by NGOs and committed individuals who have formed partnerships and lobbied for change. For example, in Taiwan in 1998 a group of political scientists and educators from Soochow University and Taipei Teachers' College organised a workshop to raise awareness of human rights education among teachers and teacher educators. They invited a number of international guests to speak. By 2004, following a change of government in 2000 which ended one-party rule in Taiwan, HRE was incorporated into the formal school curriculum as a subject.[13] In April of that year, the group of Taiwanese educators and activists hosted a number of conferences across the country to publicise local and international initiatives in HRE.[14] Their intention was to gain the support of school principals and politicians in implementing HRE as a newly recognised subject in the Taiwanese school curriculum. Not only did they invite their international guests back to participate and share in their success, but they also arranged a meeting between these guests and the Minister of Education. Having worked to get HRE onto the formal curriculum, the next stage was to lobby government for support and training so that teachers and school leaders will be in a position to implement HRE in Taiwanese schools. In Britain, the Education in Human Rights Network (EIHRN) was set up in 1986 to disseminate the work of the Council of Europe in the field of human rights education, in the absence of government efforts to promote HRE. A small group of educators working in teacher education and in NGOs

---

[11] Keet / Carrim, loc.cit.

[12] UN Convention on the Rights of the Child, adopted and opened for signature, ratification and accession by General Assembly resolution 44/25 of 20 November 1989, http://www.unhchr.ch/html/menu3/b/k2crc.htm.

[13] Hwang, K-K., Introducing Human Rights Education in the Confucian Society of Taiwan: its Implications for Ethical Leadership in Education, International Journal of Leadership in Education, 4 (1) 2001 , pp. 321-332.

[14] Osler, A. 'Preface', in: Osler, A. (ed.) Teachers, Human Rights and Diversity: Educating Citizens in Multicultural Societies, 2005, xv-xxiii.

met twice a year to share good practice and to build up support for this work. I was a member of this group. We began by organising a human rights fair and followed this with a series of conferences and other activities over a period of some fifteen years.

In 1998, again following a change of government, draft proposals were published to introduce citizenship education to schools in England. There was no mention of human rights in the draft report. EIHRN lobbied the Chair of the government-appointed working group, Bernard Crick, responsible for drafting the report. We invited him to a conference on Human Rights and Democracy in Schools, where we argued that human rights principles should underpin the citizenship curriculum. At the same time the UK Economic and Social Research Council (ESRC) sponsored a series of seminars at which scholars and other interested parties, including members of the EIHRN, were able to explore in greater depth the significance of HRE for UK schools.[15] Following this process of lobbying, the final report of the citizenship working group, while not placing human rights at the heart of the new proposals for citizenship education in England, acknowledged that students should learn about key human rights documents.[16]

Education for Democratic Citizenship, Shared Values and the Needs of Minorities

Over the past decade there has been a considerable growth in interest in education for democratic citizenship (EDC) from both nation-states and from a range of international organisations, including UNESCO, the Council of Europe, and the Organisation for Economic Cooperation and Development (OECD). A review of research literature and official policy documents has identified six key contextual factors which go some way to explaining this growth in interest, namely: concern about global injustice and inequality (linked, since 2001, to concerns about global security and terrorism), processes of globalization and migration and their impact on local communities and schools, concerns about levels of civic and political engagement, a perceived youth deficit, the end of the cold war and anti-democratic and racist movements.[17]

Following the work of the Council of Europe, there is a growing recognition of human rights as the underpinning principles of EDC at the level of the nation-state. Human rights were identified as one of 4 key principles (along with diversity and unity, global inter-connectedness and experience and participation) which an international consensus panel convened at the University of Washington's Centre for Multicultural Education argued should underpin citizenship education programmes in contexts of diversity and in our global age.[18] Human rights principles tend to be explicit in the EDC programmes of newly democratised states, such as those of Latin Ameri-

---

[15] Qualifications and Curriculum Authority, Education for Citizenship and the Teaching of Democracy in Schools (Crick Report), 1998.

[16] Osler, A., Citizenship and Democracy in Schools: Diversity, Identity, Equality, 2000.

[17] Osler, A./ Starkey, H., Education for Democratic Citizenship: a Review of Research, Policy and Practice 1995-2005, Research Papers in Education, 21(4), 2006, pp.433-466.

[18] Banks , J.A. et al,. Democracy and Diversity; Principles and Concepts for Educating Citizens in a Global Age, 2005.

ca and of eastern and central Europe and (as our recent European Commission-funded transnational research project INTERACT indicates) in countries such a Spain and Portugal, which experienced a period of dictatorship during the latter half of the twentieth century.[19]

However, not all countries make explicit the values base underpinning EDC. Britain, for example, does not acknowledge human rights as the values base for citizenship education within the National Curriculum for England. Indeed, recent media debates have tended to focus on the need to emphasise British values and Britishness as part of the preparation of young people for living together in a society characterised by ethnic diversity.[20] These debates have been particularly strong following the terrorist bombings of London on 7 July 2005. In December 2006, the then Prime Minister Tony Blair identified British values as 'belief in democracy, the rule of law, tolerance, equal treatment for all'.[21] Earlier the same year Gordon Brown gave a widely reported speech on 'The future of Britishness' in which he listed shared British values as 'liberty, responsibility, fairness'.[22] Citizens of other nations might well ask, as have many British citizens, what is peculiarly British about these values? They are in keeping with international human rights principles and might be the expressed values of any modern democracy.

The processes of introducing and implementing citizenship education into the National Curriculum for England provide us with an interesting case study of how EDC may neglect the specific needs and interest of minorities. My own analysis of the Crick Report on EDC in England, *Education for Citizenship and the teaching of democracy in Schools*[23] suggests that the images and understandings of multiculturalism within this official document are problematic and that the ways in which it deals with questions of difference, equality and justice are inadequate.[24] A key aim of any programme of citizenship must be to enable young people to understand the barriers to citizenship, including that of racism, and equip them with the skills to challenge and overcome such barriers.

Yet the Crick Report adopts terminology which reflects a lack of familiarity with the everyday realities of multicultural Britain. For example, it refers to the

---

[19] For more information see the INTERACT homepage:
http://www.education.leeds.ac.uk/research/cchre/projects.php?project=66&page=1
http://www.ces.fe.uc.pt/interact/workstatus.htm.

[20] In 2005 the government ordered a review which set out to examine ways in which diversity might be addressed within the citizenship curriculum and the role of British history in teaching for citizenship. Department for Education and Skills, Curriculum Review: Diversity and Citizenship (Ajegbo Report) PPSLS/D35/0107/14.

[21] Tony Blair 'Our Nation's Future: Multiculturalism and Integration', speech given at 10 Downing Street, 8 December 2006. http://www.education.leeds.ac.uk/research/files/31.pdf.
See for the full text of this speech http://www.number10.gov.uk/output/Page10563.asp.

[22] Brown, Gordon 'Who do We Want to Be? The Future of Britishness' speech given to the Fabian Society, 16 January 2006.
http://fabians.org.uk/events/new-year-conference-06/brownbritishness/speech.

[23] Qualifications and Curriculum Authority, op. cit.

[24] Osler, A. 'The Crick Report: Difference, Equality and Racial Justice', The Curriculum Journal, 11 (1), 2000, pp. 25-37.

'homelands of our minority communities'[25] a phrase which is not only patronising in tone but which effectively serves to question and even undermine the Britishness of students of colour and their right to identify with Britain as their home country. Hybrid and multiple identities mean that many students at school in England, and not just those from visible minority communities, are able to identify with a number of places, including Britain, but also with their locality and often other countries with which their families have a direct link.[26]

The language of the Crick Report also reveals some negative stereotyping of minority communities within Britain. For example, it states:

Majorities must respect, understand and tolerate minorities and minorities must learn to respect the laws, codes and conventions as much as the majority – not because it is useful to do so, but because this process helps foster common citizenship.[27]

According to those who drafted the report, one of the keys to a successful multicultural society is tolerance. But this tolerance is seen as a one-way process; majority society's norms are left unquestioned. There is no recognition that minorities are also exercising tolerance in living alongside a supposedly homogeneous majority. The behaviours, cultures and values of this majority community are taken as standard. This is not a model of multiculturalism where we all learn to live together and in which these processes of learning are seen as enriching, but one in which difference remains problematic, even as it is tolerated. Tolerance, by all parties, may be an essential first step towards the development of a multicultural society and the development of a multicultural form of citizenship, but it is unlikely to be a sufficient requirement. It needs to be balanced by guarantees of equality of rights, and the absence of discrimination not just at the level of inter-personal relationships but also within the structures of government at national, local and community levels, in the workplace and in key services such as housing and health.

The second part of the above quotation also presents some difficulties. Minorities are asked to 'learn and respect the laws codes and conventions' of British society. It is not clear whether minorities are perceived to have cultures and values at odds with the laws and conventions or whether they have not yet been socialised into these conventions, perhaps because they are recent migrants. There is no statistical or other evidence which suggests that individuals from minority communities break the law more often than do individuals from majority communities? However we seek to explain these references to 'minorities', it is apparent that, from the perspective of those drafting the report, minorities are seen as 'other' and that these minorities suffer from a deficit.

---

[25] Qualifications and Curriculum Authority, op.cit. p. 30. Interestingly, research by Jessica Pykett, which included interviews with members of the Crick committee, revealed a desire among those involved to play down the political implications and assumptions of the report, with one member even denying the use of this phrase 'homelands of our ethnic minorities'. See Pykett, 'Making Citizens Governable? The Crick Report as Governmental technology' Journal of Education Policy, 22(3), 2007, pp. 301-319.

[26] See Osler, A./ Starkey, H., Learning for cosmopolitan citizenship: theoretical debates and young people's experiences, Educational Review, 55 (3), 2003, pp. 243-254 and Osler, A./ Starkey, H., Changing Citizenship: democracy and inclusion in education, 2005.

[27] Qualifications and Curriculum Authority op. cit., 3.16. pp. 17-18.

Bernard Crick has defended the report against criticisms that it fails to address racism as a barrier to citizenship, arguing that explicitly anti-racist approaches are likely to be 'inflammatory – just what the racist white lads will look forward to in a classroom discussion'.[28] Crick wishes to promote free and equal citizenship, yet it is not clear how this will be achieved if we are unable to engage directly with racism as a barrier to equal citizenship, examine ways in which it serves to deny citizenship, and identify strategies for overcoming it. Thus government support for EDC does not necessarily mean that the needs of minorities will be met or that students from all backgrounds will be provided with skills to challenge the inequalities and discrimination which hinder the full citizenship and participation of many from minority communities.

Rights To, In and Through Education

Government support for EDC does not necessarily guarantee that children or adult learners will be able to access HRE, which is a right guaranteed in Article 26 of the Universal Declaration of Human Rights (UDHR) and which has later been repeatedly confirmed in binding legislation, as for example, in Article 13 of the International Covenant on Social and Cultural Rights 1966.[29] The CRC identifies, in its Article 29, detailed provisions of the right to education, including an education in human rights:

> 1. States Parties agree that the education of the child shall be directed to:
> (a) The development of the child's personality, talents and mental and physical abilities to their fullest potential;
> (b) The development of respect for human rights and fundamental freedoms, and for the principles enshrined in the Charter of the United Nations;
> (c) The development of respect for the child's parents, his or her own cultural identity, language and values, for the national values of the country in which the child is living, the country from which he or she may originate, and for civilizations different from his or her own;
> (d) The preparation of the child for responsible life in a free society, in the spirit of understanding, peace, tolerance, equality of sexes, and friendship among all peoples, ethnic, national and religious groups and persons of indigenous origin;
> (e) The development of respect for the natural environment.[30]

This implies not only the right *to* education, but rights *in* education and rights *through* education.[31] All children, including children from minority communities, are equally entitled to a quality education which enables them to achieve their 'fullest potential'. The principle of non-discrimination implies that the nation-state has taken adequate steps to prevent school drop-out and to address problems such as truancy and exclu-

---

[28] Crick, B., Friendly Arguments, in Essays on Citizenship, 2000.

[29] UN General Assembly, International Covenant on Economic, Social and Cultural Rights, adopted by resolution 2200A (XXI) of 16 December 1966 http://www.unhchr.ch/html/menu3/b/a_cescr.htm.

[30] UN Convention on the Rights of the Child, loc.cit.

[31] Verhellen, E., Children's Rights and Education, in: A. Osler (Ed.) Citizenship and Democracy in Schools: Diversity, Identity, Equality. 2000, pp. 33-43.

sion from school. So, for example, evidence of differential exclusion rates between children from different ethnic groups[32] and differentials in examination outcomes between these groups,[33] are key human rights issues relating to the right *to* education.

School exclusion also undermines rights *through* education, that is to say, it threatens access to an education in human rights. Rights in education include the right of the student to participate and to be consulted in school processes and decision-making, which implies the introduction of democratic structures and basic legal provisions to guarantee learner participation.[34] It can be seen that the development of EDC within curricular frameworks provides an opportunity for the development of HRE or rights through education, but that such initiatives need to be matched by policy developments and legal safeguards which also protect children's right *to* education and rights *in* education. These safeguards are critical when considering the needs of children from minority groups, who in many contexts experience some difficulties in accessing these rights.

Some Challenges Facing Human Rights Educators

The Council of Europe has not always distinguished between education for democratic citizenship and human rights education; the unspoken assumption is that they cover the same core ground and both are concerned with strengthening human rights and democracy. Yet, in practice, programmes of EDC and HRE may differ considerably in the ways in which they characterise the relationship between the individual and the nation-state. It is this issue which I believe needs to be addressed if EDC is to be an effective vehicle for human rights education. I have already discussed how EDC may fail to address the needs of learners from minority groups on the basis of equality, and how it is not guaranteed that such programmes will necessarily prioritise the dismantling of barriers to full citizenship for minority citizens - something which I would argue is a key responsibility of all, regardless of whether they are themselves from a minority group or from the mainstream.

One serious limitation of citizenship education programmes as a vehicle for HRE is that they do not generally encourage learners to be critical of government. National programmes of citizenship education may have, as one of their goals, the encouragement of allegiance to the nation-state and a sense of patriotism. Our research suggests that teachers in England may feel uncomfortable with such an approach, and may wish to avoid reference to national symbols, such as the national anthem or the flag.[35] Nevertheless, regardless of national contexts teachers need to remember that:

---

[32] See, for example, Osler, A./ Hill, J., 'Exclusion from School and Racial Equality: an Examination of Government Proposals in the Light of Recent Research Evidence', Cambridge Journal of Education, 29 (1), 1999, pp.33-62, and Osler, A./ Vincent, K., Girls and Exclusion: Re-thinking the Agenda, 2003.

[33] Tikly et al., 'The Ethnic Minority Achievement Grant: a Critical Analysis', Journal of Education Policy, 20 (3), 2005, pp. 283-312.

[34] Osler, A./ Vincent, K., Citizenship and the Challenge of Global Education, 2002.

[35] For further details on our projects, see http://www.education.leeds.ac.uk

Patriotism is a double edged sword ... The accusation of 'unpatriotic behaviour' can intimidate teachers and students into self-censorship. They may bow to conformist pressure from powerful media, clergymen and the government as to what is legitimate and what is out of bounds. (...) To guard against abuses of patriotism, teachers should emphasize critical patriotism. This approach eschews the irrational 'My country, right or wrong!' Critical patriotism encourages reasoned loyalty; pride in the 'rights' of the nation alongside a commitment to correct its 'wrongs'.[36]

Our research suggests that in France, programmes of civic education are more likely to encourage this critical assessment of certain aspects of national policy. For example, civics courses address the right of workers to strike and to take action against policies of which they disapprove. By contrast, it is inconceivable that learners in England would be presented with an official programme of study in which the right to strike would be emphasised.[37] One analysis of the citizenship education initiative in England, based on interviews with the Crick committee, examines how efforts to erase politics from policy-making risks placing citizenship education policy beyond political critique.[38] There is a danger that subsequent interpretations of citizenship education policy may encourage processes of teaching and learning which foster compliance rather than critical thinking.

One key difference between HRE programmes and citizenship education is that effective human rights education necessarily requires learners to be made aware of the need to hold governments to account. Governments are responsible for securing our human rights. While we may only be able to claim our rights if others are prepared to defend them, we should not see human rights as an exclusive contract between individuals. Some HRE programmes in schools might be criticised for placing too much emphasis on the responsibilities we owe to each other (horizontal ties) and insufficient attention to the responsibilities which nation-states have towards their citizens and towards others living under their jurisdiction. So, for example, a programme which encourages young people to address bullying, stressing the need of young people to look after each other's interests, is emphasising the horizontal obligations of citizens to defend each others' rights. If the programme fails to explain how specific forms of bullying are abuses of human rights and how the law has been developed to protect the individual from such abuse; how teachers, schools and other agencies have specific legal duties to protect young people from racist, sexist or homophobic bullying; and that failure to protect young people leaves authorities open to processes of legal redress; such a programme would be ignoring the duties of the State to protect and guarantee rights.

As we have seen, governments have an obligation to ensure that the promotion of human rights is a key educational goal, with the requirement that HRE be integrated into national education policies. Across Europe, it would appear that the most common response among governments to ensuring that HRE is a part of the formal school curriculum is to integrate human rights into the citizenship curriculum. Yet, as Verhellen points out:

---

research/cchre/projects.php?project=66&page=1.

36 Banks , J. A. et al., op. cit., 2005.

37 Osler, A. / Starkey, H., 'Citizenship Education and National Identities in France and England: Inclusive or Exclusive?', Oxford Review of Education, 27 (2), 2001, pp. 287–305.

38 Pykett, J., loc. cit.

Spending an occasional hour or two on the subject of children's rights in schools would clearly fall short of the obligation States Parties have taken upon themselves. Essentially, there has to be a shift in fundamental attitudes on respect for children's rights. Theoretical teaching on the values of human rights and democracy serves little purpose if these values are not also put into practice.[39]

If EDC is to be the vehicle for HRE then human rights, or children's rights, cannot simply be another topic within an overcrowded citizenship education programme. Human rights principles need to underpin both the content and the practice of citizenship teaching and learning. As the quote from Malcolm X, which introduced this chapter, reminds us, citizenship and education for democratic citizenship must be premised on recognition of our shared humanity. This implies a cosmopolitan approach in which EDC is extended so that learners are able to develop a vision of an interdependence in which they recognise their common interests and interdependence with others, in their local communities, the nation and the world. It requires recognition of the strengths of cosmopolitan and diverse communities as an asset to democracy, as practiced at local and national levels. It is through engaging with difference at these levels that democratic practices will be strengthened and renewed. After all, it is difficult to see the point of practising democracy and democratic dialogue if we all agree, and have no differences to resolve. The human rights project is a cosmopolitan one, in which nationality and citizenship are not privileged over our common humanity. This vision of our shared humanity and of our interdependent world is at the heart of the theory of education for cosmopolitan citizenship which we have been developing.[40] Education for cosmopolitan citizenship, which is underpinned by human rights and which emphasises our shared humanity is a potentially powerful framework and model enabling governments to meet their obligations in ensuring the promotion of human rights as a key educational goal.

The basic concepts of human rights (from Starkey, 1992)

[39] Verhellen, E., loc. cit., p. 42.
[40] Osler, A./ Starkey, H., 2003 loc. cit., and Osler, A./Starkey, H., Changing Citizenship: Democracy and Inclusion in Education, 2005.

Turning Walls into Doors: Challenges and Opportunities for Human Rights Education

Carolyn Kissane

Introduction

I titled this article, Turning Walls into Doors to highlight the tension between the great strides taken to expand human rights education around the world, and the gradualness of moving human rights education out of the periphery and into the forefront of educational policy across the curriculum, both at the informal and formal levels of schooling.[1] For over half a century human rights activists and advocates have sought to promote and improve human rights through advocacy and by working tirelessly to improve human rights through education. Some people question the urgency of pushing human rights education, especially when so many other educational problems exist in the world. Why should we care about promoting human rights education? The reasons, of course, are many, and the imperative behind human rights education is that it ultimately falls within our obligations as humans to protect, promote and actively work to secure human rights for all. Addressing and expanding human rights education is one important way of improving society; where human rights education exists there are greater opportunities for full rather than exclusionary citizenry participation and the presence of a more vibrant and active civil society. This answer I believe is illustrative of why the work of the UN Decade of Human Rights Education was so critical to addressing the need to support human rights education, and also why we must continue to advocate higher level policy change, follow through on policy implementation and support grassroots efforts.

This article aims to highlight the challenges of human rights education, and also the new opportunities that are emerging as a result of the amazing and courageous work of so many who have pushed human rights education onto the forefront of educational conversations and practice. The first section addresses the complex issue of defining human rights education, and then moves into an overview of the challenges and opportunities facing human rights education today. The region of central Asia is presented as a snapshot look to highlight the incredible challenges associated with moving human rights education policy onto the agenda in countries which are slowly beginning to understand human rights both in theory and practice. The purpose of including this region in the chapter is to illustrate the continuing challenges facing human rights activists and advocates in countries where rule of law, freedom of the media and respect for civil and political rights are weak or non-existent. Authoritarian countries which both regularly disregard and threaten human rights are particularly glaring examples of the obstacles to getting human rights education into schools and into the higher policy level discourse. Finally, the chapter provides a brief summary of a sampling of standout human rights education programmes that are

[1] Formal schooling refers to primary, secondary and tertiary education, while informal refers to education in settings outside of any official school system (public or private). Settings such as community associations, cultural forums and non-formal workshops and training fall under the category of informal schooling.

setting new standards and pushing boundaries towards greater inclusion of human rights throughout different areas of education.

Supporting Initiatives

Since the signing of the Universal Declaration of Human Rights in 1948, human rights education has been a right deemed vital to human beings.[2] More recently, and several decades later, there were two intergovernmental frameworks created to move forward with the work started with the ratification of the UDHR. The UN Decade for Human Rights Education (1995-2004) represented the first attempt to promote human rights education on a broad and systematic scale. Governments established national committees for human rights education and some went on to develop national plans of action for the implementation of human rights education. The UN Decade for Human Rights Education brought advocates, practitioners, governments and non-governmental organisations together to work towards expanding human rights education. The decade was pivotal for moving HRE beyond rhetoric and into more widespread practice across the globe. In addition to drawing attention to human rights and the need to further advance educational initiatives, it also focused necessary funding into programmes and projects. Governments, intergovernmental organisations, non-governmental organisations, private foundations and individuals all made important financial contributions to the success of the decade. UN decades are critical for bringing people together under a common banner, but there is also the unfortunate reality that funding cycles do not usually allow for long term investments. Many organisations that launched programmes during the UN Decade are struggling for resources and support. The second framework commenced in 2004 when the General Assembly of the United Nations announced the World Programme for Human Rights Education (2005-ongoing). The UN World Programme seeks to advance the implementation of human rights education programmes that developed momentum during the HRE decade. The UN World Programme for HRE seeks to promote understanding of the basic principles and methodologies of teaching human rights, and to provide a more concrete framework and plan of action, and to do more to forge critical cooperative partnerships from the international to the grassroots level. A vital challenge for both of these UN driven initiatives is to achieve the effective sustainability of what has been done to date.

Framing Human Rights Education

Let us first examine the definition and purpose of human rights education. A human rights education perspective places a categorical priority on the internationally defined standards of human dignity and social justice as encapsulated in the Universal

[2] Article 26, paragraph 2 of the UDHR states that Education shall be directed to the full development of the human personality and to the strengthening of respect for human rights and fundamental freedoms. It shall promote understanding, tolerance and friendship among all nations, racial or religious groups, and shall further the activities of the United Nations for the maintenance of peace.

Declaration of Human Rights. It is based on the premise that states undertake legal obligations to protect the human rights of all those living within their borders. International human rights standards are conceived as an interrelated, complex web of universal rights, namely civil, political, economic, social and cultural. States are obliged to integrate these rights into social policy at all levels; the human rights movement identifies and advocates for those human beings suffering from the violation of those standards and who are unable to help themselves; the international human rights system is used as a primary tool in advocacy, the enforcement of legal obligations on states and builds international advocacy alliances among governments, international organisations and civil society.

I view the international consensus represented in the Universal Declaration of Human Rights and its associated treaties as the most widely accepted normative code of social justice.[3] This definition however, is not definitive or static. International human rights are an evolving field with the possibility and scope for change and improvement in norms and practice. The present diversity and major debates within the field of human rights make it important to define what are, and what are not, human rights. This is made possible through education.

Defining human rights education is important for the effective implementation and evaluation of programming. According to Amnesty International, "Human Rights Education (HRE) is a deliberate, participatory practice aimed at empowering individuals, groups and communities through fostering knowledge, skills and attitudes consistent with internationally recognized human rights principles."[4] The organisation also highlights the importance of teaching human rights as a necessary means of increasing respect and the promotion and defense of human rights. The World Programme, Plan of Action for Human Rights Education defines HRE as, "education, training, and information aimed at building a universal culture of human rights."[5] Felissa Tibbits, Director of Human Rights Education Associates (HREA) and a vocal advocate and prolific writer on human rights spoke before a U.S. Congressional Human Rights Caucus in February 2007, and drew attention to the demand for human rights education materials and training by pointing out that, "her organisation alone has provided training for over one thousand human rights defenders from 75 countries and that over 1.6 million training documents were downloaded from the HREA website in 2006."[6] Ten or twenty years ago these numbers would not have been as high, and the rapid increase in demand for resources is a testament to the incredible will on the part of many educators around the world to push the teaching of human rights into their professional practice. Human Rights Education Associates

[3] The Universal Declaration of Human Rights and other relevant documents are available at: http://www.ccnmtl.columbia.edu/projects/mmt/udhr/ and Office of the High Commissioner for Human Rights, Geneva: http://www.unhcr.ch.html/intlinst.htm. Educators and programme planners can also obtain materials related to core content in J. Paul Martin, 25+Human Rights Documents. New York: Center for the Study of Human Rights 2001.

[4] Amnesty International, "What is Human Rights Education?" http://web.amnesty.org/pages/hre-intro-eng .

[5] World Programme for Human Rights Education (2005-ongoing). http://www.ohchr.org/english/issues/education/training/docs/planaction-inbrief.pdf.

[6] HREA Director testifies before U.S. Congressional Human Rights Caucus" hrea.org http://www.hrea.org/US-Congress-testimory-Feb-2007.html.

also argues that, "education about human rights is closely related to the right to education. International and human rights noted in various documents (declarations, resolutions, and conventions) emphasize that the knowledge of human rights should be a priority in educational policies."[7] Many school systems do not or cannot formally support human rights education and rely on the work of nongovernmental organisations and other organisations and institutions dedicated to supporting human rights who are vital partners both in and out of the classroom.

Challenges and Opportunities

Today, more international laws protect and promote human rights, yet, even with these laws, norms and campaigns in place, and (at least on paper) with the rhetorical support and official ratification by governments, there is still a great deal of disagreement over how to engrain human rights concepts. This represents just one area of difficulty in promoting more expansive and inclusive human rights education. Mary Robinson, former United Nations High Commissioner on Human Rights, commented, "Making the language and approach of human rights accessible to wider audiences has proven difficult. Problems of precision in how human rights standards can be applied in different situations remain."[8]

A challenge facing educators is the lack of attention and basic understanding of human rights that exists amongst populations that have not received exposure to human rights issues. In the United States, a national poll inquiring about the level of knowledge of the Declaration of Human Rights, demonstrated that, "only about 8 percent of the American population was even aware of the existence of this foundational document, let alone its contents."[9] This dismal statistic begs for attention and action and requires much greater participation from the government. There are many individual organisations working in the area of human rights education in the United States, but the government does not always match the rhetoric of support for human rights with actual practice. While governments may indicate verbal support and may even develop special commissions and departments dedicated to human rights, there are often obvious violations of human rights on the parts of these same governments, making it hard to determine the sincerity of their commitment.

In formal education, human rights education might often be part of the civic or social studies curricula at primary or secondary levels. At university level, it typically takes the form of courses in law, the social sciences and humanities such as international organisation, law, women's rights and theories of rights, and international human rights in global affairs to name but a few. There are certain common principles based on the unique content and characteristics of human rights education. Human rights education differs from most other traditional classroom subjects because of the issues it covers, its substantial normative content and the resulting dependence on the

---

[7] Study Guides: The Right to Education: Human Rights Education Associates. Pp. 1-9. http://www.hrea.org/learn/guides/right-to-education.html.

[8] Robinson, Mary."Advancing Economic, Social, and Cultural Rights: The Way Forward". Human Rights Quarterly: 2004. Vol. 26. p. 168.

[9] HREA Director testifies before U.S. Congressional Human Rights Caucus, 19 Feb. 2007.

complexities of both moral and legal obligations. As David Suarez in his examination of human rights education in Latin America and the Caribbean explains, *"as a curricular reform, human rights education is expanding and struggling to become institutionalized in national education systems... Despite the obstacles facing human rights education, such curricular reforms now have made considerable inroads."*[10]

In his work he also explains how both domestic advocacy and the international human rights movement have helped to accelerate these developments.

Today, a critical focus is that of funding and the evaluation of on-going programmes. Without funding for project implementation and evaluation many projects never get off the ground remaining ideas only, and in order to increase the sustainability of previously implemented programmes, schools and organisations need to have secure funding in place, which can at times seem like a Herculean effort. In many developing countries, funding for programmes comes from abroad largely in the form of European, American and private development funds and philanthropic assistance. Examples of this include funding from the Ford Foundation, Soros, as well as the European Union, USAID and others. Advocates struggle to get national governments to do more in the area of committing financial and material resources for in-country (HRE) programmes. Greater resources are required in order to expand HRE content, materials development, teacher training, participatory development methods and partnerships to accomplish the desired goals of sustainability, as well as to institutionalize grassroots and higher level efforts towards improving human rights education in classrooms throughout the developed and developing world.

As HRE expands in schools as well as within advocacy organisations, it is important to increase evaluation capacity and to see it as an integral part of any programme and not an isolated activity.[11] Formal evaluation offers the opportunity to assess the educational objectives and goals of HRE programmes for the purposes of future curriculum development, planning, policy-making and resource allocation. As evaluations are performed and made public, the results will provide the basis needed for more comprehensive research on HRE and on how they are best designed, implemented and sustained.[12] HRE is multi-pronged and is therefore more complicated than most types of evaluation because of the difficulty of determining if learning is applied outside of the classroom. Assessing the societal (out-of-classroom) impact of a given human rights programme requires a more substantial social science methodology. Cause-effect relationships are difficult to establish and there are many more, out-of-classroom factors at work. To date, research on evaluating human rights programmes is limited. However, it is possible to assess effectiveness through the types of initiatives students involve themselves in outside of the classroom. A new area of human rights education is connecting content taught in the classroom to service learning in the community. Another evaluation approach is to build in an action research component into the class or programme. This involves equipping students with basic

[10] Suarez, David, "Human Rights and Curricular Policy in Latin America and the Caribbean," in Comparative Education Review, vol. 51, no. 3, pp. 1-18.

[11] Wandersman, A. Imm, P., Chinman, M., and Kaftarian, S., "Getting to outcomes: A results-based approach to accountability." Evaluation and Program Planning 23 (2000), pp. 389–395.

[12] For an evaluation of a Women for Women's Human Rights Program please see http://www.wwhr.org/id_843.

research skills and asking them to design a human rights research project where they can perform 'in class' and 'out of class research'. Before the start of the research a basic survey of human rights knowledge and understanding can be conducted, and following the completion of the action research, students can be re-evaluated for a more enhanced understanding and practical knowledge of the promotion and practice of human rights in action.

Challenges for educators committed to human rights are especially large for those working in environments where there exists either limited or no space for human rights education, debate and practice. There are regimes in the world which completely ignore the rights of its citizens and where there is no recourse against human rights violations because the government makes it impossible to challenge the will of the state. One such place is Turkmenistan, a former Soviet Socialist Republic, which emerged as an independent state in 1991. Its trajectory since 1991 has been one of growing repression and rampant disregard for safeguarding the rights of its citizens. Turkmenistan is used here as a part of a larger regional case to illustrate the grave challenges faced by educators and human rights promoters in countries which do not support an environment for human rights education to exist alongside an oppressive state.

Human Rights Education: Central Asia in Focus

The central Eurasian region is engaged in a difficult process of transition, renewal, and redefinition. The former Soviet Socialist Republics of Kazakhstan, Kyrgyzstan, Tajikistan, Turkmenistan and Uzbekistan provide provocative cases from which to examine the relationship between political transition and its impact on the access to and promotion of human rights education. The year 1991 marked a significant shift for the region, when each of the five republics which had formerly existed as part of the larger Soviet Union became independent. At the time of writing, sixteen years into the "post-Communist transition" open society is still not a term that would aptly describe the current political or societal landscape of the countries under study. The former Soviet system has disintegrated in name only; many of the same structures remain in place, and this is especially true in the area of education.

Regional Educational Snapshot

	HDI[13]	GER	Expenditure on Education (Yr. 2005) (% of GDP)	Freedom in the World (2006)
Kazakhstan	80	85	3.4	Not free
Kyrgyzstan	102	79	3.1	Partly Free
Tajikistan	122	71	2.4	Not Free
Turkmenistan	87	81	*	Not Free
Uzbekistan	111	76	6.4	Not Free

According to the Freedom House Survey, Freedom in the World, not one of the five republics is considered to be free and all illustrate a very poor record in the area of civil liberties and political rights (Freedom in the World 2005). Data from four of the five countries under scrutiny show a decline in government expenditure on education as a percentage of GDP and the Freedom in the World rankings indicate weak to non-existent civil societies, as well as the continuation of authoritarian governments. The table above, though not specifically addressing human rights or human rights education in the region, indicates the challenges of implementing a human rights education programme in a region devoting fewer resources to education, and with governments that aim to impede citizen participation.

A look at the worst performing country in the region, with the most difficult challenges facing education and human rights advocates, provides a better understanding of the unique challenges of human rights education in an almost closed society. It is quite difficult to imagine the societal landscape that is present-day Turkmenistan. The country and its policies challenge all rationality and warrant serious attention by the international community. The Open Society Institute & Soros Foundation network and other NGOs including Human Rights Watch and Amnesty International monitor the deteriorating economic, political and social conditions in the country, admit that the republic is intentionally debilitating a whole generation of people who are being denied their rights to an education and basic health care, and are having their human rights all but disregarded in both theory and practice. In 1991 the educational system was a good one; and though not at the level of Russia, it did boast a literacy rate above 90% and an established programme of higher education. Today, the literacy level is falling sharply, schools are closing, and teachers are required to devote 15 minutes of every lesson, whether the subject is science or the arts, to reading one book, Turkmenbashi's *Rukhnama.*

The situation in Turkmenistan is one example of an educational landscape that has been confronted with a forced drought in terms of access to human rights education and any type of programming allowing citizens access to information. The government has, in effect, stifled all progress and movement for change, but there is hope that with a new government and increased access to other parts of the world the peo-

[13] HDI – United Nations Human Development Index: http://hdr.undp.org/hdr2006/statistics/.

ple will experience more positive developments in the future. The movement for human rights education is prohibited from mobilizing in Turkmenistan but there are more positive examples of active human rights training and education in other areas of the region, such as in Kyrgyzstan and to a lesser extent in Kazakhstan. In these two countries, activists, though threatened by both governments, have been working to tilt the balance towards greater awareness of human rights and to utilize the international human rights community to support their work and the more active integration of human rights education into different areas of education.

Human Rights Education: A Movement for Positive Change

It is true that the challenges confronting human rights education's expansion may seem daunting. Though formidable obstacles remain in increasing access to human rights education and training, the situation should not arouse pessimism. Instead, we must acknowledge the great strides taken over the last twenty years, and gauge the incredible increase in opportunities for people to engage themselves in human rights issues. Whereas at the start of the human rights movements it would have been hard to imagine having the opportunity to specialize in human rights at the undergraduate or master's level, today it is possible to find human rights concentrations and degrees in universities in many different parts of the world. When one of the world's most active advocates for human rights education, Dr. Paul Martin, launched the Center for Human Rights at Columbia University it was a struggle to get support for courses, but today, due to Professor Martin's extraordinary accomplishments introducing human rights courses into the curriculum, and establishing an advocacy programme that brings human rights activists from around the world to learn about programming and fundraising, Columbia offers not only classes but also specializations in human rights education, law and advocacy. The demand for more courses only gets greater each year, and this is true not just for Columbia University but also for New York University where I teach, and other universities around the world.

The demand for more human rights education is coming from many directions. Students with exposure to human rights education are better informed to understand the complex dynamics of our world and are also better equipped to change it for the better. They also understand the practical realities and imperatives of understanding human rights. Regardless of the area of work, human rights are today part of the dialogue. The discourse has changed, and today whether we speak of multinational corporations, nongovernmental organisations, governments, and other individual sectors, the issue of human rights is part of a broader set of issues that are being integrated into more international working norms. It is therefore crucial to expand opportunities within and beyond human rights education and for human rights education to be further integrated into the curriculum at the secondary and tertiary levels, as well as within government and nongovernmental agencies that can wield effective influence over educational policy and ultimately to permanently establish human rights education into the mainstream of educational programming in both theory and practice. These types of changes and the movement towards greater opportunity at all levels of education to learn about and from human rights cannot be underestimated and is a testament to the demands from international and grassroots level for more exposure to human rights language, laws, and practice.

Conclusion

Vernor Munoz, UN Special Rapporteur on the Right to Education expresses the view that, "human rights education is an integral part of the right to education".[14] An ongoing challenge for educators and activists is to make this statement a reality across the globe. As noted in the introduction, in comparison to two decades ago, human rights education has come a long way, but it still has a long way to go in order for students in Turkmenistan as well as in the more developed parts of the world to have the opportunity to study and understand human rights as a part of the core curriculum.

The observation of Richard E. Neustadt and Ernest May, "that the future has no place to come from but the past, hence the past has predictive value,"[15] is both true and false when thinking about human rights education. Today, an array of human rights education programmes exist in many parts of the world which were not as available or known to people outside of the human rights education community two or more decades ago. However, we are still grappling with the crimes of the past and injustices continue to be committed even though governments who commit themselves to action against these violations continue to disregard or show minimal will towards committing resources and policies to achieving larger scale change to protect human rights. In this regard, the words of George Santayana remain potent, *"Those who cannot remember the past are condemned to repeat it."*[16] Human rights education ultimately seeks to challenge all of us to prevent history from repeating itself by providing the knowledge, tools, resources, networks and vital voices towards a more equitable and peaceful world. The challenges are many, but this is also an opportune time to re-imagine the possibilities for human rights education and to take the progress and achievements of the UN Decade into the next chapter of the human rights education movement. It is a fair assessment to acknowledge how far beyond tinkering we have come with bringing human rights education into the larger educational dialogue, and with the continued commitment, energy and passion that has provided successes throughout the human rights education movement, we are sure to see many of the challenges overcome and opportunities prevail.

---

[14] United Nations World Programme for Human Rights Education - ongoing from 2005 Amnesty International. http://web.amnesty.org/pages/hre-unwphre-eng.

[15] Richard E. Neustadt and Ernest May, Thinking in Time: The Uses of History for Decision Makers. New York: The Free Press, 1986, p/ 251.

[16] George Santayana, The Life of Reason (1905-1906), vol. 1, Reason in Common Sense.

Education and Human Rights – Kind Intentions and Brutal Realities

Sia Spiliopoulou Åkermark

Introduction

Education as a field of activity and the school as its main spatial location are often presented as loci for peaceful interaction, mutual understanding, respect and focusing on the interests of the child. This is also the impression given to us by Article 29 of the *Convention on the Rights of the Child.* It provides that:

'1. State Parties agree that the education of the child shall be directed to:
(a) The development of the child's personality, talents and mental and physical abilities to their fullest potential;
(b) The development of respect for human rights and fundamental freedoms, and for the principles enshrined in the Charter of the United Nations;
(c) The development of respect for the child's parents, his or her own cultural identity, language and values, for the national values of the country in which the child is living, the country from which he or she may originate, and for civilizations different from his or her own;
(d) The preparation of the child for responsible life in a free society, in the spirit of understanding, peace, tolerance, equality of sexes, and friendship among all peoples, ethnic, national and religious groups and persons of indigenous origin;
(e) The development of respect for the natural environment [...]'

Education is here understood as a human right and in that it is also understood as a primary task of the state. The Universal Declaration of Human Rights included an extensive provision on education (Article 26) which states that education shall be free (at least at the elementary and compulsory stages) and 'directed to the full development of the human personality and to the strengthening of respect for human rights and fundamental freedoms'. I will not give in this paper a definition of terms such as 'human rights education', 'education for democratic citizenship' and 'political education'. This has been done by other authors in this publication.[1] Instead, I will focus on current debates on the right to education as a human right and in particular the right to, and rights in education for minorities.After an overview of some of the main challenges concerning minority education today, I have used the work of the Advisory Committee of the Framework Convention on National Minorities of the Council of Europe as my main point of reference.[2]

The Challenges of Education Today

The idea of education as a human right also includes the idea that education is to be understood as the responsibility of the state. This idea is of course not something new which appeared first in human rights documents. Adam Smith argued in several chapters of *Wealth of Nations* that education was one of the core tasks of the state, e.g:

> After the public institutions and public works necessary for the defence of the society, and for the administration of justice, both of which have already been mentioned, the other works and

[1] See also the chapters by Audrey Osler and Elena Ippoliti in this publication.
[2] The work of the Advisory Committee is found at www.coe.int/minorities, including state reports, opinions of the Advisory Committee and other relevant documents.

institutions of this kind are chiefly those for facilitating the commerce of the society, and those for promoting the instruction of the people. The institutions for instruction are of two kinds: those for the education of youth, and those for the instruction of people of all ages.[3]

Rousseau emphasised the crucial importance of education – at least for boys – in his *Emile,* for the whole of the 19th century in Europe which meant the introduction of general schooling and the creation of universities where the officials necessary for the newly established nation-states' administrations were to be educated.[4]

The inherent tensions in the multiple goals of education will be addressed below, but at this stage we can assert that this benevolent conceptualisation of education is in disharmony with many of the things we can see around us today. Among them one may mention the phenomena of segregated education on the basis of ethnicity, residence, language, religion or other grounds in many countries; the exclusion of considerable parts of the world's population from access to education; the exclusion of girls from education and in particular higher education; harassment and bullying of children and young persons sometimes on the grounds of ethnicity, race or language; the abandoning of the state task of education into the hands of private actors operating outside any regulatory framework and beyond state control and monitoring.

Here, as with all human rights, we find the paradox of the relationship between human rights and the state. Human rights are introduced in order to control and limit the power of the state vis à vis individuals, but at the same time the fulfilment and protection of human rights depends completely on the existence of a strong and well functioning state. Still, the Organisation for Economic Co-Operation and Development (OECD) reports that in half of the OECD countries, the private sector share in education increased at all levels of education, e.g. with an increase of more than 3% in tertiary education, while that increase exceeds 9% in Australia, Italy and the United Kingdom between 1995 and 2003 again at the level of tertiary education.[5] Of course the issue of funding is not alone in defining control and responsibility, but there is an obvious declining trend in state involvement in the field of education in OECD countries, i.e. the countries which at the same time consider themselves as defenders of human rights.

A second challenge in the field of education, as in many other fields where human rights are of immediate relevance, is the effect of decentralisation leading to strengthened local governments. In many states today, certainly in Europe, basic education is the responsibility of local authorities. While human rights rules have a centralising logic in implying the responsibility of, and monitoring and control by states' central governments, in practice entire fields are the responsibility of local authorities. There are many positive sides to this, since local authorities are assumed to know local conditions and the wishes of the inhabitants in their region better than the central government and parliament. Decisions are taken 'closer to the citizens' following the general principle of subsidiarity as found in EU law where it entails that decisions should be taken at the appropriate level and as close to the citizens as possible. On the negative side, however, is the weak knowledge of human rights norms

---

[3] Adam Smith, An Inquiry into the Nature and Causes of the Wealth of Nations, City publisher, 1776, (chapter 1).

[4] Jean-Jacques Rousseau, Emile ou De l'éducation, 1762, Paris: Garnier, 1961.

[5] Education at a Glance, OECD Indicators 2006, Paris: 2006, pp. 215-216.

at the local level. For minorities, this may be particularly sensitive as they may be in very weak positions at the local level and thus depend upon parliamentary, governmental or international rules and decisions in order to defend their rights. As we shall see below, the OECD has also found that there is insufficient information and monitoring with regard to spending on pupils with social disadvantages in many of the countries it monitors.

Finally, education today in many countries and regions takes place in environments where conflict and hate dominates. In the age of al-Qaeda and of perceived massive migration flows 'we have grown accustomed to thinking of the world as divided among warring creeds, separated from one another by chasms of incomprehension' as aptly put recently by Kwame Anthony Appiah.[6] Recent violent clashes in cities around Europe, e.g. in Athens, Budapest, Copenhagen and Paris have become commonplace as we begin to realise that a part of the population and youth in all countries seem to be marginalized and distancing itself from parliamentary deliberation and the state. While education as a human right is thought of as a sphere of constructive and peaceful coexistence, for very many children and young people, education is a battlefield or a space of degradation and oppression.

The Right to Education

Education is today considered as a goal in its own right as well as a forceful tool for transmitting knowledge, attitudes and values. For this reason, issues of education are always crucial in the relationships between majorities and minorities in all societies. This was already the case during the League of Nations period, when the Permanent Court of International Justice gave its Advisory Opinion in a matter concerning minority schools in Albania.[7] In this case the Permanent Court discussed the difference of equality in law and equality in fact, or, as the Court said, how to bring about 'an equilibrium between different situations', and it accepted the necessity of differing treatments and the right of minorities to operate their own institutions, i.e. schools, churches and associations.

It is not surprising therefore, that no other issue is given such prominence in the Framework Convention for the Protection of National Minorities (FCNM) adopted under the auspices of the Council of Europe, with three specific provisions (articles 12-14) on education, as well as explicit references to education in general provisions concerning equality and intercultural dialogue. This is so because the right to education can be seen not only as a right in itself but it is also instrumental as a precondition for the full enjoyment of many other rights, such as the right to participation, expression and association. Some of the aims of education, such as the development of the linguistic capabilities of the child, are understood as primarily instrumental. In

[6] Kwame Anthony Appiah, Cosmopolitanisn. Ethics in a World of Strangers. London: Penguin Group, 2006 (cover text).

[7] Case concerning the Minority Schools in Albania, Advisory Opinion, PCIJ reports, Series A/B No. 64 (1935). For an evaluation of minority protection by the League of Nations see, Athanasia Spiliopoulou Åkermark, Justifications of Minority Protection in International Law, Dordrecht/Uppsala: Kluwer Publ., 1997, pp. 101-118.

these cases education is seen as a tool for the achievement of other goals (e.g. finding employment or participating in decision-making). Other aims of education are perceived as primordial in that they are felt as important *per se* even if there is no other rational or economic justification for this. This is the case with the development of respect for the child's identity.

The aims of education in a diverse society allow us to look at education as having multiple and occasionally contradictory aims which need to be reconciled and balanced. There are many different stakeholders in education: those educated, the educators, parents, minority groups, local, regional and central authorities. Their needs and aspirations may vary and need to be constantly assessed and accommodated to the greatest extent possible. The Convention on the Rights of the Child (see above) has placed in a paramount position the needs and wishes of the child, something which was lacking in earlier documents. This is of great importance in the field of education where other international legal precedents and case law have given preference to the interests and options of parents or educators at the expense of the views of the child, as is for instance, the case in the Universal Declaration on Human Rights and the European Convention on the Protection of Human Rights and Fundamental Freedoms. This shows that our understanding of the role and goals of education has been and is still changing over time.

From the fact that the right to education is recognised as a human right, it follows that the *right to education* and the *rights in education* for minorities, as guaranteed by the Framework Convention, are also an integral part of education rights as entrenched in a number of specific provisions in international instruments, including the Universal Declaration of Human Rights, the International Covenant on Economic, Social and Cultural Rights, the Convention on the Rights of the Child, the Convention on the Elimination of All Forms of Discrimination against Women, the UNESCO Convention against Discrimination in Education, the European Convention of Human Rights and Fundamental Freedoms and the (Revised) European Social Charter.[8]

A number of different rights are covered in these provisions, including:

- the principle of a free and compulsory primary education;
- equal access to education;
- the liberty of parents to choose the kind of education that shall be given to their children according to their own religious, moral or philosophical convictions;
- the right of individuals and legal entities to establish and direct their own educational institution;
- the right to language education for migrant workers and their families.

Much guidance in matters concerning the education rights of minorities can also be found in the OSCE Hague Recommendations Regarding the Education Rights of National Minorities (1996).[9] With regard to issues of minority languages in education, additional guidance is found in the European Charter for Regional or Minority Languages where the levels of obligations for the different stages of education are clearly outlined.

---

[8] These are very basic HR documents. In an article of this kind, I would not expect to find full references to documents. Do you need the year of adoption/entry into force, an UNTS number, or something else?

[9] The Hague Recommendations can be found at:
http://www.osce.org/documents/hcnm/1996/10/2700_en.pdf (visited on 30 October 2007).

Education Denied

The former UN Special Rapporteur on Education, Katarina Tomasevski, has consistently argued that problems in access to and the quality of education can be explained by conscious decisions made by governments.[10] Among the evidence is the long list of countries in which allocations for defence exceeded those for education in the central government budget in the period 1992-1999. Among them we find OECD and European countries including for instance Bulgaria, Canada, Russia, Switzerland, United Kingdom and United States.[11] Using a longer perspective, allocations for education in central government budgets have decreased in many countries in the period 1972-1986, e.g. from 14,8% to 8,9% in Sweden and from 20% to 6% in Argentina.[12] In the former Soviet Union there was a strong decline in schooling for 15-years-olds in the period 1989-1997, with a retrogression of 24% in Georgia and 26% in Tajikistan.[13]

Gender disparity is another longstanding problem in the field of education with girls enrolment being overall far lower than that of boys, even though even the opposite situation does occur and is of course equally problematic.[14] Social practices such as early marriage and the ending of schooling for girls after the compulsory years of schooling are sometimes explained with reference to culture and tradition and may therefore be of particular relevance to girls belonging to minorities.

The relationship between the average performance of students and social equity is a new area of interest and research, and much remains to be done, but some results indicate that there is a correlation of social equity and the level of performance.[15] What is clear by now, however, is that the objective of ensuring that all children have access to good quality primary education is far from easy to achieve.[16]

Funding in Minority Education

Very few states provide details about the funding of minority education. The State Report of Poland indicates that local authorities running schools for national minorities receive additional (as compared to non-minority education) state subsidies (20% supplement per pupil in larger schools and 50% in smaller schools).[17]The State Re-

[10] For her reports see http://www.ohchr.org/english/issues/education/rapporteur/annual.htm, last visited August 15, 2007.

[11] Katarina Tomasevski, Education denied, London, Zed Books, 2003, p. 12 (drawing on UNICEF statistics).

[12] Ibid., p. 86 (with reference to the World Development Report 1988).

[13] Ibid., p. 90.

[14] Ibid., p. 164.

[15] OECD, Policy Brief, Education and Equity, February 2004, Figure 1.

[16] See the most recent reports of the Millennium Project which monitors the UN Millennium Development Goals adopted in the year 2000 at:
http://www.unmillenniumproject.org/reports/tffindings.htm.

[17] State Report of Poland to the Advisory Committee on the Framework Convention on National Minorities, ACFC/SR(2002)2. All documents on the FCNM can be found at:
www.coe.int/minorities, last visited October 4th 2006.

port of Hungary reports that a local government operating minority educational institutions receives extra subsidies.[18]

Many States provide no information on methods and levels of funding affecting minority and intercultural education. It is instructive that this also seems to be the experience in the education work of the OECD. In the Education Policy Analysis of the year 2003 the OECD had no information on the percentage of students with social disadvantages (including minority affiliation) receiving additional resources in compulsory education. Sweden, Switzerland, the United Kingdom, (all well resourced countries), were not able to supply the OECD with such information. Finland and the Netherlands were among the countries with the highest levels of additional support.[19]

The State Reports received so far by the Advisory Committee provide no information on the participation of minorities in budgetary decision making with regard to education at central, local or school level.

As regards kin-state support in the field of education, the Advisory Committee has dealt with such issues under Article 12 of the Framework Convention. Article 4 is, however, also relevant when kin-state support creates differential treatment that may amount to discrimination which enhances the vulnerability of groups with no kin-states. The Advisory Committee has indeed emphasized in several of its statements that over-dependence upon kin-state support may place some groups in a disadvantaged position, and has established that 'the authorities should ensure that all the national minorities, particularly those that are numerically smaller or do not enjoy the support of a kin-state, benefit equitably from the special government programmes for national minorities'. If used prudently, kin-state support can be an asset for the minority concerned, other minority groups and for the majority population. When discussing kin-state support in the field of textbooks and other teaching materials supplied by kin-states, it needs to be taken into account that such materials may not in some cases reflect adequately and correctly the experiences and aspirations of minorities concerned since they are produced in and by the kin-state by persons who do not live in the country of the minority at issue. The knowledge and experience of Finnish-speakers in Sweden, for instance, is not entirely identical to the experiences of Finns in Finland, so that books produced for Finland often need to be adapted or complemented with other materials when used in other countries.

Here, one should refer to the guidelines developed by the European Commission for Democracy through Law, of the Council of Europe, better known as the Venice Commission, in its *Report on the Preferential Treatment of National Minorities by the Kin-State* in 2001, which discusses in detail the advantages, disadvantages and limits of Kin-State support.

The Advisory Committee Commentary on Education

In order to summarise its experiences in the field of education during the first monitoring cycle, and in order to give guidance to states and non-governmental organisa-

[18] State Report of Hungary ACFC/SR(99)10 at www.coe.int , last visited October 4th 2006.

[19] OECD, Policy Brief, Education and Equity, February 2004, available at http://www.oecd.org/dataoecd/17/10/29478774.pdf.

tions in the preparation of reports under the monitoring system of the Framework Convention on National Minorities (FC), the Advisory Committee adopted, in March 2006 a *Commentary on Education.*[20] Its aim is thus to be a practical tool in the hands of decision makers at central and local level.

The Commentary concludes that there are three types of core questions which need to be addressed explicitly in issues of minority and multicultural education:

Why? What are the precise goals of educational policies?

As already indicated, the Framework Convention requires not only the protection of minority cultures and languages, but also the dissemination and development of intercultural contacts and dialogue, the encouragement of a spirit of tolerance in all educational efforts and even an ethos of bilingualism and plurilingualism. Different situations and different groups may need to be treated differently in order to ensure effective equality and access to good, quality education for all individuals.

Who? Who are the involved and concerned actors?

State Parties need to have access to adequate basic information concerning the situation of different minority groups with regard to their needs and aspirations. Differences in geographic concentration, historical status and experience, kin-state support, level of organisation and gender disparities require different responses from the State and local and regional authorities. The particularly disadvantaged position of the Roma and Travellers needs to be taken into account in all countries that have ratified the Framework Convention. Many other actors influence the availability and quality of education. Decision-makers at central and local level, teachers and school heads are among the most important. Parents and those receiving education (pupils or adults) are other crucial actors. The wishes of these groups and individuals need to be heard and the right of effective participation, as enshrined in Article 15 of the Framework Convention, should be kept in mind in all decision-making processes, including in the field of education.

How? What tools are available and feasible?

The form and content of education needs to be adapted to the aims discussed above. The introduction of multicultural and intercultural elements in all curricula is one step. Alternative types of schools and classes are other methods to address the varying needs. The training of bilingual and plurilingual teachers with an expertise of working in multicultural environments is another important step. These aspects are not exhaustive, but they are crucial in offering access to good quality education to all persons living in a country in a way which supports a climate of tolerance and intercultural dialogue.

This list of core issues is complemented by an inventory of the issues that have been raised under the various substantive provisions of the conventions and which are inspired by the "*Four-A scheme*" developed within the United Nations.[21] The scheme offers some basic quality criteria from a human rights perspective.

Planning and evaluation of all education, including minority education, can be guided by reference to this scheme. While the first two A-factors are of equal rele-

---

[20] ACFC/25DOC(2006)002 available at www.coe.int/minorities, last visited October 4th 2006.

[21] General Comment 13 (1999) on the Right to Education of the Committee on Economic, Social and Cultural Rights, and Preliminary Report of the UN Special Rapporteur on Education E/CN.4/1999/49.

vance to all children and students, the Advisory Committee finds that the notions of acceptability and adaptability are of particular relevance for persons belonging to national minorities.[22] According to the *Four-A-scheme*, education in all its forms and at all levels shall exhibit the following interrelated and essential features:

Availability: Functioning educational institutions and programmes have to be available in sufficient quantity. The availability of trained teachers and teaching materials, issues of buildings, sanitation facilities for both sexes and safe drinking water are among the most crucial elements under this criterion. The Framework Convention includes different levels of obligations for States with regard to availability in the different levels of education.

Accessibility has three overlapping dimensions: non-discrimination, physical accessibility (appropriate geographic location, transportation, modern technology) and economic accessibility. Primary education must be 'free to all' under human rights instruments.[23] In Europe, Article 17 (2) of the Revised European Social Charter requires State Parties to provide children and young persons with 'a free *primary* and *secondary* education'.[24]

Acceptability: the form and substance of education, including curricula and teaching methods, have to be acceptable (e.g. relevant, culturally appropriate and of good quality) to students and parents. Acceptability is thus relevant for the whole physical and social environment of education. While this criterion is of particular importance for national minorities, it does not exempt them automatically from the objectives and standards defined in the educational system of the State.

Adaptability: education has to be flexible to adapt to the needs of changing societies and communities and to respond to the needs of students within their diverse social and cultural settings. This must be kept in mind as both minorities and majorities are developing entities as are individuals belonging to them. Minority and majority identities need to be constantly discussed and re-assessed as they are not fixed. Nor are languages and religion frozen phenomena and this has also been the view of the Advisory Committee in its work.

Conclusion

There is some tension between the discourse of the human right to education and programmes on 'human rights education', 'education for democratic citizenship' and 'political education'. The human right to education emphasises the right of each individual, and in particular of each child, to good quality, free and compulsory educa-

---

[22] See also Duncan Wilson, report on education in "Filling the Frame: Five years of monitoring the Framework Convention for the Protection of National Minorities", Council of Europe, Strasbourg, 2004, pp. 161-226.

[23] General Comment 11 (1999) on Plans of Action for Primary Education of the Committee on Economic, Social and Cultural Rights elaborates on the notions of 'compulsory' and 'free-of-charge' education.

[24] The full text of the European Social Charter and the Revised European Social Charter can be found at:
http://www.coe.int/T/E/Human_Rights/Esc/1_General_Presentation/

tion. Its goal is the development of the capacity, the qualities and abilities of individuals. As such, its goal is empowerment with an individually oriented emancipation potential. Human rights incorporate an unavoidably critical element, as they require the constant questioning of the state, and of existing distributions of power and resources. Human rights education, education for democratic citizenship and political education are all directed towards societal interaction, democratic decision-making and peaceful co-existence. However, these goals cannot be achieved if the basic right to good quality primary education, an education adapted and appropriate for children from minority groups and children with various disadvantages is fulfilled. It is here that our priority should lie.

The remaining paradox is that the current universal interest in, and reference to human rights norms coincides with a decrease in confidence in traditional democratic and parliamentary institutions (political parties, voting, parliamentary debate and decision-making). How this paradox will evolve will be one of the challenges for the coming decades. Any development will surely have an effect on the inclusion or exclusion of minorities in public life.

The State, Politics and Human Rights Education during the UN-Decade for Human Rights Education: The Case of Spain and Armenia

Anja Mihr

Introduction

In this article I argue that first, political actors and state authorities are pivotal players in democracies in order to promote human rights education at all educational and societal levels. Secondly, the more political actors get involved in supporting human rights education, human rights become political and thus human rights education turns into civic education or education for democratic citizenship with less of a holistic approach. The two arguments will be based on the findings of my research in the project "Teaching Human Rights in Europe" and will concentrate on the time frame of the UN-Decade 1995-2004 in Europe. I will provide examples from Spain and Armenia and will further elaborate on the pros and cons of involving politics and in particular, governments, in the promotion of human rights education in democracies in the case of Spain and in countries of transition, in this case, Armenia. I will refer here to NGOs as the traditional main drivers in the field of human rights education on one hand and to national authorities, political entities and international organisations on the other, such as ministries of education, secondary and higher education authorities or the UNO.

Human rights education becomes formal when the state or the government takes responsibility for implementing human rights education programmes in the national education curricula and school education system. It remains informal if done mainly by NGOs, private initiatives, foundations or even international organisations such as the United Nations or the Council of Europe. Whereas NGOs and private initiatives express greater independence but also a single issue interest in setting up a human rights curricula, seminars or workshops, the formal education sector depends on many more societal, state or political interests regarding what to teach. Even though the formal education sector turns human rights education into civic education, it nevertheless reaches by far, more people in a society than if done solely by NGOs. The formal education sector has the most impact when disseminating the idea of human rights through education, but because state programmes have the tendency to become civic or focus mainly on "democracy education" this can turn into a controversial matter among human rights education experts. This is the case, for example, when education programmes show evidence of dealing only with selected human rights issues. These can be based on specific political rights such as the human right to free and fair elections, the right to participate or freedom rights. It becomes problematic if only some human rights are taught selectively without putting them into a broader context. In other cases, as in Armenia for example, human rights education programmes represent specific family or Christian values. Other programmes can have the intention of training people to become loyal citizens who obey national laws and constitutions even if these norms are in opposition to universal human rights values such as the case of educational programmes in the Basque Country in Spain.

Politics and Human Rights Education

Without political and governmental engagement there is no overall human rights education in society. Without the commitment of governments and public administration there is no implementation and dissemination of human rights for the wider public. If the idea, notion and meaning of human rights is meant to be disseminated into society as a whole it needs public administration and implementation, otherwise human rights will stay only at an elite level, for example at the academic and higher education level or it will be accessible only for elite groups or a limited number of people. This is the case in the NGO sector and non-formal education sector. Here NGOs, due to their limited resources, can offer training programmes only to small sized groups and/or only to those who are already interested in the subject of human rights and therefore sign up for classes in human rights education. It is a very selective process. Contrary to this, once governments and state authorities such as ministries and national institutions get involved in human rights education they can determine the extent to which human rights is an integral part of the formal education sector, for example in schools, life long learning programmes and higher education institutions such as universities. They affect large parts of the population. Consequently, governments and state authorities are pivotal players in terms of the dissemination of human rights and they also determine what kind of human rights are taught or learned. The impact and success of human rights education programmes therefore is inherently connected to the degree to which political actors commit themselves to it.

The UN Decade for Human Rights Education 1995-2004 had an impact in this respect.[1] Unanimously decided by the UN General Assembly in 1994, governments of more than 190 member states made a pledge and commitment to set up national action plans for human rights, to educate and integrate human rights in the formal education sector in all countries. At the same time human rights education was seen as a tool to transport and disseminate not only human rights values but also political values, such as tolerance, democracy and the participation of minorities and others.

The declaration of the UN-Decade was the result of a long process when human rights education entered national policy arenas in the early 1990s. It was at this point that the term and notion of human rights education shifted from the NGO sector and thus non-formal education sector to slowly become part of state education policies and practice. After the World Human Rights Conference in Vienna in 1993 it became officially included in many international documents or declarations such as those of the UNO or Council of Europe.[2] It was seen as one way to finally promote the notion of the Universal Declaration of Human Rights (UDHR) of 1948. This had been almost impossible for four decades from the Cold War until 1990 during which period human rights were held "hostage" and state powers of the east and the west claimed their sole interpretation of the meaning of human rights as the only true interpretation. From the perspective of western states this meant that rights of political freedom were more relevant than social and economic human rights. Socialist countries proclaimed that social and economic human rights had to be realized first before

[1] See also contribution by Elena Ippoliti in this book.
[2] Mihr, Anja, Die UN-Dekade fuer Menschenrechtsbildung, Eine Bilanz, in: Frech, Siegfried/ Haspel, Michael (Eds.), Menschenrechtre, Schwalbach/Ts., 2005, p. 189-210.

political freedom could be guaranteed. Consequently, during the Cold War there was no time to promote a holistic view of human rights through human rights education. At the end of the Cold War, expectations of many actors in the human rights community increased, in particular in the NGO sector who hoped that with the UN-Decade the time to finally promote and disseminate all human rights in equal terms would arrive. Governments and state representatives were in a euphoric mood regarding human rights in the early 1990s and they ratified every human rights document they could sign. This was particularly true for newly independent countries in central and Eastern Europe such as Estonia and Armenia.

Human rights education and the UN-Decade for Human Rights Education was therefore one factor amongst others for political actors and state representatives to show to the international and NGO communities that they adhered to the human rights principle. Not without self-interest, their expectations were that their credibility would increase the more they supported international documents and declarations of human rights. This "euphoric" wave, which blinkered many NGOs and civil society actors in the 1990s into believing that human rights were finally more respected than ever before, soon lost ground to the reality. Consequently, the 1990s are today known as the decade of signing, ratifying and approving human rights documents, regardless of the consequences and ignoring human rights realization. Conversely, the 1990s was also a decade of gross human rights violation with genocides in the former Yugoslavia and Rwanda and the outbreak of civil wars which led to failing and corrupt states particularly in countries undergoing transition. One can also argue that human rights standards lost their credibility during these years. Governments ratified international human rights standards and then they violated and corrupted them. What appeared to happen was that they embraced human rights norms and reinterpreted these norms in their own ways. The same happened in the field of human rights education. Whereas the former UN-special Rapporteur on the Right to Education, Katarina Tomashevski, branded the slogan "human rights education is the tool to unlock human rights", the reality was that in far too many cases it had been used to transport political messages. It had been misused as a tool to disseminate certain particular values in the interest of corrupt governments and not in the interest of people and human rights.

But regardless of how the political reality was during the UN-Decade of Human Rights Education, at the same time the concept of holistic human rights education programmes was developed. NGOs like the Boston based Human Rights Education Associated (HREA), Amnesty International, the Peoples Decade for Human Rights Education (PDHRE) and the International Center for Human Rights Education in Montreal (EQUITAS) soon became important actors in the field of promotion of human rights. Individual human rights activists and smaller NGOs who for years had tried to lobby governments on the importance of human rights education were also successful. For them the proclamation of UN-Decade was a useful tool to lobby governments, national authorities and other international organisations since governments had committed themselves to the Decade. What NGOs wanted was that states would adhere to their commitment and set up national action plans for human rights education in their countries, including the formal and non-formal education sector. Thus, governments officially recognized and agreed to enhance their efforts and cooperation with all possible actors to promote the full document of the UDHR. However, the reality was more complex as we will see in the case of Spain and Armenia.

Democratic Values and Human Rights Education

Many authors argue that the higher the degree of democracy, the higher the possibility that human rights values are respected and implemented. Numerous comparative studies have shown that this correlation exists because people in free democracies vote for political representatives more if they respect and safeguard their human rights. Peoples votes are linked to the level at which governments are held accountable to the implementation of basic human rights. In countries with a lesser degree of freedom and a higher degree of corruption and authoritarian leadership, people ask for different values and sometimes do not even know what freedom rights are.[3] Likewise, they don't see human rights as being a tool to protect their personal safety, but rather as something that is unreachable or a utopian dream. Human rights are perceived as a luxury only for an elite group of people, because governmental institutions, police, courts and administration do not work sufficiently to protect human rights, as it will be seen in the case of Armenia.

Is it possible to differentiate whether human rights are implemented because democracies are established or whether the claim for human rights will lead to more democracy? Authors like Donnelly and Howard-Hassmann find no evidence that democracy is necessarily the best political system to protect or promote human rights.[4] Without a doubt it can be stated that democracies aim to empower the people in order to ensure that they aim at guaranteeing a good standard of living and a political system which includes human rights.[5] However, it can also be stated that the struggle for human rights is independent from any political movement or democratization efforts. The struggle for justice and thus for human rights and values is as old as mankind under any regime and consequently, whereas democracies tend to please and to listen to their citizens and voters, the concept of human rights aims to empower individuals and therefore controls, or limits governmental intentions to the benefit of all.

The holistic concept of human rights as proclaimed in the guidelines of the UN-Decade is "blind" to any political regime and has no preference for any particular political system. It cares less about a political regime as long as all human rights for, and by the people are respected and protected. But contrary to that, not every political system "cares less" about human rights and "what" kind or human rights are taught at schools or universities.[6]

---

[3] For example: UNDP (Ed.), Human Development Report, Human Rights and Human Development, 2000.

[4] Howard-Hassmann, Rhoda E., The Second Great Transformation: Human Rights Leapfrogging in the Era of Globalization, in: Human Rights Quarterly, Johns Hopkins University Press Vol 27, 2005, p. 1-40.

[5] Donnelly, Jack, Human Rights, Democracy, and Development, in: Human Rights Quarterly, Johns Hopkins University Press, Vol 21, 1999, p. 619.

[6] For this see also: Reardon, Betty A., Education for Human Dignity, Learning about rights and responsibilities, University of Pennsylvania Press, 1995.

Regardless of this, today we find that the modern concept of a liberal democracy is the most likely qualified to implement, promote and protect all human rights. Therefore, human rights education will find greater acceptance in societies and amongst political actors in democracies than amongst authoritarian regimes.

Human Rights Education becomes Education for Democratic Citizenship

Human rights education becomes education for democratic citizenship to an even greater extent when governments make an official commitment and spend financial and human resources to promote civic or citizenship education programmes. Civic education or Education for Democratic Citizenship is meant purely in a political sense and it is not intrinsic to learn a holistic human rights approach which includes all human rights at equal levels and balanced.[7]

With the commitment to the UN-Decade, governments have set up educational programmes in human rights. Education for democratic citizenship was not excluded or even understood as a part of the larger human rights education picture. But in many cases these programmes reflect a particular political agenda or governmental interest rather than the aims of the UN guidelines for the Decade.

In Europe it was the Council of Europe and later the European Union that took the initiative in order to promote the UN-Decade. In 1997 the Council of Europe began to promote a programme called Education for Democratic citizenship (EDC) which was followed by numerous smaller and short term training programmes by the European Union. At the end of the UN-Decade in 2005, the Council of Europe proclaimed the European Year of Citizenship through Education. Under the slogans of “Learning and Living Democracy” and “Live Long Learning” the Council of Europe and the European Union promoted the educational programmes among their member states throughout Europe from the 1990s to the present day.[8] Only later did the Council of Europe add the notion of human rights education to its programme of Democratic Citizenship.[9] Nevertheless, the Council clearly determines its policies as programmes by which students and scholars learn how governments work, how elections take place, how to participate in communities or to file a petition to the European parliament.[10] It is quite clear that these educational programmes are aimed at citizens of European member states. What has been criticized by the former UN-Special Rapporteur on the Right to Education, Katharina Tomashevski in one of her earlier writings, is the fact that EDC and citizenship education is “exclusive” because it excludes all those people living and working in Europe who are, for example, not citizens of these countries, such as immigrants, guest-workers or even minorities such as the Russians

[7] Beaumont, Elizabeth/ Battistoni, Richard M., Beyond Civics 101: Rethinking what we mean by civics education, in: Journal of Political Science Education, Vol 2, Routledge 2006, p. 241-247.

[8] European Commission, Furthering Human Rights and Democracy across the globe, Office for Official Publications of the European Commission, 2007.

[9] Council of Europe, Adopted texts on education for democratic citizenship and human rights, Council of Europe Publishing, Strasbourg, 2003.

[10] Cecchini, Michaela, Education for Democratic Citizenship in Europe: Concepts and challenges for action, (unpublished paper) Networking European Citizenship Education, 27 October 2004.

in Baltic countries who are denied citizenship.[11] These groups are literally excluded from civic education but would never be so under the terminology of human rights education.

Thus, human rights education is aimed at all people living in a society – in Europe or elsewhere. Human rights education is therefore "inclusive". It includes all people regardless of their citizenship or status. It was intentional that the UNO proclaimed the UN-Decade for Human Rights Education and not for democratic education only. Needless to say, democratic values are also an important part of human rights education and that through democratic participation people exercise their basic human rights as declared in the UDHR.

To assess the impact of human rights education programmes in Europe it is important to understand the main differences between the "exclusive" educational programmes promoted by European institutions and the "inclusive" programmes proclaimed by the UNO. The differences arose when the Council of Europe and the European Union started sponsoring long and short term projects over the past decade. Many human rights NGOs and initiatives which preferred to promote a holistic human rights approach through educational programmes had to change their applications for money and grants to the title of 'citizenship education'. At the same time, national governments throughout the European member states displayed their commitment to citizenship education rather than to human rights education. They supported programmes and added into their national school curricula elements of civic education. As a consequence some curricula and national programmes fostered citizen rights, electoral rights and "loyalty towards national constitutions and governments" instead of increasing citizen's critical awareness of the full spectrum of international human rights norms and standards.[12] The idea of these state owned programmes was the adherence to state norms and values instead of shaping the analytical mind of people to analyse their environment, to detect unjust behaviour and to speak out when a violation of human rights takes place. NGOs like Amnesty International and the HREA, who preferred a holistic educational approach and the empowerment of individuals and therefore human rights education rather than citizenship education, had only limited influence. In the end, it was in the hands of governmental and state representatives to decide what kind of rights to promote during the UN-Decade for Human Rights Education. Since human rights education has been on the political agenda it has been a dilemma for the actors involved. On the one hand it was the ultimate goal of the human rights community, the educators and NGOs that governments finally commit to the concept of human rights education and include it in their national curricula; on the other, it became clear that the moment governments take ownership of human rights education it would not be about educating people to become critical and in many cases disobedient citizens. Human rights became political rights and they were shaped the way governmental authorities preferred them to be.

---

[11] Tomashevski, Katerina, Education denied, Costs and Remedies, New York, 2003.

[12] A good example of material which was used as part of human rights education is the book by: Beetham, David/ Boyle, Kevin, Introducing Democracy, 80 Questions and Answers, UNESCO Publishing, 1995.

Using the example of two very different countries in Europe, Armenia and Spain, I will show that the success and outcome of human rights education during the UN-Decade can be very different with similar impacts. Both countries have in common the fact that in 1994 they supported the declaration of the UN-Decade for Human Rights Education (1995-2004) at the General Assembly of the United Nations and both governments were open to the implementation of the means of the UN-Decade. However, in both countries it took external players such as NGOs in the case of Spain, and special agencies of international organisations like the UNDP or the Council of Europe Decade for Citizenship Education in the case of Armenia, to cause political reactions and hence the involvement of political actors in the country. Spain is a particular case, because the different states, the *autonomias,* create their own state action plans for education. The Basque Country for example, with a nationalistic government is promoting its own civic education programmes which do not refer much to human rights on the whole.

Spain

Spain is one of the success stories of the UN-Decade for Human Rights Education. The Spanish government initiated at the end of the Decade a law and curricula reform for secondary schools to implement human rights education. It is worthwhile taking a closer look at the actors who initiated it and where the obstacles lay.

In Spain, 55% of the formal curricula is set up by National Agencies and the Ministry of Education and the remaining 45% is left to the independent states with educational autonomy. States like Catalunya and the Basque Country make wide use of this freedom. Most of the other states adhere to the proposals made by the central government and Ministry of Education in Madrid. As a result, when talking about revision and school book reform in terms of human rights, it affects a minimum of 55% of the curricula content. Nevertheless, Spanish human rights NGOs played a main role and took the initiative of the UN-Decade for Human Rights Education. It was Amnesty International Spain (AI) and the *Asociacion Pro Derechos Humanos de Espana* (APDHE), who started the initiative in 2004. They were encouraged by the call of the UN-Decade. Amnesty International together with APDHE evaluated some school curricula and books based on their expertise in this field.[13] The two NGOs published the results and then lobbied the Ministry of Education to ask for more im-

---

[13] Amnestia Internacional, Educación en Derechos Humanos, Propuestas didácticas, Madrid 1995; and Amnestia Internacional, Educar en y para los Derechos Humanos, Dinámicas y actividades, Seminario de Educación para la Paz, Asociación Pro Derechos Humanos, Madrid, 1996. Other actors in this field in Spain were: Helsinki Foundation Spain, Memoria del proyecto de voluntariado universitario, la educacón de derechos humanos en centros escolares de la communidad de Madrid, 2003; and Universities: Tuvilla Rayo, José, Educación en Derechos Humanos, hacia una perspectiva global, Bilbao, 2000 (2nd); Jares Xesús R., Educación y Derechos Humanos, Estrategias didacticas y organizativas, Madrid 2002.
Confederación Espanola de Asociaciones de Padres y Madres de Alumnos (CEAPA) (Ed.),50 anos de derechos humanos? Guía para padres y madres comprometidos, Madrid, 1995.

plementation of human rights elements into the curricula.[14] Their initiative and results led to wide media coverage and their representatives were received by the Ministry of Education in 2005 who promised to change national legislation in favour of human rights education.[15] The result was that the government again made a commitment to the new UN-World Programme for Human Rights Education and introduced a law reform on education and a revision of school books to start in 2006.[16] At the same time however, the NGO representatives emphasized that part of this success had to do with the 2004 national election and the subsequent change from a conservative government, who had apparently ignored their appeals for school reforms since 1998, to a socialist government, the *Partido Socialista Obrero Espana* (PSOE), which was more likely to be open to the idea of the UN-Decade and human rights. The previous government whose majority party was the conservative *Partido Popular* (PP) had nevertheless promoted value education in terms of Christian values which was no longer a priority after the political change in 2004. But still today, many school books in Spain keep the focus on Christian values as the basis for solidarity and societal peace in the country. Authors like Naval Duran and Ugarte Artal emphasize these values as the basis for human rights education in Spain.[17] The electoral programmes of the political parties reflected this division, although none of the political parties made a clear commitment to the UN-Decade. Only the PSOE mentioned the importance of civic education and human rights in Spain and the creation of a department of human rights in the Ministry of Education and to undertake more research in universities.[18]

During the UN-Decade, Spain was not subject to any external funding or international pressure by the UN or other international organisations to implement human rights education programmes. As a full member of the UNO, the Council of Europe and the European Union, it was up to its own assessment how to and whether to implement the measures of the UN-Decade. As a result, in Spain it needed 'the bottom up' approach by civil society actors and NGOs who brought the issue and the deficits in terms of human rights education on to the political agenda using media coverage and lobbying.

---

[14] Asociación Pro Derechos Humanos de Espana (ed.), Implantar en Espana una major educación en y para los Derechos Humanos, 2004; and: idem, Derechos Humanos, Una Mirada, Madrid 1994.

[15] Amnesty International meeting with Ministry of Education, 10 January 2005, Letter to the Ministry of Education and Sciences, Maria Jesús Sansegundo Madrid 26 January 2005. See also: EL MUNDO, Los Maestros no estan preparados para informar sobre derechos humanos, segun denuncia Amnestia Internacional, 4 March 2003;
www. elmundo.es/elmundo/2003/03/03/solidaridad/ EL MUNDO, 4.500 profesionales de la educacion solicitan que los derechos humanos sean una asignatura obligatoria, entrega firmas en el Ministerio de Educacion, 5 May 2005;
www.elmundo.es/elmundo/2005(05/05/solidaridad/ .

[16] Interview with Manuel Ollé Sesé, Chair of APDHE and Luis Acebal, Monfort, Vice-Chair 7 February 2005, Madrid.

[17] Naval Durán Concepción, Educación y Derechos Humanos, in: Humana Iura de derechos humanos, Persona y Derecho, Vol 10, 2000 p.43-59; and: Ugarte Artal, Carolina: Las Naciones Unidaa y la Educacion en Derechos Humanos, Universidad de Navarra, Pamplona, 2004.

[18] PSOE, El programa de la mayoria, Madrid, 1993; PSOE, Electoral Program, Espana como tu la harias, Madrid 2000 and PSOE-EE (Basque Country), Electoral Program in 2005.

But in Spain, as in many other countries, it made a difference whether one lobbies for human rights in the capital or in the regions, because if human rights education was hardly known at the national level it was even less known at the local state level of the *autonomias*. The UN-Decade was, if at all, known only to a few private actors, most of whom were NGOs active in Madrid and Barcelona. In the case of the Basque Country it was the UNESCO Commission, which at least by its title had heard of the UN-Decade. The Commission made some efforts to establish human rights training courses, but it only reached an elite group and people in the Basque Country who were already interested in human rights training anyway.[19]

The Case of the Basque Country

The efforts of NGOs the Basque Country is a case apart. Nevertheless this makes it more interesting for investigation particularly in terms of human rights. The Basque state became autonomous in 1976 and since then has increased its powers and responsibilities either in terms of taxation or education. The formal education system is a delicate issue for politicians of all parties in particular the ruling party, *Partido Nacionalista Vasco* (PNV) which has been in power for more than 30 years.

The Basque government learned to use education as a tool to communicate ideologies, language and values. It established a three tier school system in which the elite and best schools taught mainly in the Basque language. What on the one hand had a positive effect in preserving the Basque language, created on the other a very exclusive school system excluding for example migrants from other parts of Spain or abroad who struggled with the Basque language. For more than thirty years the predominant issue of human rights and politics in the Basque Country has been connected with the *derecho a decider*, the right to decide or the right to self-determination. Both rights have been unfortunately interpreted incorrectly by the Basque government as the human right to become an independent, separate state whenever the government proposed it. It is the most disputed human right among Basque politicians and elites. Consequently, when dealing with human rights education one cannot escape the questions, "What human rights?" and "What about the right to decide?" and so setting up a human rights education programme that matches the needs of Basque society remains a challenge. Any researcher is intrigued by the fact that the discussion on human rights starts with the question "What human rights? " and has to make a standpoint on the right to decide before going on in his or her research. Although, as mentioned in my introduction, human rights are likely to be used by all political powers and democracies to achieve the goal of loyal citizens, it is striking in the case of the Basque Country.

Basque NGOs like BAKEAZ, El Karri, Bake Orin, IRSE and GEURNIKA GOGORATUZ have made numerous efforts since the "Basta ya" and Basque peace

[19] UNESCO ETXEA, Introducción a las Naciones Unidas, Estructuras y areas de trabajo, Govierno Vasco, 2002 and: Leah Levin, Derechos Humanos: preguntas y respuestas, UNESCO publishers/ BAKEAZ, 1999 (also in Basque language: Giza Eskubideak) in ENGLISCH "Human Rights, Questions and Answers, 4th edition, UNESCO Publishing, 1982, 1989, 1996,2004.

movements started in 1998.[20] Jointly, the compromise between human rights education and education for democratic citizenship has been *educacion para la convivencia y paz*, peace education. Peace education comes before human rights and citizen rights education and some would even call it elementary or basic education. But what it really shows is the fact that Basque society struggles very much with democracy and human rights due to the immense pressure of terrorist attacks by ETA, which is the nationalistic independence movement who have killed over 500 people including politicians and civilians since the 1960s in order to achieve independence for the Basque Country. Whoever opposed the idea of independence or the right to decide was under threat. Such is the culture of "fear" in the Basque country, which it seems, does not leave much space for a holistic educational approach to human rights for all.[21] Politicians, opposition leaders, NGO representatives and police forces are under threat and some, including peace activists, need bodyguards 24 hours a day. "Human rights are no reality in the Basque country" said Victor Urrutia, PSOE-EE Senator for the Basque Country in the Senate in Madrid. [22] Because of the constant fear and threat of violence people think about safety first and human rights come last. The programme of the Basque Government, the PNV, mentions the UDHR but highlights only one right, the right to decide and self-determination.[23] This human right, however, when it was first mentioned in the 1950s was meant only for decolonization efforts during this period. It would be hard to apply the terms of international law to the case of the Basque Country.

The UN-Decade and the private actors in Spain who felt they wanted to foster human rights education for all, did not find much understanding in the Basque Country. When talking to NGO representatives in Madrid about the case of the Basque Country, one received irritating looks. Spanish NGOs considered it a success to reach the national government on that issue, but the Basque government seemed unreachable. Even democracy education would not fit into the concept of the Basque government. The most to expect is peace education. Nevertheless, the Basque government published the UDHR in Spanish and Basque and also an introduction to freedom rights and rights of the European Union. Both were of little use for educational purposes but at least showed a willingness to inform the public.[24]

---

[20] After the assassination of conservative politician, Miguel Angel in 1998 by the ETA the majority of the Basque people was tired of violence and terrorist attacks. With "Basta ya!" many movements and manifestations started to seek for peace and non-violent conflict resolution in the society. Many NGOs started to set up offices and campaigns to unify the society and combat ETA.

[21] Interview with Txema Urkijo, Human Rights Commissioner of the Basque Government/ Founder of Peace Movement BAKEAZ, 14 February 2005, Vitoria.

[22] Interview with Victor Urrita, PSOE-EE Senator for the Basque Country in the Senate in Madrid, 28 February 2006, Bilbao.

[23] Govierno Vasco (Ed.), Estatuto Politico de la comunidad de Euskadi, propuesta de reform de Estatuto Politico de la Comunidad de Euskadi aprobada por la mayoria absoluta del Parlamenta Vasco en el Pleno celebrado el 30 de noviembre de 2004, p. 18-19, and 23-24, Vicotria-Gasteiz, 2005.

[24] Govierno Vasco, Departamento de Justicia, Empleo y Asuntos Sociales, Direccion de Derechos Humanos y Cooperacion con la Justicia: Todos los Derechos Humanos para todos, empezando por el Derecho a la vida, Victoria Gasteiz, 2001.

School books in the Basque country keep strictly to the quota of 55% coming from the central administration in Madrid and 45% from Basque authorities. Sometimes the Basque part exceeds the quota. This division has been a matter of dispute for many years between the central government in Madrid and the Basque government in Vitoria. Even though the Basque government is nationalistic, it does adhere to major democratic principles. Nevertheless, there has been no serious effort in revising Basque school books and introducing human rights education for all. Only the peace educational programme *convivencia y paz* is discussed as a serious next step to be introduced in the formal education sector.[25]

Spain is seen as one of the states which complied with the UN-Decade for Human Rights Education. This is due to the fact that NGOs invested resources to lobby the central government in Madrid. However, formal education and human rights are highly politicised as can bee seen in the case of the Basque Country. There, NGOs are only successful if they introduce peace as an educational goal which means solving political problems with peaceful means in a society in which there are those who support the violence of ETA and those who oppose it.[26] Whether the anticipated school book reform and a holistic human rights concept will also reach pupils in the Basque Country remains to be seen.

Armenia

Armenia, very much in contrast to Spain, is a country which has been in democratic transition since the 1990s. Under international pressure the Armenian government made all political commitments to international organisations such as the UNO, the Council of Europe and the OSCE to implement human rights standards and to set up educational and school book reforms after its independence from the Soviet Union in 1990.[27] But these commitments stayed at the elite level. They were made between the government and international organisations such as the UN-Development Programme (UNDP) and its office in Yerevan.[28] During the period of the UN-Decade for Human Rights Education, the strongest actors were the Ministry of Education, the UNDP and the World Bank who provided the relevant credit for the necessary school book reform in 2001. Overall, the UNDP office in Armenia had the resources and means to publish and translate international human rights documents such as the UN-Charter or Human Rights instruments into Armenian and the resources to train, for example

[25] Interview with Konrado Mugertza Urkidi, Director for Innovative Education at the Basque Government, Ministry of Education and Neli Zaitegi, Advisor, Basque Government, Ministry of Education, 15 February 2005, Vitoria. See also: Govierno Vasco (Ed.), Jornadas, educar para la convivencia y la paz en Euskadi, hoy, Bilbao, 2005.

[26] For example: Aranguren Gonzalo, Luis A, Educar en el sujeto solidario, Bakeaz, 2004; Fernandez Sola, Susana, Actitudes y comportamientos hacia la educacion para la paz en Euskadi, Bakeaz, 2004.

[27] Libaridian, Gerard J, Modern Armenia, People, Nation, State, Transaction Publisher, New Brunswick et al, 2004.

[28] About co-operation and developments in Armenia see for example: UNDP-Armenia (Ed.) Development Co-operation Armenia, 1998 Report, Tigran Mets, Yerevan, 1999.

teachers to understand what these documents meant.[29] Nevertheless, the UN-Decade was a side show that clashed with the interest of the Armenian government in undertaking necessary educational reforms to enable the country to be an eligible candidate and political partner for the Council of Europe, the EU, the UNO and other states in general. In 1998, under the pressure from the international community, the government of Armenia passed a resolution to decentralize school administration, undertake teacher training and to introduce civic education into the curricula.[30] The Ministry of Education was open to any suggestions and proposals from outside. Due to the lack of financial resources they accepted a grant from the World Bank to finance a school book reform in 2001. The content of these school books, which significantly carry the titles of human rights and civic education, was developed mainly through NGOs and individuals such as the Armenian Rights Protection Centre (ARPC) and the US based NGO Junior Achievement. "Human rights education is almost completely funded by donor agencies outside Armenia" was a conclusion drawn in the baseline study on human rights education financed by the UNDP in Armenia in 2006.[31] On the one hand external engagement and pressure from international agencies released the Armenian government from its responsibility to establish its own funds to secure reforms in the education sector during the transition and transformation period. On the other, external interference, the monitoring eye of the World Bank, the UNDP and donors from other countries were meant to guarantee that the reforms were aimed at the goals of international education standards and to anticipate the introduction of at least some human rights issues into the curricula. However, the reality was much more complex.

First, governmental officials and the Ministry of Education had no real interest nor did they know what civic education or human rights education really meant. As Razmik Martirosyan, member of the National Assembly and the governing Republican Party in Armenia till 2007, pointed out, "People are passive about their rights in Armenia; there is no culture of human rights. Armenians do not know what to do with these rights".[32] So in 1999, when the Council of Europe demanded the government set up an educational reform to fulfil the requirements of becoming a member of the Council, the government had little time to react and consequently its membership was terminated in 2001. Within a few months, governmental authorities applied for a grant at the World Bank, invited national and international NGOs to contribute and by 2001 they had the first school books ready. At the end of the UN-Decade this was a major contribution for the fulfilment of the UN World Programme for Human Rights Education. What was not mentioned was the fact that the content of the books was a mixture of old soviet style lectures and a description of international organisations such as the UNO or the Council of Europe. The book on civic education dealt

[29] UNDP-Armenia (Ed.), Human Rights Compilation, Charter of United Nations, Human Rights Instruments, Millennium Declaration, Yerevan, December 2003.

[30] Center for Educational Reforms Armenia (Ed.), Justice normative documents, Yerevan, 1999.

[31] UNDP-Armenia (Ed.), Baselines Study on Human Rights in Armenia, Yerevan 2005, p. 5. See also the article by Theresa Khorozyan in this book.

[32] Interview with Razmik Martirosyan, representative of the Republican Party of Armenia (RPA) in the National Assembly of Armenia, Yerevan 3 May 2005.

solely with national legislation and laws and therefore not necessarily in conformity with international human rights standards.

Even though the best intentions by many private actors were anticipated, due to the lack of knowledge on what human rights education is and the fact that almost all initiatives and activities in Armenia depended on external donors and organisations, the outcome of the UN-Decade was "civic education". Civic education or education for democratic citizenship was more in the interest of state agencies and actors, while at the same time international donors like the Council of Europe or the European Union fostered short term projects in the form of training seminars, targeting democratic and civic values rather than human rights. What has been underestimated in countries of transition such as Armenia is the fact that "civic" in most cases means loyalty towards the political system. As Valery Poghosyan, UNESCO-Chairholder at Brusov-University in Yerevan and Judge of the Constitutional Court of Armenia, pointed it out,

"(...) even after some years, students still behave very passively and hopelessly towards human rights and do not believe they can actually change anything. This is similar to other post-soviet countries. In all these countries people still have the soviet mentality of little or no respect for other people or human rights at all."[33]

Matching the demands of the UN-Decade and the international human rights community with the reality in Armenia remains a challenge. The government has been the most dominant actor in this field by first making the commitment and secondly allowing external actors to determine the curricula reform under the auspices of overall civic education. It was partly due to ignorance and partly intentional because the desire to please the international community was bigger than the desire to have a self assessment to see what was needed in terms of human rights in Armenia. The lack of a needs assessment by international donors and the lack of a political will by state agencies to transform from the soviet-style obedience thinking towards human rights awareness affected a large number of the NGO community in the country. Surveys in Armenia have shown that people are mainly concerned about the abuse of social and economic rights, health care, electoral rights and the issue of corruption.[34] But many NGOs follow external policies in order to get international grants rather than implement so called human rights programmes from outside Armenia. An exception to this is the Armenian NGO ACRPC, who since the late 1980's has undertaken continuous training programmes and is now in the process of establishing the first Armenian Human Rights School (AHRS). Although supported by international donors the centre and school has continuously being led by Armenians only who did a needs assessment first before they set up their educational programmes.[35]

---

[33] Interview with Valery Poghosyan, UNESCO-Chairholder on Human Rights and Democracy, Brusov University Yerevan/ Member and Judge of the Constitutional Court of Armenia, Yerevan 22 April 2005.

[34] UNDP Armenia (Ed.) What we know about human rights, National Survey 2004, Armenia, Yerevan, 2005.

[35] Manoukyan, Gevork, Two Priorities and Two Suggestions in Leading the Way to Human Rights Protection, in: Mihr, Anja/ Mkrtichyan, Artur/ Mahler, Claudia/ Toivanen, Reetta (Eds.), Armenia: A Human Rights Perspective for Peace and Democracy, Human Rights, Human Rights Education and Minorities, Potsdam University Press, 2005, p 31-35.

The case of Armenia, unlike Spain, is typical for a country in transition. On the one hand there is the bottom up approach of a few NGOs and private actors who are ready to change and start initiatives soon after the change of regime. On the other there is the government under pressure from the international community to adhere to international standards and human rights agreements and therefore has to implement a number of law or educational reforms under the surveillance of international organisations. Being under so much scrutiny to act quickly and being accountable to external donors like foundations and the World Bank, the Armenian government has had to pass laws and reforms quickly. It was the main actor but did not conduct the work itself. This was left to international organisations and NGOs, and overall the UNDP so the government had no clear human rights policy on what to expect from the curricula. And even though NGOs published by far the most training and educational material concerning civic and human rights it was the formal education sector which made the biggest difference in the country. And as a consequence, it is mainly the EDC which is promoted in these curricula.[36] That, combined with the fact that the post-soviet mentality and obedience to state law prevails, to introduce a holistic approach towards human rights learning and thinking could hardly have been achieved until the end of the UN-Decade in 2004.

Consequences

The commitment of governments and state policies are important factors when implementing human rights education programmes. This can be shown by looking at the commitments made by governments in 1994 when proclaiming the UN-Decade for Human Rights Education and the results from 2004. Even though NGOs and private actors are in many cases the pivotal and crucial factors, and without them the UN-Decade wouldn't even have been observed, it is the government and the state which takes the overall responsibility to communicate human rights education into the formal education sector. NGOs can by no means replace this responsibility or take up the task to train and educate a population in human rights.

Turning the commitments of a government into realization and fulfilment can take different ways. In the case of Spain it was a number of NGOs and in the case of Armenia it was the pressure from international organisations such as the Council of Europe and the UNDP. Whereas one case is the bottom up approach, the other case is the top down approach. In both cases a school book reform was initiated (in Spain in 2005 and in Armenia in 2001). And in both cases the involvement of the state or inter-governmental organisation in human rights education meant that the curricula is civic education and EDC orientated rather than towards education for democratic citizenship. This is in the interest of the state even though it is highly disputed among the human rights community.

The outcome of the school book reform seems to be similar but the impact may still be different. In Spain, NGOs such as Amnesty International will watch the re-

[36] For example: Khazinyan, Gagik (Ed.), Human Rights, Textbook for 8th grade, Tigran Mets, Yerevan 2001; Vagharshyan, Artur (Ed.) Civic Education, Textbook for 9th grade, Tigran Mets, Yerevan 2001.

form process and observe whether or not the changes of law and reforms will be implemented; in Armenia the responsibility to watch and monitor will remain in the hands of the international community which is less likely to be as quick and responsive to necessary changes in the curricula as NGOs.

III Teaching Human Rights in Different Political and Cultural Contexts

Educating Citizens for Democracy - Changes in the Estonian Education System

Sulev Valdmaa

Out of Communist Indoctrination

Since the late 1980s, when the collapse or at least unavoidable dramatic change of the Soviet system was evident, the first signs of the forthcoming changes in the education of Estonia started to take form. In order to understand the essence of today's compulsory education of Estonia, it is necessary to know the general aims, goals and features of the Soviet education system. This is indispensable to understand better the challenges which emerging democracy in Estonia has faced.

Soviet society placed most value on collective ideas and the collective good. It meant neglecting individual rights in theory and in practice. (For example, it was almost impossible to find and to read the original text of the Universal Declaration of Human Rights of the United Nations during the Soviet time). In the Soviet Union and in Estonia as in a part of it, where in a small country more than 100 different ethnic groups lived[1], an idea of unity, solidarity and friendship was propagated. But the unity was seen as embedding the recognition of the supremacy of Russian culture and Russian language, which in practice meant russification and assimilation of the different nationalities to a Soviet identity model. The Soviet Union was an example of a society with a developed personal cult. The economy was based on the principles of a planned economy. People were indoctrinated by Soviet propaganda, which declared church and religion to be the enemies of the people; historical events and personalities were classified into good and evil etc.

Education in the Soviet Union had to implement this type of ideology and social order among the fellow citizens, indoctrinating generation by generation. For this purpose there was a wide range of compulsory subjects in the Soviet curriculum. For example there were special courses for teaching the fundamental values of the Soviet socialist order and ideology which were taught in grade 8 (one lesson per week) and grade 11 (two lessons per week). Subjects such as history, the mother tongue, foreign languages, geography and even music were also carriers of ideology. The efficiency and results of this totalitarian influence can still be seen today, if we observe, to which extent the same patterns are followed or are visible in the hemisphere of the previous Soviet empire. Some of the countries of the previous communist block have made significant progress in the societal transition while some are more modest. Estonia's desire at the end of the 1980s, after half-a-century of Soviet occupation, was to restore the democracy lost in 1940.

---

[1] http://www.nationalities.ee/EST/art/viikberi_taabel.shtml.

The task appeared to be extremely difficult. All the fundamental concepts of democracy were unknown in Estonian society because they had been replaced with the contrary ideas described above. A couple of generations had been born in Estonia under communism and generations of teachers had been prepared in the Soviet education system the only aim of which was to reproduce the dominating values and attitudes of the 'Soviet multiplicators'. Estonia's inheritance from the Soviet system was a 12-grade compulsory education system for 7–19 years-olds consisting of primary, secondary and upper-secondary levels, a curriculum which determined a list of compulsory subjects, and a set of obligatory subject syllabuses, created, formed and developed under the communist regime and in the interests of it.

What gave hope to the people and to the new leaders to manage the societal change? There were two main agents: among the elderly people existed memories and knowledge about democracy in pre-occupation Estonia and continuous support during the years of Soviet occupation for the dreams of Estonians of a fair society on behalf of Estonian refugees living in exile and western democratic governments. The changes in society and in education had nevertheless to be made by the generation of people and educationalists living in Estonia whose upbringing and education took place under the communist system.

To draw a true picture of the situation in society during the days and months of the collapse of communism it is obligatory to mention that Estonian society (as in all the previous Soviet republics) was not monolithic in its future perspectives. The population of the former Estonian SSR was roughly divided into 2/3 of native Estonians, preferring overwhelmingly the restoration of a democratic free market society and 1/3 of non-Estonians (Russian-speakers)[2], who had entered the country as "civil occupants" under the years of Soviet occupation and who were afraid of the changes dreamt of by Estonians[3]. The term "civil occupants" may sound rather crude, but it reflects in its essence the nature of the people who entered Estonia during the years of Soviet occupation when there were no Estonian authorities to regulate immigration. Civil occupation was designed by the Soviet government to raise the percentage of Russian-speakers in the occupied territories to russify and connect forever the areas to USSR/Russia. From the 1950s to the 1980s people from other areas of the Soviet Union voluntarily used the freedom of movement inside the USSR to establish a home in the best developed Baltic countries which were Estonia and Latvia. Many people, who were considered to be valuable specialists in different areas were recommended/sent by the Soviet authorities from other areas of the USSR to Estonia and Latvia to "strengthen and develop" these countries economically, culturally etc. A special legion of civil occupants and military officers including family members were sent to the service of Estonia. At the end of the service period, the families attempted to stay in the country. The opinion that people entered Estonia from the other areas of

[2] The term non-Estonians was taken into use in the beginning of nineties of the last century to identify those people living in Estonia, whose home language was not Estonian. By ethnicity they were (and are until today) mostly Russians, but very often also rather diverse group of people, rather often mixed-ethnic families (Russian-Ukrainian, Byelorussian –Uzbek Kazakh-Udmurt etc), whose home language was/is Russian.

[3] http://www.estonica.org/eng/lugu.html?menyy_id=62&kateg=38&alam=45&leht=2

the Soviet Union were forced to do so is only partly true as the majority of immigrants entered Estonia voluntarily. The reason for their fear was the threat of losing the positions and privileges in everyday life. Those privileges were 1) the universal right/ability to communicate with anyone anywhere in Russian, expecting that everybody else speaks and understands naturally the language referred to as "the language of people's friendship" which in effect diminishes the aboriginal people's right to use their mother tongue, 2) often the higher and more responsible positions in the political, cultural and economical structures were filled with non-Estonians (like the puppet ministers of the Estonian SSR e.g. minister of education Elsa Gretshkina and others), 3) on entering Estonia, Russians were immediately provided with brand-new living accommodation or were settled into very prestigious apartments built in 1920s-1930s and taken away from their legal owners during the process of nationalisation, while Estonians waited for better living conditions for decades.

During the years of Soviet rule the use of the Estonian language in practical communication became narrower while the usage of Russian became more common. Potential changes in society may have meant a need to be able to communicate in Estonian in the near future, which non-Estonians couldn't speak. Official Soviet propaganda had also created a picture of the importance and very high standard of Russian culture, which had caused restrictions on the exercising of other nations' culture. Non-Estonians felt uncomfortable due to the threat of losing the "gained" dominating positions in all of aspects of everyday life. It was much better for them to maintain the status quo.

Under these circumstances, one of the most urgent needs for the new education system was the "purification" of the contents of education from the communist ideology and indoctrination. At the same time it was considered vital for the development of the new system that the people's historical memory about their "true past" be restored. Restoring awareness of the "true past" in reality meant after five decades Estonians were able to speak honestly about the nations' history, including telling the truth about relations with neighbours (including Russia) throughout the centuries, about achievements of the period of independence (1918 to 1940) and the process of the incorporation of Estonia into the Soviet Union (1939 to1940). These issues were prohibited during the years of Soviet occupation, because this knowledge could raise Estonians' self-consciousness too much and diminish the myth of the Russians as the saviours and big brother. In general, Estonia was willing to start a societal transition from totalitarianism to democracy and had to pass paradigmatic changes in the field of educational life. The question of the national capacity for identifying the needs for that change and the ability to plan and carry out the processes rose at the end of the 1980s.

The preconditions for the change in Estonian education meant in practice, that the Estonian government had to rely solely on existing teachers (no replacement of teachers as in Germany after the fall of Berlin wall was possible). In the interests of preserving a feeling of social security for teachers, it was necessary to ensure that every teacher could continue teaching their own subject and earn their salary.

Along with emotional feelings concerning the historical chance to restore independence and join the society of free democratic countries, practical steps were needed to be taken. The agent of these educational changes at the end of the 1980s

was a state institution called Eesti Hariduse Hariduskeskus (Estonian Education Centre - EEC), which employed specialists in content and teaching methods in all school subjects. This institution became the main body for educational change.
The staff of educationalists in EEC started the renewal of Estonian education from an intensive study of the educational systems of democratic countries. Contacts had already been established at the end of the 1980s with Estonia's closest neighbours - Finland and Sweden. Each subject specialist tried to find out the most important differences between the particular subjects taught in Estonia and abroad, and to determine the issues for immediate change for their subjects. Understandably there were no dramatic findings for natural sciences or language teaching, but differences in social sciences were dramatic.

EEC specialists in history and civics at first started to make efforts to "cleanse" the existing teaching content from communist indoctrination and adding other values and issues which were considered essential for democratic society but which was missing from Estonian content. It meant that in history teaching, simply to start speaking about the events which had taken place in the past as they actually had taken place and not to teach theories and versions useful for the Soviet authorities. It also meant increasing the part of Estonian national history, which had been minimal in the Soviet history syllabus. Civics however, was much more complicated. With the collapse of the Soviet state there was no sense to continue teaching the content of the 9th grade syllabus which concerned the basics of the Soviet state and law. The Soviet syllabus of civics in upper secondary school consisted of theories of "scientific communism", "scientific atheism", Marxist-Leninist philosophy and Marxist political economy. None of those theories were appropriate for emerging democracy in Estonia. To enable teachers to maintain their teaching quota immediate decisions were needed about what to teach instead of Soviet indoctrination courses. The solution offered by the Estonian Education Centre was teacher's freedom, "teach what you can, but not the old contents". Alternative syllabuses were offered by specialist's including ethics, logics and a course in world religions. Teachers were also allowed to compile their own teaching contents to replace the Soviet syllabus.

The EEC specialist came to realise that Soviet education didn't teach the basics of democracy, the concept of the rule of law, principles of market economy, human rights. The concept of the individual didn't exist in Soviet education. Realising those deficits, the first experimental syllabuses as alternatives for grades 4, 9 and 12, containing the basics mentioned above, were created following the foreign examples before the official collapse of the Soviet Union. The most crucial question arose which was how can we train teachers in-service to teach the alternative syllabuses if there is not enough intellectual capacity for that in the country?

International Aid

Luckily, emerging democracies were not left alone by the international democratic community. Western countries followed with great interest the steps for further societal development the east European countries were taking. As mentioned above, the closest neighbours to Estonia, especially institutions in Sweden started to offer professional aid to Estonian education. Among the various Swedish institutions offering intellectual and practical aid to Estonian education were the national agency Skolverket, the higher educational institutions of Malmö University, the Stockholm Teacher Training Institute (Lärarhögskolan i Stochkolm) and the Swedish Institute. Direct cooperation, targeted at the development of civic education was first offered by the United States. In 1992, in connection with the first democratic parliamentary elections in Estonia, a US organisation, the International Foundation for Elections Systems (IFES) sought partners in Estonia to cooperate on in-service training for teachers in civic education. An in-country partner was found in the Jaan Tõnisson Institute, a non-governmental organisation established in 1993 to foster democracy in Estonia. The Jaan Tõnisson Institute (JTI) was the first non-governmental organisation established in the emerging democracy (containing a steering committee and around 10 employees) matching the commonly recognized classification of NGOs. As a consequence, several western donors were found during the following years as cooperation partners for supporting democratic changes in Estonia, especially through education. From 1993 to 1997, the IFES provided financial support and sent specialist staff and lecturers who provided a series of five-day seminars for up to 100 participants[4]. The initial thirst for new knowledge on the basics of democracy such as the concept of the rule of law, principles of market economy and human rights was satiated. The majority of teachers involved in teaching civics throughout Estonia participated in those seminars and each time after the new experiences they were wiser and better prepared to educate their students about the essence of a democratic society. From the very beginning, society's division into Estonian and Russian-speaking groups was taken into account by the training providers and both sets of teachers were educated equally. Equal treatment of the Russian-speakers was necessary and nobody was truly forcing the civil occupants to leave the country. Some did it voluntarily, but others, who had over the decades lived in Estonia, started their families in Estonia and practically lost all ties to Russia or other areas of the former Soviet Union had no alternative. Many chose to stay in Estonia because they believed in Estonia's faster development and better living standards compared with Russia. Non-Estonians staying on, teachers among them, were seen as co-inhabitants of Estonia, whose teaching to function in the new democratic society was seen as beneficial to everybody. Equal attitudes and treatment of non-Estonians was easier to practice for non-governmental organisations than for official bodies, who had to solve the difficult question for a country being occupied for a half of century: Who is a political citizen of the country and who is not, which can also be interpreted as who has besides human rights, political rights?

Therefore, the initiative of developing civic education in Estonia went into hands of the emerging third sector. Non-governmental organisations appeared to be more flexible in using foreign support and working with foreign countries' NGOs. At the beginning of the nineties official structures behaved with a kind of suspicion towards the aid programmes offered to Estonia from the West, and they also tended to emphasize the differences between Estonians and non-Estonians, which restricted officials in their usage of the Russian language. Many new donors appeared in Estonia

---

[4] http://www.jti.ee/kodanikuharidus/en/projects/pro_civiceduprogram.html.

and offered different types of development assistance. No doubt the most influential agent of educational changes since the beginning of new era was the Open Society Institute (the Soros Foundation in Estonia) which paid attention to the issues of educational policy, renewal and modernisation of teaching methods, establishing contacts with foreign colleagues and creating different networks etc. Civic education also benefited from the programmes offered by the Soros Foundation. For instance attention was paid to the introduction of the teaching of human rights and law. International organisations like the National Endowment for Democracy (NED), Constitutional and Legal Policy Institute (COLPI), Freedom House, the Citizenship Foundation (Great Britain), The Hansard Society for Parliamentary Democracy (Great Britain), the movement of Helsinki Committees etc enabled applicant organisations from Estonia to apply for grants for cooperation in the field of democracy education.[5]

During the years 1993, 1994 and 1995 not only the above mentioned organisations and donors, but also the PHARE/TACIS programme and the OSCE mission allowed under four bigger programmes, the implementation many more projects for supporting civic education in Estonia. All of the projects provided teachers with knowledge and familiarized them with active teaching methods. Usually special written materials were compiled and handed out to the participants. We can say, that during the first half of the nineties Estonian teachers of civics got a valuable chance to become familiar with the basic concepts of democracy. Educationalists working for curriculum development enriched their professional skills and knowledge. Everybody realised that civic education is not something that a young person can simply learn on the streets, from the parents, on television and so forth, as had been previously thought. The general understanding that a society, which moves out of totalitarianism to democracy and personal freedoms, should learn about the fundamentals of that new society.

Surprisingly, some resistance towards the innovations was received from the Ministry of Education. For instance, the Ministry did not pay any interest towards the work carried out by the JTI and its partners which had produced new resources like Human Rights textbooks and methodical handbooks for teaching social subjects. The official position was that it was all additional alternative material for voluntary creative use by the teachers, as there was already a fixed curriculum to be taught, which according to the official opinion, did not require any supplementary resources. It was also evident that not all teachers attending the active teaching methods seminars and new textbooks courses were fond of the changes offered. Today we can find the consequences of that low level enthusiasm in the modern teaching of social sciences in Estonia where the national curriculum still doesn't put any effort to the innovative methods.

The result of this intensive offering by donors and its reception by the Estonian educators of the achievements of contemporary civic education concepts and practices was that in the first national curriculum of the Republic of Estonia, adopted in 1996, civics didn't appear as a random bunch of different alternative syllabuses, but as an obligatory systematic course in grades 4, 9 and 12[6]. It was also decided that

See examples of the programmes and contents on the website of the Jaan Tõnisson Institute http://www.jti.ee/kodanikuharidus/en/projects/.

6 http://www.ibe.unesco.org/curriculum/Balticpdf/vilnius10e.pdf, p 73, 74.

schools teaching in Estonian and Russian, despite the cultural differences of the two communities, should work following an identical curriculum and syllabus. Today, looking back at the activities and achievements of those days those can be assessed as the fundamentals for a transitional society. The characteristics of these innovations and changes were basic and general, not relaying on deeper analyses or expertise, but on empirical observations. The time for assessing the impact of changes and innovations made in Estonian education in general and in civic education in particular, had to follow.

Self-Recognition

After the 1996 national curriculum was enacted, the testing period for the civics syllabus started. The in-service training in cooperation with foreign partners brought teachers regularly together and the information about how the teaching was going was therefore accessible from primary sources. There were several complaints. First, teachers lacked deeper knowledge about some of the basic concepts they had to teach. They felt a lack of methodical skills to provide the contents in attractive ways. Also mentioned as a weakness was the low number of civics subjects: one per week in class 5 and two per week in classes 9 and 12. In some schools it resulted in lesson time being handed over to other subjects like mathematics or foreign languages. It was against the spirit of the national curriculum, but as there was no "danger", that such a "tiny" subject could ever be controlled by final examinations or by other serious assessments, that kind of practice was exercised. A compulsory course of civics in the national curriculum didn't appear to be very prestigious among students and teachers.

Curriculum developers and NGO training providers saw that the civics syllabus appeared to be too encyclopaedic; trying to inform learners about many things, but not teaching particularly anything. During the second half of the nineties, the understanding grew that a fundamental concept around where civics could be placed should be found. It guided educationalists to analyse what kind of civics was actually needed for Estonia as an emerging democracy, a society in transition. A specific characteristic of Estonian society (it's multicultural nature) was recognised as a dominant task for civics. Together with the issues of human rights, it rose into the focus of attention. The issues of human rights in Estonia (and in Latvia as well) were brought into the centre of discussion by the officials of international organisations, mainly by the mission of the OSCE to Estonia. The violation of the human rights of non-Estonians living in Estonia was publicised in the international press. The cited violations were mostly connected to political rights such as why Russian-speakers must have a knowledge of, and be able to speak Estonian and why they can't get Estonian citizenship without any special requirements. Not knowing the language of the country and not having political citizenship naturally caused some restrictions in the field of employment and also in the access to higher education for instance. On the other hand, Estonian teachers of civics let educationalists know about their needs of which the weakest issues taught by them were those concerning economics.

Teachers from Estonian language schools didn't share the view that the human rights of some particular groups of people in Estonia were being violated. Furthermore, when talking to them about human rights the general attitude was opposition. Usually, Estonian teachers argued that living in Estonia and not being able to communicate with Russian-speakers (e.g. regarding medical care and supermarkets) in their own language, Estonian, is discrimination of Estonians. They connected the whole range of problems concerning human rights in the world to people with different ethnic backgrounds and people in the less developed parts of the world. For them, it was an issue of the slave labour of women and children, wars in different parts in the world etc. Europe and Estonia were not considered as areas where violation of human rights took place. Speaking about the multicultural nature of Estonian society and specific needs of the representatives of different ethnic groups quite often met with the reaction that those who didn't like living there were free to leave the country. The comments expressing that idea still appear today, for instance in the newspapers' internet editions after articles reflecting problems concerning Estonian society's integration.[7] That kind of attitude was the result of long-lasting oppressive Soviet occupation which made Estonians victims of the Soviet system. People entering Estonia during the years of Soviet occupation were after the restoration of independence, legally recognised as occupants. The legal status of people being citizens of the Estonian Republic before the occupation in 1940 was restored under the principles of legal continuation. Those who entered the occupied country after WWII did it naturally without any legal permission of any Estonian authority.

The state launched campaigns and programmes for the integration of society. In the beginning even the term "multiculturalism" and "integration" were almost unknown. Under the guidance and observation of European structures, Estonian officials made attempts to bring those concepts into practical circulation. The Jaan Tõnisson Institute was continuously one of the main protagonists in the field. In 1995/96 a larger project of the Institute supported by EU PHARE/TACIS programme allowed Estonia to implement a project named "Education of a multicultural society"[8]. That particular programme brought different prominent specialists and researchers such as the internationally renowned, Professor John Rex from Great Britain to Estonia. Through the seminars and conferences, Estonian teachers, researchers, administrators and journalists explored the concepts of multiculturalism and international examples of education-building in multicultural societies. The project produced thee publications[9] on the issues of education in the multicultural society and two educational videos - "What is democracy?" and "What is multicultural society?" A good start for the deeper analysis of Estonian society as a multicultural one was made. These steps

[7] On January 12, 2007 an author under the nickname "M" says about Russians in the rubric of comments after an article handling Russian youth organization "Night Guard": "If they think they are discriminated in another cultural hemisphere – LET THEM GO HOME!" http://www.postimees.ee/120107/kommentaarikeskus.php?ARTIKKEL_ID=238902&TASK=KOMMENTAARID.

[8] http://www.jti.ee/kodanikuharidus/en/projects/pro_educmulticultural.html.

[9] Mitmekultuurne ühiskond: probleeme ja lahendusi". Tallinn, 1996; "Eesti koolid ja eesti keele õpe välismaal". Tallinn, 1996; "Estonian Schools abroad and Educational Institutions for Ethnic Minorities in Estonia". Tallinn, 1996.

helped Estonia to apply for membership to the European Union and to obtain EU candidate country status.

Additionally, during 1995-1997, the Netherlands Helsinki Committee supported the Jaan Tõnisson Institute in creating an original Estonian Human Rights syllabus and textbook together with a teachers' manual and a series of teacher in-service training and implemented a larger cooperation project[10]. All Estonian schools with Estonian and Russian language tuition were equipped with 30 free copies of the textbooks, written for the grades 6 and 8. The syllabus for teaching human rights using the above mentioned textbooks and teachers' manual is available in Estonian on the website.[11]

In 1995 in Prague, with the initiative of the United States of America, a wider international network of institutions CIVITAS International[12] dealing with civic education in the former Eastern Europe was launched. Estonia, represented by the Jaan Tõnisson Institute became a member of the network. At the same time the international partners continued cooperation with Estonian NGOs in fostering democracy in Estonia and developing civic education.[13]

For the development of civics in Estonia the second half of the 1990's saw a compulsory school follow-up of the implementation of the 1996 national curriculum and civics syllabus. Together with the mapping of the problems mentioned above and attempts to find solutions, continued a project-based development of content and methodical support of the subject teaching. For instance, in 1999-2000 an optional practical law course for upper high school was created starting from syllabus to textbook and teachers' manual to teacher training[14].

Civics in the Estonian National Curriculum 2002

In 2002 Estonia adopted a new national curriculum which was actually a revision of the 1996 national curriculum and the syllabus of civics in it was compiled in 2001. For civics, some content changes were added into the syllabus[15]. The main change for the subject teaching, however, was the underlining of the practical approach to it. Civics was not considered to be an encyclopaedic selection of different social knowledge, but as a subject giving the students' skills for orientation and participation in society and the ability to make critical decisions.

How was this change of approach put forward to the teachers? In 2000-2001 the Jaan Tõnisson Institute together with Indiana University surveyed Estonian civics teachers'[16]. The questionnaire not only included quantitative data such as the teachers age, years of teaching, amount of teaching lessons per week etc, but also self-

[10] http://www.jti.ee/kodanikuharidus/en/projects/pro_humanrights.html.
[11] http://www.ise.ee/oppekava/valikava/inimoig.htm.
[12] http://www.civiced.org.
[13] About all the projects of JTI see: http://www.jti.ee/kodanikuharidus/en/projects.
[14] http://www.jti.ee/kodanikuharidus/en/projects/pro_manlaw.html.
[15] http://www.ibe.unesco.org/curriculum/Balticpdf/vilnius10e.pdf,p.79 TABLE 4: Changes in the syllabuses of civics in 1992, 1996 and 2001.
[16] http://www.jti.ee/kodanikuharidus/en/projects/pro_survey.html.

assessment e.g. to what extent do teachers feel familiar with the syllabus content areas, how well do they know different active teaching methods, what do their lessons look like etc. The picture which came out of the collected data, highlighted that civics was taught mainly by history teachers, whose average age was over 40 and teaching experience was around 20 years.[17] Teachers complained continuously (as 5-6 years before) about weak knowledge in economics. They listed quite some active teaching methods known to them, but while they described the typical lesson, it resembled Soviet times: a 45 minute period of teaching dominated by a teacher narrative and a textbook reading. It was a strong signal to teacher in-service training that more methodical help was needed. According to the survey data, teachers in Estonian schools were slightly older. Russian teachers were better educated. If among Estonian teachers there was considerable amount of people without either higher education or without proper specialisation similar to the needs of civics, then this record was much better among Russian teachers. The phenomenon of the difference in the Estonian and Russian pedagogues' professional qualities discovered by the survey is explained by the following: after the shift of the societal order, life offered to most entrepreneurship-minded and talented teachers a challenge to start a new business in other, more financially lucrative areas of life. (For instance, English teachers left the schools, as there was a need for English speakers in the very well paid written translation and interpretation business.) The schools lost their best specialists and to replace them the schools had to hire less able or unprepared staff. But it was true only for Estonian and not Russian teachers because the Russians generally lacked Estonian language skills and were unfamiliar with the options in the society where they lived due to weak integration. For even the highly talented Russian teachers the school often remained the best working place.

Since 2002, JTI has started to offer civics teachers Project "Citizen" which was developed in the United States. Project "Citizen" is a universal project method making activities into attractive and exciting creative work for students aged 11-18.[18]

By that time a lot of research was done about the multicultural nature of Estonian society. According to the population census there were 1,372,071 people living in Estonia in January 2000. The number of Estonians among them was 935,884 (68%). The remaining 32% of the population consisted of around 120 different nationalities. Only four nationalities out of those 120 exceeded 10,000: Russians 354,660, Ukrainians 29,259, Byelorussians 17,460, and Finns 11,974.[19] The questions asked about that composition were: how/to what extent do those nationalities differ from each other?

Research was conducted by the Jaan Tõnisson Institute among Russian teachers and students asking questions about the cultural characteristics and preferences of non-Estonians, for example about food habits, attitudes to religion, principles of

---

[17] The research outcome was introduced at the US – Baltic Civic Education conference in Riga in 2002. The material has not been published.

[18] http://www.jti.ee/kodanikuharidus/en/projects/pro_citizen.html, http://www.civiced.org/index.php?page=introduction last visited 7 January 2008.

[19] http://pub.stat.ee/pxweb.2001/I_Databas/Population/01Population_indicators_and_composition/02Main_demographic_indicators/02Main_demographic_indicators.asp.

bringing-up children and of future perceptions.[20] Many respondents concluded that despite the linguistic differences, the Soviet past instilled similar features in all people of that society which today make us more similar than different. The main attitude was that the difference maker is not ethnicity or national belonging, but the amount of money in your purse. Partly this is true, but it doesn't mean that we do not have problems stemming from multi-ethnicity in society. According to different opinion polls and surveys Estonians and non-Estonians assess history differently and also future perceptions are different. The areas of disagreement mostly concern the issues of the events in Estonia between the years 1939 and 1940: was it occupation or Estonia freely joining the Soviet Union? About the future, the biggest difference among the two groups was that Russians quite often do not see their future in Estonia, but they dream about emigration to Canada, Germany or some other well-developed western country for instance.[21] This directly is an area for civic education to diminish such kinds of different value orientations which make the population of the country weakly integrated. Therefore, shortly after the adoption of the new 2002 national curriculum the possibility to pass a national examination in civics to graduate from secondary school was implemented. The institution of a national examination for graduating from secondary school was implemented in Estonia in the late 1990s in subjects like mathematics, mother tongue and foreign languages. It was observed, that in those subjects which offered a chance for taking national examination the teachers' and students' interest towards learning was much higher.

As soon as the same became possible in civics in 2002, a greater interest towards the subject from the students appeared and the teachers' responsibility toward the subject teaching rose accordingly. We have followed the rapid growth year-by-year of those students choosing civics for graduating from upper high school. If in 2002 the exam was taken by around 1000 students (out of 12000 annual graduates), then the figure was in 2003 around 2000, in 2004 around 2500, in 2005, 3600 and in 2006, 4300.[22] The explanation for such a rapid growth in participation can be simply students' love of the subject. And this is partly true, as in their evaluation lists at the back of the test paper students are giving positive feedback about it. The second argument is that for non-Estonian students the national examination is the examination which applies for Estonian citizenship. (This benefit is nevertheless used not by many students, because majority of them have taken the citizenship examination already at the end of grade 9.) The truest explanation for the popularity of the national examination in civics is its relative easiness if compared to what is needed for passing national examinations in mathematics or in history. Taking history as a national examination fell between the years 2001 (when there was no civics national examination) and 2006 from 5200 to 2200 pupils. It meant that the number of students taking history decreased by 3000 as the students decided to take civics instead.

To give an essence of what the national exam in civics is (the exam is in written form), it should be stated that it consists of three parts: essay writing, analysis of

---

[20] http://www.meis.ee/files/est_raamatukogu_uuringud/Eesti_yhiskonna_mitmekultuurilisus.pdf.
[21] See for instance: Integration of Estonian Society: Monitoring 2000, http://www.meis.ee/book.php?ID=100; Integration of Estonian Society: Monitoring 2002, http://www.meis.ee/book.php?ID=101.
[22] Data found: http://www.ekk.edu.ee/statistika/index.html.

documents and solving of different tasks/answering questions. For instance, in the first ever national exam in civics in 2002, the students were given optional themes for a minimum one A4 page essay:

Can a newsboy become a millionaire in Estonia?

The aging population as a problem of the society.

The example of an exercise in the national examination for analysing sources could be the following:

Compare the provisions of the Constitution of the Republic of Estonia as of 1920, 1933, 1937 and 1992 in terms of participation of the people in exercising the authority, i.e. find out how the people exercised the authority. Indicate the similarities and differences and enter them in table.

Excerpts from paragraphs of those constitutions named above were given in the paper. Students had to read the different paragraphs, compare and analyse them. Finally they had to write the conclusions about the similarities and differences into a table drawn in the paper. The example of a task in the national examination could be the following:

a) In your opinion, what is positive and negative for Estonia in the four freedoms of the European Union (1. free movement of labour, 2. free movement of capital, 3. free movement of goods, 4. free movement of services). Show your judgements in the assessment scale:

Negative ←—— *0* ——→ *Positive*

b) Indicate on the contour map the countries that were the candidate states of the European Union in 2002.

Challenges for Civic Education Today

In his paper *Democratic Multiculturalism: a New Model of National Integration* Mr. Raivo Vetik, speaking about multiculturalism in Estonia, wrote: "The essence of integration of Estonian society is specified in the definition of integration by two processes: social homogenization of the society based on knowledge of Estonian language and acquiring Estonian citizenship on one hand, and by preserving ethnic differences through recognizing the minorities cultural rights on the other. The Estonian version of multiculturalism, comprising the principles of cultural pluralism, strong common ground and preserving Estonian cultural space, based on the given definition, is formulated in the national programme of integration. Although the concrete content of the integration programme rests on the Estonian context, it can be assumed that the ideas it is based on are applicable to other multi-ethnic countries as well. [...] The aim of integration of Estonian society is to create an internally coherent entity ready to face the global challenges of the 21st century. The question in Estonia is no more set in a manner where the alternatives in ethno-policy are either national purity or complete blending. Instead, the ability to remain yourself while in change, is becoming a keyword for a successful development. In a democratic multicultural model of society this applies both to the majority and minority cultures."[23]

---

[23] Raivo Vetik, Democratic Multiculturalism: a New Model of National Integration. Åland Islands Peace Institute, 2000.

The conclusion in Mr. Vetik's paper concerning multiculturalism in Estonia is that our case doesn't fit well with any of the known models of multiculturalism. Estonia has worked hard on the issue including arranging international conferences, launching research projects, consulting with international researchers etc. The common understanding created is that Estonia's becoming multicultural has a certain and unique historical way. Today's ethnic composition of the population is rather unique as well. (Estonia's case is similar only to Latvia's.) The country cannot follow directly the international recommendations and models of multiculturalism.

Recognising the importance of the issues coming from the multicultural nature of Estonian society and the fact that there is lot to do for integration in society, an office of the Ministry of Population Affairs has been established in the government. The minister's responsibility is observation, research, planning and implementing processes supporting integration.[24] In Estonia there is also a special organisation, the Integration Foundation, which in its way deals with the issues of integration of society from various aspects. Through different campaigns and projects it supports education, research, mass media and several other fields of the life of society. The foundation practically influences the integration processes in the society[25].

The Ministry of Education and Research, responsible for the curriculum development, takes into account the ideas and points-of-view of both institutions; the Ministry of Ethnic Affairs and the Integration Foundation. Since the fall of 2000 there has been an ongoing process of remodelling of the Estonian National Curriculum. The leading body in the process is (since summer 2005) the Estonian National Centre for Examinations and Qualification (from 2000 to 2005 it was Tartu University). As indicated above, there were only NGO-based achievements made during the second half of the nineties for introducing the ideas of multiculturalism and also human rights to the teachers and to society more widely.

The explanation of why human rights seem not to have been highlighted in Estonia (and not only in education!) is, that human rights do not have such an emancipative connotation in the Estonian context. This is why civic education sounds more appealing as citizenship education was for a long time seen as something favourable because the decision makers tended to see "the Russians", the non-citizens, as the biggest challenge.

Nevertheless, HRE has now slowly started to become an easier topic to address. It is partly due to Estonia's European Union membership. The EU highlights human rights issues quite often and quite intensively and Estonian members of the European Parliament have themselves become activists raising the question of human rights, for instance in Chechnya and in several areas of the Russian Federation.[26]Ad-

---

[24] See: http://www.rahvastikuminister.ee/en/home/plans/integrationprogram.html; see: Action Plan of the Estonian Government: Integration of non-Estonians into Estonian Society, March 1999.
[25] See for instance report from 2003:
http://www.meis.ee/files/est_sihtasutusest_loppenud_nordic/Multi1_lopparuanne.pdf.
[26] See: Education in Vernacular Biggest Concern of Finno-Ugric Peoples - Estonian PACE Member. Estonian Review. VOL. 16 NO 45 NOV 15 - 22, 2006.
http://web-static.vm.ee/static/failid/045/ER_45.pdf;
Estonian Member of European Parliament on discussion with Russian parliamentarians on Russia's minorities, see http://www.kelam.ee/?mainID=45&newsID=130.

ditionally, Estonian teachers have become used to the issues during the past few years while the topic of human rights has been represented in the civics syllabus. In-service training courses on the content and active teaching methods training has made teachers more dedicated. Human rights are not considered to be a "problem of Russians living in Estonia" anymore, but as a global one. International terrorism, war in Iraq, asylum seekers all effect Estonia and makes human rights more meaningful.

One import change in curriculum development in Estonia in 2006/2007 was that of the separate teaching of civics in the grades 4 and 8/9[27] and teaching about human nature in the grades 1, 2, 3, 5, 6 and 7 will be integrated according to the concept of Life Skills (Health Education) and spread to all of the grades of elementary school from grades 1 to 9. The combination of civics and health education gives us a chance to form a new integrated course of social sciences, which deals in more complexity with human society and in doing so, the aim of the curriculum developers is to give human rights in the curriculum a more adequate meaning and better space for teaching.

Challenges for Human Rights Education and Civic Education

Today the problems of teaching civics and human rights are still there. One of the major problems is related to the teachers. As mentioned above, according to the research the teachers (not only teachers of civics) are aging. The numbers of young teachers graduating from the two pedagogical higher education institutions – Tallinn University and Tartu University are not sufficient for the country's needs. Even worse, after graduating from university the fresh, highly educated teachers do not proceed to the schools where they are urgently needed. They choose better-paid and easier jobs.

Old-fashioned teachers and schools in bad condition are still today a stereotypical image of the challenge for education. We really can speak in general about the problem of teachers being underpaid. But the situation with teachers' salary is not as bad as five years ago. At the beginning of 2007 the raise in salary was 20%. Teachers having an average amount of lessons (18-20) per week earn around 500-600€ per month, which is comparable to the average salary in Estonia. Also the renovation of schools (which belong to the local communities) continues.

One of the reasons why teachers graduating from the universities do not go to work in school might be in the existing system of the pre-service training and organisation of the training process itself. There are two ways of becoming a teacher of civics at Tallinn University:

1. Studying a 2-year, 30 credit points (CP) supplementary course called Social Theory, which gives to the teachers of history an additional competency to teach civics in elementary school and upper secondary school.[28] The curriculum contains 8 obligatory courses/subjects: Basics of Law, History of Civil Society, Concept of Civil

[27] The schools have the right to teach Civics either with one lesson per week in the grade 8 and one lesson per week in the grade 9, or with two lessons per week in the grade 9.

[28] See syllabus:
:http://www.tlu.ee/files/arts/5506/EST_K92ac6b3b61b0b4a8fb4471c5ced08b0e.rtf

Society: Meaning and History, The Models of Welfare State, Political Sociology, Basics of Economics, History of the World Perception, Understanding and Handling of the Main Problems of Philosophy. Those courses make 22 CP and the conclusions will be made through 3 CP Special Seminar. To cover the remaining CP the curriculum offers 19 different courses/subjects.

2. Studying a 2-year, 80 CP Master Degree course called Teacher of History and Civics giving primary professional competency for starting teacher's career.[29] The following components of knowledge and skills concerning Civics are taught to the students following this curriculum: Contemporary Economics (3 CP), World Religions (3 CP), Basics of Law (3 CP), Basics of Economics (3 CP), Political Sociology (3 CP). Also there are three blocks of Didactics of History and Civics in the curriculum (9 CP altogether).

Tartu University offers an 80 CP curriculum called Teacher of History and Civics.[30] The students graduating from the university will become masters of Humanities (Teachers of History and Civics for secondary and compulsory school). The curriculum is composed of the following parts: studies in general pedagogy, psychology and subject methodology (30 CP), master's thesis in pedagogy and/or subject methodology (20 CP), studies in the subject (lecture courses in Estonian, contemporary and general history, 26 CP), optional subjects (4 CP).

If investigating the above mentioned curricula to find out how human rights are taught to future teachers, we discover hardly any particular content. But we do find a 3 CP course of Human Rights and Human Development in the curriculum of Tallinn University for preparing class teachers for elementary grades.

In general, the teachers, who get their education at Tallinn or Tartu University, do not seem to have a fair chance of including human rights education in their training. There is more chance for the teachers to have an in-service training offered by the NGOs. NGO-based training has certain weaknesses such as: it is not systematic, it is not always oriented to the needs of the compulsory school curriculum, some seminars will remain too theoretical and do not offer the learners methodical elaborations etc. Most known NGOs teaching human rights are for instance the Estonian Institute of Human Rights (www.eihr.ee)[31], Estonian Union of Child Welfare (www.lastekaitseliit.ee) The Jaan Tõnisson Institute Civic Education Centre (www.jti.ee). The Office of the Council of Europe in Tallinn provides information about the Human Rights on their website (http://www.coe.ee/) and also supports seminars on the topic. Some activities informing about human rights have been provided by Amnesty International Estonian Group (www.amnesty.ee). Other organisations, such as Humanitarian Aid offers teachers events on the human rights topics.

The situation of the under-representation of human rights education in teacher pre-service training and it's random (unsystematic) character in in-service training follows into the classroom and appears there as a weakness of teaching about human

---

[29] See syllabus:
http://www.tlu.ee/files/arts/5188/EST_Afc6a1a205513e429c1a268f9656c38bd.rtf

[30] See syllabus: https://www.is.ut.ee/pls/ois/tere.tulemast

[31] See about EIHR seminar on Human Rights in 2002:
http://www.eihr.ee/Eng/seminar3eng.html and
http://www.koolielu.ee/pages.php/0705,5725

rights. The concrete case at each school level is of course always individual, as the teachers have access to the resources and they are free to include Human Rights education on the school syllabus.

Current Developments in Civics and Human Rights

In July 2005 the Estonian Ministry of Education and Research started a process of modernising the Estonian National Curriculum for elementary and high school. One of the guidelines given for this process was to integrate the interests of learners' better and to optimise the learning contents for similar and related subjects. As the guideline specifies, it concerns social subjects. Since 2005, the Estonian National Centre for Examination and Qualification, the leading organisation for curriculum development, has made efforts to integrate existing (so far separated but having similar contents and aims) subjects of Civics (grades 4, 9 and 12) and Teaching about Human Nature (grades 5-9) into one logical entity.

There is also a plan to integrate in the first three grades, social studies content and natural studies content into one subject which would allow a more united discovery of society for the young learner. The approach of teaching without subject boundaries (general studies) has been a part of Estonian pedagogical culture since the first half of the 20th century.

The approach of integration of social studies and related subjects so far has been received in society as a kind of surprise. In the mind of curriculum developers, the approach is promising. For integration, the concept of International Health Education has been used. It draws the attention of all educationalists to the necessity of teaching about human values and health issues throughout the students' school career such as hygiene, drugs, psychological aspects of human life, sex education, safety etc. Generated on the basis of the above mentioned idea of integration the subject for Education of Democratic Citizenship will allow learners to obtain a better knowledge, skills and attitudes for living in a democratic society. For curriculum developers, textbook authors and of course teachers the new approach will allow for much more flexibility in planning, including engaging human rights more intensively into classroom practices.

Democratic Reforms and Human Rights Education: Are the Education Reforms Directed to shape New Democratic Political Culture in Armenia?

Theresa Khorozyan

Introduction

During the past 15 years the educational system in Armenia has passed through considerable changes. The important question is whether the reforms in this sector have been directed at building a new democratic and human rights culture in Armenia through the successful introduction of Human rights education at all levels of the education system.

Human rights education is considered a human right and as being an integral part of a right to education[1]. Therefore, its realization is an important aim in itself. It is also a means to other important ends. Human rights education for all sectors of society is considered a crucial instrument to promote respect for, and protection of all human rights because it contributes to building a universal culture of human rights through the imparting of human rights knowledge and skills and shaping of attitudes. Such knowledge and skills will also contribute to *"the promotion of understanding, tolerance, gender equality and friendship among all nations, indigenous peoples and racial, national, ethnic, religious and linguistic groups"*[2].

In 1993, the United Nations World Conference on Human Rights (Vienna Conference) acknowledged that the principal role of human rights education was *"for the promotion and achievement of stable and harmonious relations among communities and for fostering mutual understanding, tolerance and peace"*[3].

Therefore, human rights education plays a crucial role in conflict prevention and resolution, and peace building and peace making. It is widely acknowledged that education in general, and human rights education in particular, can play a crucial role in strengthening civic engagement, conception of citizenship and sense of political efficiency. Human rights education can influence political and social behaviour[4] and thus, it can foster empowerment and participation in the democratization and policy processes. Thus, human rights education can also have a big impact in the process of building durable democracy in a country through knowledge and skills aimed at *"the enabling of all persons to participate effectively in a free society"*[5]. Bearing this in mind, intergovernmental organisations at international and regional level, namely the

---

[1] The United Nations Decade for Human Rights Education (1995-2004) No. 3 The Right to Human Rights Education: A Compilation of Provisions of International and Regional Instruments Dealing with Human Rights Education, United Nations, New York and Geneva, 1999

[2] "Human Rights Questions: Human Rights Questions, Including Alternative Approaches For Improving The Effective Enjoyment Of Human Rights And Fundamental Freedoms United Nations Decade for Human Rights Education (1995-2004) and Public information activities in the field of human rights", Report of the Secretary-General -- Addendum Guidelines for national plans of action for human rights education A/52/469/Add.1.

[3] Vienna Declaration and Programme of Action, A/CONF./157/23, 12 July 1993, paragraph. 78-82.

[4] A. Mihr (2004) "Human Rights Education: Methods, Institutions, Culture and Evaluation," Magdeburg, http://www.anjamihr.com

[5] Fn. 2.

United Nations (UN), the Council of Europe (CoE), the European Union (EU) and the Organisation for Security and Cooperation in Europe (OSCE) stressed the importance of human rights education on various occasions such as at events and in official documents urging its member/participating states to take relevant measures to provide human rights education. As a specific measure, UN called upon its member states to develop national plans of action for human rights education by the resolutions of the General Assembly and the Commission on Human Rights[6].

Democratic Reforms and Political Culture in Armenia

Since independence in 1991, the Republic of Armenia, one of the 15 republics of the former Soviet Union, has been carrying out various reforms in social, economic and political sectors which have involved the adoption of new policies and laws and the transformation of old institutions and the building of new ones. Armenia ratified major human rights instruments at international and regional levels as well as having carried out key legislative reforms to promote the realization of human rights. Yet, little attention has been paid to what people feel and believe about government, how people act towards the government and what their understanding of and attitude towards human rights values and principles are. Democratic institutions are a prerequisite for the establishment of durable democracy. At the same time, the democratic, political culture of a society is crucial for the progress of political development. Western democracies depend on the existence of an active civil society, in particular the informed and meaningful participation of citizens and civil society organisations that are the upholders of human rights and democratic values. It is hard to imagine a country becoming easily democratic when its society has continued to carry the legacy of a totalitarian regime. Likewise, serious improvements in human rights protection is less likely to happen in a society if members of that society do not appreciate the importance of the rule of law and share human rights values. The failures in implementing institutional reforms in Armenia are often caused by the existing "*mismatches between the new realities and people's mindset*" and could have a simple explanation that "*confronting new challenges based on the old practices and mindset will not only hinder the progress, but also make some segments psychologically opposed to change*"[7]. Furthermore, education reforms should have been directed at molding new skills and behaviour which are essential for a democratic society. In all those long years of the transitional period, the policy makers in Armenia, especially those working in the education sector, had to keep in mind that "*to choose an education system is to choose a kind of society we wish to be*"[8].

In centuries past, several factors hindered the process of building a national democratic culture. The nation lived without statehood and was oppressed by the Ottoman Empire for centuries. In the 20th century, Armenian society was deeply traumatized by over seven decades of communist totalitarianism. What is the current state of the

[6] GA resolution 1994/184, A/RES/49/184 6 March 2005.

[7] The National Development Report 2006: Educational Transformation in Armenia, UNDP Armenia, Armenia 2007, p. 22.

[8] Ibid, p. 16.

Armenian political culture? No systematic studies of the existing political culture have been carried out in Armenia. Various public opinion surveys were commissioned by international organisations to design strategies and programmes to assess the impact of the implemented education programmes. Obviously, such studies are not sufficient to thoroughly assess changes and developments in the political culture over the past few years. Nevertheless, the findings of the existing studies reveal certain tendencies in values, attitudes and civic knowledge and skills of the Armenian public. The following observations are noteworthy of consideration:

1) Armenian citizens exhibit democratic values in some aspects. According to the findings of the USAID/Armenia 2005 Democracy and Governance Indicators Survey, aimed at understanding, "how the democratic political culture in Armenia has been strengthened"[9], more than half of Armenian citizens exhibit tolerance toward political pluralism – 65 percent of respondents believed that the Armenian citizens have the right to belong to different political parties. 79 percent of the survey respondents agreed that media in the country should be free to criticize the government. But less than one fifth of respondents are tolerant to religious pluralism[10].
2) Armenian citizens demonstrate a low level of political efficiency. The USAID and IFES public opinion surveys indicate that citizens of Armenia do not have the confidence to believe that they can influence how things are run in Armenia and appear lacking civic skills. According to the IFES 2004 Survey, less than a third of respondents believe that people like them do have some influence and the 64 percent of the respondents asserted that people like them have no or little influence in decision making[11]. Significantly less than one seventh of the population considers that people themselves can have a determining impact on reducing corruption in Armenia[12].
3) For the Armenian, public elections seem to be the main form of citizens' participation in political activities. According to the 2005 USAID/Armenian Survey, 67.4 percent of all respondents surveyed and 68.9 percent of young adult respondents surveyed have not participated in any other forms of political action, except voting. According to the findings of the 2004 IFES survey, a majority of Armenians have never discussed their community or state budget (76 percent), signed petitions (77 percent) or attended community council meetings (90 percent)[13]. Armenian citizens demonstrate reluctance to contact elected or appointed officials with an issue or problem. According to the 2005 USAID Survey about half of the survey respondents have never contacted their National Assembly

---

[9] USAID/Armenia Governance Indicators Survey, Final Report, conducted by Development Network, December 2005, Armenia, p. ii.
[10] Ibid, p. i.
[11] "Citizens' Awareness and Participation in Armenia: Survey 2004" prepared by the International Foundation for Election Systems, Yerevan 2004, page 5, at
http://www.ifes.org/publication/9ae776581eb88e76e3448a40c707a1e1/2004_Armenia_CitizenParticipation.pdf.
[12] "The 2006 Corruption Perception in Armenia" conducted by the Centre for Regional Development/Transparency International Armenia with financial support of UNDP Armenia, Yerevan 2006, p. 31.
[13] Fn. 11, p. 24.

deputies but 18.6 percent of respondents and 18.2 percent of young adult respondents have done it very often[14]. Moreover, Armenians are less likely to contact appointed officials[15].

4) An Armenian citizen lacks the capacity to claim his or her rights or to seek redress. Half of Armenians would not go anywhere or did not know where to go if they or a family member believed there was a violation of their human rights[16] .
5) The Armenian public is not familiar enough with the work of the NGO sector in the country and demonstrates poor understanding about the role of NGOs in democratic society. The IFES surveys conducted in 2002, 2003 and 2004 have shown that most Armenians cannot name an NGO working in Armenia - about one quarter of respondents could name an NGO[17].

As a result of a few surveys commissioned by international organisations working in Armenia, general reflections can be also drawn on the level of the Armenian public's understanding of human rights. The 2004 Survey conducted in the framework of the UNDP/Armenia Project provides interesting findings on the understanding and level of knowledge amongst the public concerning human rights[18]. Overall, the Armenian public does not have a sufficient understanding about the modern concept of human rights and information about human rights standards and mechanisms. According to the 2004 UNDP Survey the Armenians believe in the universality of human rights and that individuals have human rights because human rights are natural rights that belong to all humans. At the same time, about a half of the survey respondents believe that people have human rights only because governments give them to people. The study revealed that the Armenian public lacks adequate information about internationally recognized human rights. Respondents had difficulties in identifying what a universal human right was, for example, nearly all respondents believed that driving on safe roads qualifies as human right (96 percent)[19]. At the same time, the freedom of religion was considered a human right by only 70 percent of the respondents. Overall, respondents tend to recognize socio-economic rights as a universal human right but were less familiar with civil and political rights[20]. Similarly, people tend to think that socio-economic rights are violated more than civil and political rights in Armenia. Forty percent of the respondents have indicated that their

---

[14] The 2004 IFES Survey has similar figures. According to the Survey less than a quarter (22 percent) of survey respondents has contacted elected officials to help with an issue or problem. The main reason for citizens' reluctance to approach elected officials as explained by the Survey participants is that it would have done no good – see Fn. 11, p. 26.

[15] Fn. 11, p. 27.

[16] "What we know about Human Rights: National Survey 2004, Armenia", prepared by the Turpanjian Center for Policy Analysis, American University of Armenia , UNDP Armenia, Yerevan, 2004, p. 9.

[17] Fn. 11, p. 28.

[18] Fn. 16.

[19] Fn. 16, p. 11.

[20] To the question 'can you please tell me if you think that the item is a universal human right that should be guaranteed for all people everywhere? " access to quality education, adequate housing, food, clothing, health care, fair employment opportunity received higher percentage of 'yes' answers (over 95 %) than freedom of movement, humane treatment of prisoners and freedom of religion (about 80 %).

rights to work had been violated in the past two years. The other two rights mentioned most by respondents were the right to social security (34 percent) and health care (22 percent). In contrast, about 18 percent of respondents stated that their right to participate in governance through free and fair elections had been violated. This figure was especially disappointing in view of the fact that those answers were recorded a year after the 2003 Parliamentary and Presidential Elections in Armenia which were criticized by local and international observers and were not considered to be in line with international standards of free and fair elections. Furthermore, the year the survey was conducted, the unified Armenian opposition demonstrated against election frauds and gross human rights violations during opposition rallies. Additionally, less than a quarter of the population believed that the Presidential (22 percent) and Parliamentary (24 percent) elections in 2003 were fair or somewhat fair. Nearly half have believed that both elections were not at all fair[21].

Human Rights and rule of law are not widely accepted as important national values according to the findings of the 2005 UNDP Survey. In a measure adapted from the 1997 U.S. survey, respondents were asked to name the national values most important to Armenians. Twenty-one percent of the answers specified culture, the arts, language and architecture, followed by 15 percent who named patriotism, and nine percent who said religion. About 2 percent (17 respondents) named human rights/justice and only 4 respondents considered rule of law as a national value[22].

Education Reforms and the State of Human Rights Education in Armenia

The education system of the Republic of Armenia has been gradually reformed with some accomplishments in the decentralization of education management, the revision of curricula in many disciplines, and the publication of textbooks in line with new standards. Several key policy documents and laws were adopted to initiate new changes in this area. A few social science subjects dating from the Soviet era were excluded from the curriculum and the content of some others were revised. Furthermore, new subjects were introduced in schools and universities, including human rights. However, changes in the education system have been slow to meet the present-day requirements. The timing of the UN Human Rights Decade (the UN Decade) almost coincided with the beginning of important reforms in the education sector in Armenia. Hence, the UN Decade could have been an impetus for the Armenian authorities to put human rights education on the agenda. Many of those who follow developments in the human rights education field reckon that reforms in human rights education have not been carried out in the spirit of, and in line with, requirements of the UN Decade. Human rights education was not declared a priority area in the education policy of Armenia. The findings of the 2005 Baseline Study on human rights education in Armenia back this view with detailed evidence[23].The objective of the

[21] See fn. 11.

[22] Fn. 16, pp. 14, 27 and 28.

[23] "The Baseline Study on Human Rights Education in Armenia", UNDP Armenia, 2005.
The Baseline Study was conducted within the "Promoting Human Rights and Facilitating Public Awareness of the Public Defender's Office in Armenia" joint project of the National Assembly and

Baseline Study carried out within the framework of the UNDP Armenia project in 2005 was to assess human rights education activities in Armenia within the framework of the UN Human Rights Education Decade with a focus on existing programmes for human rights education and curricula at all levels of formal education for all groups and programmes for continuing professional development. The assessment also focused on the organisational and financial support for human rights education in Armenia, the availability of human rights publications to the Armenian public, and analyses of national plans and of all legal norms pertaining to human rights education in Armenia. The Baseline Study reveals that a few steps have been taken to introduce human rights education in educational establishments in Armenia, however, these undertakings have been accompanied by major flaws as they were not based on the Baseline assessment and the comprehensively designed plans.

By the end of the UN Decade, Armenia had not adopted any special policy and/or law on human rights education. Existing state policies and laws in the area of education, including the 1999 Law on Education of the Republic of Armenia do neither directly claim human rights education as an indispensable part of the education system nor stress a paramount need to mainstream human rights principles and values in the curriculum at all levels of formal school education. A few paragraphs exist in the law, as well as in other policy documents that could be interpreted as referring to human rights principles and standards as the guiding principle of our education system. For example, universal human values are declared as a priority of the general education system. Likewise, the State Standard for Secondary General Education has a clause which declares that education should be organised on combined national and universal human values which makes each graduate of the secondary school "*appreciate both rights and responsibilities and be law-abiding, honest, humane, responsible, an initiator and an active citizen with an interest in social affairs.*"[24].

Albeit, the policy documents are not explicit in what is meant by the terms "universal human values" and "*combined national and universal human values*". Several relevant laws such as the 1996 Law on Children's Rights, the 1993 Law on Social Protection of Disabled Persons, the 2005 Law on Education of Persons in Need of Special Education and the 2003 Law on Human Rights Defender contain no explicit reference to human rights education. Regrettably, the National Plan of Action for the Protection of the Rights of Children in the Republic of Armenia for 2004-2015[25] which consists of over seventy items referring to the education of children, fails directly to advance human rights education and to instruct mainstreaming human rights principles and values in pre-school as well as in secondary schools in spite of the fact that the UN Committee on the Rights of the Child recommended Armenia "*to*

UNDP Armenia and financed by the Netherlands Minister for Development Cooperation. The Turpanjian Center for Policy Analysis at the American University of Armenia conducted the study and presented the findings in the report entitled "The Baseline Study on Human Rights Education in Armenia" is available at www.undp.am.

[24] "State Framework for General Education, State Standard for Secondary Education", Ministry of Education and Science of ROA, Yerevan, 2004, Antares (in Armenian).

[25] Adopted by the Decree N 17 45 N of the Government of the Republic of Armenia in December, 2003.

pursue efforts to promote children's rights education in the country...".[26] Inclusion of a an explicit statement in the law or in other policy documents claiming that education of the child in Armenia should be directed to the "*development of respect for human rights and fundamental freedoms*" and to the "preparation of the child for responsible life in a free society, in the spirit of understanding, peace, tolerance, equality of sexes, and friendship among all peoples, ethnic, national and religious groups and persons of indigenous origin"[27] could be the first indication of the existence of a genuine political will in Armenia to take human rights education seriously.

The state of human rights education is very much in line with the spirit of the above mentioned policy documents. In reality, human rights education has not received adequate financial and organisational support from the government[28]. The state budget has never included special financial allocations for human rights education programmes. International organisations remain the primary funding source for human rights education in Armenia, including for school programmes.[29] Following the logic of the UN Decade, the World Programme for Human Rights Education (following the World Programme) urged governments to appoint or strengthen a relevant Department/Unit responsible for coordination with all relevant actors and to serve as a national focal point for human rights education in the school system in the first phase (2005-2007) of the World Programme. According to the 2005 Baseline Study, no special state coordinating body or a focal point for human rights education was in place to identify national needs and to provide policy advice in this area. A section of the website of the Office of the High Commissioner for Human Rights which provides information on the existing focal points for the national implementation of the first phase (2005-2007) of the World Programme contains no information about a human rights education focal point in Armenia[30].

The Plan of Action for the UN Decade listed national human rights institutions as a principal actor in human rights education.[31] As the Office of the High Commissioner of Human Rights (which reports experiences from several countries) demonstrates, national human rights institutions can function as a key actor in coordinating and facilitating the provision of human rights education to various sectors of society. The Human Rights Defender of the Republic of Armenia, established in 2004[32] has not been empowered by the law with the mandate to "*assist in the formulation of*

---

[26] Concluding Observations of the Committee on the Rights of the Child: Armenia, CRC/C/15/Add.225, 30 January 2004.

[27] Articles 17 (a, b) 19 (1) and 29 (1: a, b, c, d, e) of the Convention on the Rights of the Child, 1990.

[28] See fn. 23.

[29] For example, the publication of textbooks on human rights and civic education for secondary schools was funded by the World Bank project and the first training of teachers for these subjects is implemented by Junior Achievement and funded by USAID/Armenia.

[30] http://www.ohchr.org/english/issues/education/training/initiatives.htm, last visited in July, 2007 See alsohttp://www.ohchr.org/english/issues/education/training/national-focal.htm.

[31] A/49/261-E/1994/110/Add.1, Annex.

[32] The Ombudsman institution in Armenia was created on the basis of the 2003 Law on the Human Rights Defender. Armenia is the last country in the sub-region to establish an Ombudsman institution. Furthermore, the Human Rights Defender Office is the youngest national human rights institution in the territory of the former USSR.

programmes for the teaching of, and research into, human rights and to take part in their execution at schools, universities and professional cycles" and "*publicize human rights and .. increasing public awareness, especially through information and education...*" as the Paris Principles recommend[33]. In spite of this, the first Human Rights Defender Ms. Larisa Alaverdyan expressed her strong interest in engaging in human rights education initiatives. Raising awareness on human rights was declared an important objective for the Human Rights Defender to achieve.[34] Yet, her appointment was too short to turn her words into action. No facts are available about human rights education initiatives undertaken by the present Human Rights Defender who was appointed in 2006. In the absence of another specialized body, the Human Rights Defender's office could play an important role in human rights education in Armenia.

Human Rights Education at Pre-School

Human rights education has not received due attention in pre–school education in Armenia. Existing education policies and legislation do not command human rights values and human rights principles to be mainstreamed in the pre-school education system. Consequently, human rights principles and values are not included in the pre-school education curriculum. This is very unfortunate because pre-school years are a crucial period for each person to develop values, skills and behaviour of a responsible and free citizen of a democratic society. For example the National Programme of Human Rights Education of Croatia rightly asserts that "*the foundations of life in democratic society are laid at the earliest age of a child because what we acquire at that age, we carry out throughout our lives... what we miss at that age, we cannot compensate for later in life*."[35] Therefore, the current state of pre-school education is a missed opportunity for Armenia and thus, immediate measures needs to be taken to mainstream human rights principles and values, including tolerance and non-discriminatory attitudes by integrating them in games, training and the syllabus as well as the overall process of communication at the pre-school level. This is also required by the World Programme.

Human Rights Education at Secondary School

The most considerable human rights education efforts undertaken by the Armenian authorities were the introduction of the human rights and civic education into the

[33] Paris Principles Relating The Status Of The National Institutions, adopted by the resolution of the UN Human Rights Commission 1992/54, 1992 and the UN General Assembly Resolution 48/134, 1993.

34 Annual Report: Activities Of The Republic Of Armenia's Human Rights Defender, And On Violations Of Human Rights And Fundamental Freedoms In Armenia During 2004, Yerevan, 2004.

[35]National Programme of Human Rights Education," Zagreb 1999, in Compendium of National Plans of Action for Human Rights Education (including relevant excerpts from National Human Rights Action Plans), [Unedited Version], Office of the High Commissioner for Human Rights, Geneva, 2001, p. 21, para. 2.

State Curricula for Secondary Education in 2000[36]. These subjects have been taught in grades eight and nine since 2001[37]. The Education Quality and Relevance Project of the World Bank financially supported the publication of textbooks for these subjects. Since then the textbook has been a subject of criticism by human rights community in Armenia for various reasons. The 2005 study shared the key concerns expressed by independent experts including the arguments that the textbook contains some outdated information, pays little attention to human rights issues contextually relevant to the country and lacks the use of culturally relevant examples[38]. Along with several principles which the World Programme puts forward, the human rights educational activities shall "be relevant to the daily life of the learners, engaging them in a dialogue about ways and means of transforming human rights from the expression of abstract norms to the reality of their social, economic, cultural and political conditions"[39]. There is no alternative textbook available for the teaching of the human rights subject in Armenia. A 70-page pamphlet in the teachers' manual was provided by the Ministry of Education and Science to be used for human rights, civic education and state and law subjects which fall under the 'legal chapter' in the state curriculum.[40] However, according to the findings of the 2005 Baseline Study, not all teachers received the manual and those who did use it, did not consider the manual useful for their needs because it failed to serve as "a comprehensive methodology guide as it only says "what to do" and not "how to do it...". The teaching of human rights requires interactive and participatory methods. Since such methods have not been traditionally part of our educational system, teachers need appropriate guidelines and training to apply them properly. A supplementary manual was published by the Armenian Constitutional Rights Center with the financial support of CORDAID Netherlands and approved by the Ministry of Education and Science[41]. The teachers consider the content of this manual more informative that the first manual. No doubt the second manual contains an extensive list of themes important for the human rights teacher. Yet, the volume of the manual is too small to cover all the themes in-depth. It makes references to the domestic legislation but it is again deficient in useful illustrative cases taken from real life situations in Armenia. The manual's content could be improved further by presenting more accurately the concept of human rights and to elaborate further on human rights standards in easy to understand language. A good example of concept-specific shortcomings occurs in the first chapter of the manual

[36]In spite of this the state curriculum for special needs students in special education schools does not include the human rights subject.

[37] Human Rights were one of three subjects included in the "Legal Bloc" introduced in 2000.

[38] Last two criteria are listed among sample criteria for human rights textbook review by Tibbitts F. (1997) "Evaluation in the Human Rights Education Field: Getting Started" HREA, at: http://erc.hrea.org/Library/research_evaluation/evaluation-guide.pdf.

[39] "Human Rights Questions: Human Rights Questions, Including Alternative Approaches For Improving The Effective Enjoyment Of Human Rights And Fundamental Freedoms: Revised Draft Plan of Action for the First Phase (2005-2007) of the Proposed World Programme for Human Rights Education", Note by the Secretary General, 2005, A 59/525/Rev. 1.

[40] Harutyunyan N., and A. Vagharshyan (2004) "Manual for Human Rights, Civic Education and State and Law: 8-10th Grades," Yerevan, Tigran Mets.

[41] Manukyan G., Papikyan A., Parsamyan V., "Human Rights: Manual for the teacher", Vanadzor, Armenia, Arminfo, 2002.

where the author does not mention the principle of equality and non-discrimination as one of the main principles of the modern concept of human rights alongside the other principles such as universality, inalienability, indivisibility and interdependence[42]. In the chapter "The Concept of Law" the author of the manual lists several sources of law and then concludes that, "*But the only true source of law is the Bible.*"[43]

In 2000- 2001, when human rights education was introduced to secondary schools, the imperative was to prepare an adequate number of educators to teach human rights within a year. Junior Achievement of Armenia, a local NGO carried out the training of human rights teachers in cooperation with the Ministry of Education and Science of the Republic of Armenia and financial support of USAID Armenia until 2004. Teachers of history and other social subjects were re-trained by means of a short training programme to become human rights teachers. In the period of 2002 – 2006 another local NGO, the Armenian Constitutional Rights-Protective Center reached an agreement with the Ministry of Education and Science to train 400 teachers during the period of 2002-2006 and to publish teacher manuals and other supplementary materials on human rights.[44] Despite this, human rights teachers still face serious challenges to effectively train the young generation of Armenia on human rights standards and mechanisms and to try to help school students form a new attitude and behaviour and to adopt a human rights culture. The initial short training could have only been a good introduction to the subject and would have hardly enabled a re-trained teacher specialized in other disciples, to gain adequate knowledge and be very confident in the subject. The findings of the 2005 Baseline Study revealed that "*many teachers are themselves lacking a good understanding of main human rights principles and standards*"[45].

Furthermore, a human rights teacher or educator needs to share human rights values and possess a comprehensive understanding of the practical aspects of human rights work in order to be able to change attitudes and behavior. During focus group discussions carried out as part of the 2005 Baseline Study, most of the teachers, especially those living the countryside, expressed a strong belief that some human rights, including an individual's freedom of religion and equal rights for men and women contradict Armenian culture and traditions. The question is, can we put our trust in a teacher to teach our youth about equal rights of men and women if the teacher complains that "*talking about women's rights will bring about the destruction of Armenian families and if human rights destroy Armenian national traditions then they are not justified.*"[46]

A supportive environment for human rights educators is lacking in Armenia. Human rights teachers lack access to relevant materials in Armenian, including educational printed materials and audiovisual aids and updated information on this relatively new subject. No human rights documentation libraries or resource centers exist for human rights teachers. As a result teachers find it difficult to follow new devel-

---

[42] Ibid, p. 12.

[43] Ibid, p. 9.

[44] Memorandum of Intentions between the Armenian Constitutional Right-Protective Center and the Education Reform Center of ROA Ministry of Education and Science, 24 January, 2001.

[45] See fn. 23, p. 28.

[46] Fn. 23, p. 25.

opments in the area of human rights at both local and national level. More than a year after the establishment of the post of Human Rights Defender in Armenia, the majority of teachers interviewed as part of the 2005 Baseline Study stated that they did not have a chance to "*look through*' the law on the Human Rights Defender to learn about the role and functions of this important national human rights institution[47]. Similarly, because of limited access to the internet and the absence of relevant materials in the Armenian language, teachers have a very limited possibility of getting familiarized with current developments in international organisations, work of human rights NGOs and experiences and materials of their colleagues from other countries. Several studies, including the 2005 Baseline Study indicate that media remains the primary source of information for the most of the teachers. There is no study that provides a thorough assessment of the content of media coverage on human rights issues. However, considering the fact that TV, which remains the primary source of information for the public lacks independence, objectivity of human rights reporting could be questioned even without a professional assessment. Additionally, the national media very rarely covers new developments in the area of human rights at the international level. I find it difficult to recall media coverage on the reformation of the UN charter-based human rights body, namely the Human Rights Commission or the work of the newly established International Criminal Court. The small exception is the European Court of Human Rights in Strasbourg which receives coverage from time to time. Having the above mentioned in mind, effective human rights teaching in secondary schools requires a continuous effort to produce human rights materials in Armenian both for teachers and students.

Learning to do and to be is as important as learning to know. The Armenian education system is traditionally a knowledge-based system which is less suitable for changing attitudes and developing skills to claim rights. The 2006 Human Development Report points out that,

"*In a dynamically evolving world, our education remains faithful to the delivery of ready-made knowledge and testing by recital, rather than problem-solving, application of knowledge, and development of skills*".[48]

It will take years to change this educational culture even if there is a political will to do it. Moreover, school students rarely witness in their daily life adults demonstrating civic activism and vigorously seeking redress for their violated rights. What would an average 15-year old student observe for example, if a human right of a family member was violated? Most likely an adult member of the family would decide not to take any action by concluding that,

"*We would not be in a position to change anything, so our efforts would be a waste of time*". "*I have a good friend who is very influential and can help me to address this situation so let's call him*"

– could possibly be another remark a teenager would hear in such a situation. Therefore, such behaviour of parents and neighbours would hardly have a positive influence for the formation of human rights culture amongst Armenia's youth. This situation creates an additional burden for a human rights teacher and the education system

[47] Fn 23.

[48] See Fn. 7, p. 28.

in general and makes it the primary institution to foster a positive impact on the attitude and behaviour of youth. Therefore, to be able to establish a human rights culture among school students, human rights classes need to be accompanied with human rights related extra-curricular activities in close cooperation with human rights practitioners and non-governmental organisations.

Then again, specialized human rights courses can change little if an education system still relies on an authoritarian teaching style. During the 2005 Baseline Study human rights teachers talked about 'problematic' situations where students were addressing such questions so teachers would face a dilemma if they answered based on what they taught in human rights classes or what is practiced in schools. For example, a student asked whether or not teachers could hit school students. The teacher explained, "*I realized that I could not give him a clear answer because if I answered 'no' he might not obey me any longer* and if I said 'yes' I would be contradicting what I teach during my classes."[49] Human rights education should be seen as a process of "human rights in education" that ensures the respect of the human rights of all actors, and the practice of rights, within the education system"[50]. Therefore, the learning environment in school should protect students' dignity but should not promote relations between students and teacher and compliance of the former based on fear and use of force.

Last but not least, one or two separate subjects on human rights and civic education would not be in a position to have the desired impact if other courses did not avoid stereotyping in language and illustrations, did not preach tolerance, equality and non-discrimination. Human rights education should be considered as a process of "human rights through education" which implies "*that all the components and processes of learning, including curricula, materials, methods, and training are conducive to the learning of human rights*". Would it be possible at all to promote tolerance among school students through a separate module if textbooks and teaching of other subjects implied intolerance towards other cultures, traditions and belief? No doubt a separate subject would have a very minimum impact.

Human Rights Education in Universities

The state of human rights education at the higher education level is also not yet satisfactory. One third of higher education establishments offer human rights courses and about 60 percent of those provide human rights courses for law students only, according to the findings of the 2005 Baseline Study[51]. All institutions offering a human rights course face those problems familiar to secondary schools such as the paucity of highly qualified lecturers, the absence of consistent professional training, the scarcity of literature in Armenian and outdated materials, the absence of research in higher academic institutions in this new discipline and an insufficient number of academic hours for the subject at University level for example. Furthermore, low salaries, nepotism and corruption in the faculty recruitment processes create obstacles for a new

[49] Fn. 23.
[50] See fn. 39.
[51] See fn. 23.

generation of educators to join the universities, in particular those who have received their graduate and post-graduate education in the west. Albeit, some of the private universities have proven to be more open to the involvement of prominent human rights activist as lecturers. Interaction with human rights lecturers and a review of course outlines reveals a certain misinterpretation of human rights concepts and standards. For example, the rights of women, family, children, disabled and vulnerable groups are presented as collective rights. Recently, I had a chance to gently remind a law professor who taught family and women's rights as collective rights that the international human rights law claimed differently.

Human Rights Education for Professionals

Human rights education for key professionals and state officials is another area that requires considerable efforts directed at institutionalizing human rights in pre-service and in-service training. In the past decade, various human rights training and awareness-raising events were organised for a large number of professional groups such as judges, police, defence lawyers, prison officials, journalists and military officers. A large portion of this training was organised or supported by international donors and organisations with different short term projects. The majority of the training for professionals was not provided in a systematic and on a constant basis but rather in a form of short 'ad hoc' training and to a limited number of professionals. Therefore, the existing training programmes for professionals and state officials could not have had the desired impact and could not have provided effective and constant education opportunities in human rights education.

Conclusion

As a country in political and economic transition, Armenia faces an urgent need to shape the mindset of its population in order to effectively foster substantive progress in democratic and economic sectors along with institutional changes. Desirable changes in political culture depend greatly on successful reforms in the education sector in general and the effective integration of human rights education at all levels of the education system in particular. To this end it is imperative that the respective policy documents are amended to explicitly recognize and ensure that the education system in Armenia is directed to educate a society with strong democratic and human rights values and skills. These policies should also set human rights education as a priority area for education reforms and spell out a comprehensive plan with short term and long term activities to improve the quality of human rights teaching at all levels of the education system. Furthermore, adequate state funding should be allocated to human rights education unlike in the past and the present day when human rights education has been dependent on donor funding. Human Rights NGOs can continue to be effective service providers in teacher training but their dependence on international donor funding makes their work less sustainable. Thus, advanced and regular training of human rights teachers would not be possible without state funding allocated for this purpose.

As teaching and the general environment in Armenian education continue to hold on to the legacy of the past, a separate human rights subject would hardly have a profound impact in shaping new attitudes and behaviour. One possible solution for this situation would be to mainstream human rights principles and values in the teaching of all school subjects in Armenia. The full integration of human rights in schools would require the teaching of all courses to be reviewed and revised and teachers of other subjects would have to be educated in the main principles of equality, non-discrimination and tolerance.

Bearing in mind the enormous efforts required for serious improvements in human rights education, the development of a national plan of action on human rights education could be very useful tool to effectively plan and coordinate such efforts. Unsuccessful implementation of previous national plans of action in other areas should not serve as a reason to undermine a need and effectiveness for a national action plan; rather the past experience should be seen as a possibility to learn lessons. If a national plan of action on human rights education was developed through the active and meaningful participation of all stakeholders concerned, based on the Baseline studies and assessments, based on lessons learned from successful experiences of other countries and had clearly identified the roles and responsibilities of each actor for its implementation, we would have a national action plan reflecting the true needs of the sector including realistic mechanisms for successful implementation. Constructive coordination with international donors working in the area of democracy, human rights and education could possibly result in donors providing a part of the funding for the implementation of action plans rather than carrying out separate short term projects and thus, assure more sustainable donors' contribution.

Sustainability of Human Rights and Minority Education
Reetta Toivanen

Introduction

"When it remains at the level of a recital of abstract human-rights norms, human-rights education may come dangerously close to a secular religion, a set of universal truths that pretends to be self-evident, which it might be in an ideal world, but surely is not in ours. [...] The results of such a learning process are negligible, if not altogether absent."[1]

This article tackles the question of how international initiatives to promote human rights education in the European context succeeded during the United Nations Decade for Human Rights Education (1995-2004).[2] The contents of this article are based on the research conducted for the 'Teaching Human Rights in Europe'- project described in chapter two. The success is gauged with questions regarding the sustainability of the programmes and projects. National implementation is addressed as the key issue in establishing sustainable human rights education. The paper will argue that when international support was given to national non-governmental organisations as external help without involving the governmental agencies as national partners, sustainability suffered as a consequence. It will be shown that in most cases, international organisations sought support for the implementation and monitoring of human rights education amongst the civil society of the countries. Whereas this can be welcomed as efforts of supporting civil society actors, a successful programme clearly needs a common approach taken by both the governmental and non-governmental sectors. Some national foundations, especially in the three EU member states analysed in this study, actively supported human rights education; their outreach, however, remained unclear.[3] As the empirical focus of this paper is on minority organisations' possibilities of promoting equality and non-discrimination, the case studies mainly from Germany and Estonia shall illuminate the challenges encountered by minorities in participating in the programmes as equal partners.

There are great differences in how governments and non-governmental organisations interact with each other between the post-socialist states on the one side, and the established "old" western states on the other. What they share is that human rights education in both "systems" is considered to be merely a short term problem solving tool. A government is most likely to find interest in human rights education when it is seen as a means of securing societal peace and thereby securing the existing power structures. The same attitude applies to intergovernmental organisations such as the Council of Europe[4] and the Organisation for Cooperation and Security (OSCE).[5]

---

[1] Katarina Tomaševski, at the ODIHIR/OSCE meeting on Human Rights Education in Vienna, 2004.

[2] See more in chapter 1 of this publication.

[3] The German government offered human rights education material produced by the Bertelsmann Foundation as proof for *their* human rights education actions to the United Nations.

[4] Mahler, Claudia, ‚Menschenrechtsbildungsprogramme im Bereich des Europarates' in: Claudia Mahler / Anja Mihr (eds.) Menschenrechtsbildung Bilanz und Perspektiven. Wiesbaden: Sozialwissenschaftlicher Verlag, 2004, 105-116.

Therefore, the support by international foundations and independent philanthropists is fundamental in order to guarantee a circulation of human rights knowledge with less strict ties to governmental policies. Many governments would not voluntary invest in human rights education and international funding is often the only channel financing human rights activities. This is a fact even though human rights education is a state duty laid down in numerous human rights treaties.[6]
It is, of course, not possible to measure the success of human rights education projects and equally impossible to find out in which ways the understanding (and misunderstanding) of human rights are spread and kept over a lifetime by an individual person. Our research was not designed to analyse any causal relationships between human rights education and human behaviour, so the sustainability is here gauged against the perceived responsibility taken by governments, local governments, international organisations and larger NGOs. The responsibility is reflected in the opinions and perceptions of the key persons in these institutions. The research team conducted over 200 interviews in six European countries, Armenia, Estonia, Finland, Germany, Slovakia, and Spain, and undertook several two to six weeks visits to these countries in order to achieve a grassroots understanding of how human rights education actually takes form and takes place. The team focussed especially on the question of how minority needs and issues are integrated into the framework of general human rights education.

The first part of this article discusses the concept of sustainability and its meaning for human rights education especially when dealing with the needs of national minorities. The second summarizes some international initiatives which aimed at promoting human rights education. The third part introduces how human rights education was promoted in the case study countries of Germany and Estonia. The fourth part addresses the challenges of human rights education faced by minority populations in these two countries. The final part summarizes the results of this study; human rights and human rights education has to be defined and coordinated concomitantly by the international community, representatives of states and civil society. However, the greatest challenge is how to create a more inclusive understanding of what constitutes a civil society. Members of minorities and other marginalized sectors have to be partners in this definitional enterprise in order to promote a human rights based holistic approach to education.[7]

---

[5] Toivanen, Reetta, ‚Organisation für Sicherheit und Zusammenarbeit in Europa: Menschenrechtsbildung als Mittel zum Frieden', in: Menschenrechtsbildung Bilanz und Perspektiven, ibid. Pp. 93-104.

[6] Universal Declaration of Human Rights (article 26), the International Covenant on Economic, Social and Cultural Rights (article 13), the Convention on the Rights of the Child (article 29), and, most recently, the Vienna Declaration and Programme of Action (section D, paragraphs 78-82).

[7] See also Mahler in this publication.

On Sustainability: What Does Sustainability Mean?

One of the most often cited definitions of sustainability can be found in the report by the World Commission on Environment and Development (WCED).[8] The Commission defined sustainable development as development that "*meets the needs of the present without compromising the ability of future generations to meet their own needs.*"[9] Also the rights of future generations should therefore be incorporated into the definitions of rights of today's generation. This definition, as it addresses development, is not fully practicable for human rights education purposes. Human rights education is certainly related to development, but even more so, human rights are an inclusive and expansive project which follows the aim of extending the rights-based approach to new issues and themes.[10]

Human rights education therefore must tackle the challenge that people of today are not aware which themes may fall under the human rights rubric within for example, the next ten years. The expansion and inclusion of new themes as new human rights, makes the sustainability approach to human rights education even more crucial: Human rights education has to take a human rights approach to the whole concept of what education means in the formal, informal or non-formal sectors and to stress the indivisibility and interdependence of all rights.[11] There has to be structural and financial resources to both maintain and develop human rights education on a continuing basis. Contrary to a sustainable approach is an ad-hoc approach in which resources are allocated only after a societal crises (such as racist incidents in Germany) or in order to tame socio-political needs of certain sectors of society (such as creating language education projects for Russian speakers in Estonia). The results of the research project, 'Teaching human rights in Europe'[12] showed that the ad-hoc approach is most commonly taken in European states. The research project also offers plenty of evidence illustrating that if resources are made available without pre-agreed follow-up procedures, they are likely to have no sustainable effects. The same is true if the funding does not sufficiently cover the costs of the infrastructure of the project (office, personnel). This follow-up should not be misinterpreted as state or other ex-

---

[8] It is better known by the name of its leader, former Norwegian Prime Minister Gro Harlem Brundtland, "Brundtland Commission".

[9] Brundtland, G.H. (ed.), Our common future: The World Commission on Environment and Development, Oxford, Oxford University Press. See also United Nations. 1987. Report of the World Commission on Environment and Development, General Assembly Resolution 42/187, 11 December 1987.

[10] Lohrenscheit, Claudia, ‚Zum Zusammenhang von Menschenrechten und Bildung', ZEP 25/4, 2-5. Frankfurt M/ Verlag für Interkulturelle Kommunikation, 2002.

[11] The formal education sector refers to school, vocational school and university education. The non-formal education sector refers to complementary or supplementary education forms. HRE in this sector can be part of "after school activities". The in-formal education sector is the most independent but also the smallest education sector which includes activities in youth groups, clubs, and NGOs such as Amnesty International (AI) and the Human Rights Education Associates (HREA), etc.

[12] For more details about the project, see chapter 1 in this publication.

ternal control but rather as a means of evaluation and self-evaluation which guarantee the continuity of well functioning projects and programmes.[13]

In order to be sustainable, human rights education initiatives needs to target those holding "keeper" positions in a society. Lenhart and Savolainen have listed seven professions in which human rights education is especially necessary in order to guarantee and enable human rights for all: Teachers, social workers, scientists, medical personnel, lawyers, members of police force and soldiers.[14] These professions are either potentially or actually involved in human rights problems. According to Lenhart and Savolainen, if personnel in these professions have an appropriate education which enables him or her to recognize human rights violations and raise awareness of his or her own behaviour and thereby avoiding their own contributions to the violations, the level of human rights obedience would be much higher in the society.[15]

The international human rights law states clearly that human rights education is a human right.[16] This means that in order to fulfil international legal standards a state must make human rights education an integral part of general education and the general education must be provided according to these international agreements.[17] Although states are left to implement the initiatives according to their ability, there are international monitoring bodies which establish certain benchmarks which have to be respected; education has to be organised in an inclusive and non-discriminatory manner and primary education should be free for all. During the Decade for Human Rights Education, the United Nations monitoring bodies have paid more attention to human rights education.[18]

International and European Initiatives

United Nations

When states representatives unanimously agreed to the establishment of the UN Decade for Human Rights Education in 1993 in Vienna, Austria, they underlined the importance of bringing human rights education finally onto the global agenda as a matter of state responsibility. Educational programmes and appropriate institutions in society were asked to encourage incorporating human rights education into formal and

[13] Kissane, Carolyn, 'Evaluating Human Rights Education', in: Mahler, Claudia/ Mihr, Anja / Toivanen, Reetta (eds.) Democracy, Minorities and Human Rights Education in Europe, Potsdam: Potsdam University Press 2004, 72-79.

[14] Lenhart, Volker / Savolainen, Kaisa, 'Human Rights Education as a Field of Practice and of Theoretical Reflection', in International Review of Education 48 (3-4), 2002, 145-158, here pp. 152-154.

[15] Ibid. p. 151.

[16] Mahler, Claudia / Mihr, Anja / Toivanen, Reetta, 'Teaching Human Rights in Europe and its Role for Minority Movements', in: Malte Brosig (ed.), Human Rights in Europe – A Fragmented Regime? Frankfurt M: Peter Lang Verlag, 2006, 169-183, here p. 170.

[17] Hornberg, Sabine, 'Human Rights Education as an Integral Part of General Education', International Review of Education 48(3-4), 2002, 187-198, here p. 190.

[18] Especially the Committee on the Rights of Child, see for all recent reports under www2.ohchr.org/english/bodies/crc/index.htm.

non-formal education systems respectively. The Plan of Action of the Decade envisioned the designation of national focal points for human rights education in each state which should have been charged with identifying national human rights education needs, developing a national plan of action, raising funds, coordination with regional and international bodies and reporting to the High Commissioner. Each state was also encouraged to establish a national human rights resource and training centre capable of engaging in research, training of trainers, etc.

All member states were requested by the UN to draft a national plan of action for human rights education and to make efforts to implement it before the end of the decade. However, this was not completed in any of the six states included in the study "Human rights in Europe". The Decade remained rather invisible in all states; one extreme example being Estonia where basically nobody in state institutions including the national UNESCO committee or any of the NGOs was aware of the existence of the UN Decade. The other extremes were Germany and Finland. In Finland, the national UNESCO-committee (a ministerial body in Finland) co-organised a regional conference in 1998 and the NGOs launched a joint internet site for the purposes of disseminating information on human rights education resources and even a working group to draft a national plan was set up at the National Board of Education – but it never completed its work due to higher state priorities.[19] The German Institute for Human Rights established a focal point for human rights education which actively started organising courses for 'multiplicators' and establishing national cooperation in the field and the German UNESCO-committee (which is a NGO) lobbied forcefully for a Plan of Action. However the ministries of culture (there are 16 of them in Germany) clearly had other priorities and human rights education received much less attention than for example, the Council of Europe initiatives for citizenship education.

It seems a fair assessment that the UN Decade failed in two respects: UN offices did not receive enough resources to work properly and the UNESCO office was impeded due to internal conflicts between the law sector (responsible for the human rights law) and the education sector (responsible for the educational approach). Sustainability however, may be achieved with the UN World Programme for Human Rights which followed the Decade and demonstrated that UN organisations shall continue with its efforts.[20] Ideally, it shouldn't be the task of the UN to push for HRE; the member states should hold on to the responsibility and live up to promises they made by ratifying human rights treaties. But, none of the governments in our six country study took the role of a human rights education convener.

European forces: The Council of Europe and the European Union

The Council of Europe, as a regional human rights system actively took part in preparation for the Decade. The HRE was defined as "educational programmes and activi-

[19] Toivanen, Reetta, 'Education on Human Rights – a Method for Inducing Global Critical Thinking', in: Taina Kaivola / Monica Melén-Paaso (eds.) Education for Global Responsibility – Finnish Perspectives. Publications of the Ministry of Education 2007:31, 33-45.

[20] See http://www2.ohchr.org/english/issues/education/training/programme.htm,.

ties which focus on promoting equality in human dignity, in conjunction with other programmes such as promoting intercultural learning, participation and empowerment of minorities."[21] The Council of Europe activities were manifold and focus groups ranged from Roma youth to children with disabilities. However, the main focus of its efforts was to establish a rule of law in its member states[22] and it allocated more resources to projects on "Education for Democratic Citizenship"[23] than to human rights education.[24]

In Estonia and Slovakia the European Union (EU) was the best known intergovernmental organisation. During the Decade both countries strove successfully for full EU membership. In order to comply with the membership criteria and in addition to the large amount of other political and economic changes, the so-called Copenhagen Criteria also demanded respect for human rights and minorities.[25] JOIN and EQUAL were EU programmes which were significant to our research. Both programmes aimed at fostering equality and participatory rights in EU states. The EQUAL Initiative took place between 2000 and 2006 focussing on the European Employment Strategy and the Social Inclusion process. Its mission was to promote a better model for working life by fighting discrimination and exclusion on the basis of gender, racial or ethnic origin, religion or belief, disability, age or sexual orientation.[26] In Estonia the EQUAL project did not involve any assessment or effort to address the human rights problems of minorities. The interim evaluation also stated quite clearly that "[o]ne of the main obstacles of sustainability is the low involvement of target groups".[27] The PHARE programmes[28]on the other hand, financed structural reforms without a clear human rights perspective but still contributed to many human rights efforts, e.g. by co-financing the Estonian Integration Foundation's work.[29]

---

[21] Council of Europe, Compass – A Manual on Human Rights Education with Young People. Strasbourg Cedex: Council of Europe Publishing 2003, at p. 17.

[22] In our study this was visible especially in Armenia, Estonia and Slovakia.

[23] This is the term used by the Council of Europe.

[24] Mahler, Claudia, ‚Menschenrechtsbilsungsprogramme im Bereich des Europarates' in Claudia Mahler/ Anja Mihr (eds.) Menschenrechtsbildung – Bilanz und Perspektive, Wiesbaden: Sozialwissenschaftlicher Verlag, 2004, 105-117

[25] The EU was often accused of using "double standards" as it is a well-known fact that that many older member states (France, Greece, Sweden) don't have better minority rights situations. Mahler, Claudia / Toivanen, Reetta, ‚Nationale und ethnische Minderheiten im Prozess der Erweiterung der Europäischen Union', Europa Ethnica, ½, 2004, 16-20.

[26] See http://ec.europa.eu/employment_social/equal/index_en.cfm.

[27] Talve, Siret/ Reincke, Klaas-Jan/ Lipp, Ando, Evaluation of the preparatory and introductory phase of the EQUAL programme Mid-term evaluation report for the Ministry of Social Affairs of Estonia, Cycle plan, 2005
At p. 21, http://ec.europa.eu/employment_social/equal/data/document/eva-ee-05.pdf.

[28] PHARE is one of the three pre-accession instruments financed by the European Union to assist the applicant countries of Central and Eastern Europe in their preparations (fulfilling the Copenhagen Criteria) for joining the European Union.

[29] The Phare programme allocated around 245 million euro (3.8 billion EEK) to Estonia during the period 1992-2001. In addition to the National Programme, Estonia also benefitted from PHARE-funded multi-beneficiary programmes. With PHARE funds the Estonian Integration Foundation carried out e.g, the "Social Integration and Language Training Programme for Ethnic Minorities in Estonia"-project, http://www.fin.ee/index.php?id=8104#Sector:_Education.

International Foundations and activities

It was interesting to learn to what extent different foreign ministries actually financed human rights work in Armenia, Estonia, and Slovakia. For example the Legal Information Centre for Human Rights in Estonia received financing from the Danish foreign ministry (through the Danish Institute for Human rights) and from the Netherlands Helsinki Committee (financed by the Netherlands' foreign ministry and the Embassy of Netherlands in Finland[30]), and the Norwegian foreign ministry's money was visible in the work and activities of many Estonian NGOs. The U.S. and Canadian Governments also gave money, the British Council and the German foreign ministry (partly again through German foundations and other forms of co-operation) contributed to the organisation of teacher training, human rights and minority rights conferences and activities. For example, the British Council supported teacher training by sending British experts on multiculturalism (such as the famous Professor John Rex) whose visits were expensive, but the lectures could only be understood by a few attendees.[31]

In Germany there was much less international money available for human rights education and the German NGOs could only apply for resources at German foundations and ministries. At the same time, many German human rights experts were actively involved in projects outside the country and in that sense "international funds" actually arrived or stayed in Germany, but were not spent for human rights education projects in Germany but for salaries of German experts. If international support had been as strong in Germany, Spain and Finland as it was in Armenia, Estonian and Slovakia, the position of HRE would certainly have progressed immeasurably. The reason could have been that in the EU states structures already existed which could manage allocated resources more effectively whereas in the applicant countries huge amounts of money was allocated to building structures according to the conditions of the financers who were not always up-to-date with the situation in the target country.

In Estonia the Decade was not well-known amongst the authorities working in the ministries and other public institutions. It was quite commonplace to hear that the Council of Europe and even more so the European Commission (EU) had "more to offer and were easier to cooperate with" than the United Nations.[32] The United Nations and UNESCO were generally considered by Estonians as being unaware of the Estonian situation. Even the role of Council of Europe was marginal if compared to the effects of OSCE and even more so with the European Union.[33]

---

[30] This organisation used to be responsible not only for Finland but the whole Baltic countries.

[31] Interviews with Jaan Tonisson Institute (25 May 2004), LIHR (1 June 2004), Vihalem (1 March 2005).

[32] Interview with Katrin Rein, Ministry of Education, 30 March 2005.

[33] Anu Toots, a professor at the former Pedagogical University in Tallinn was the Estonian representative in the Education on Democratic Citizenship network at the Council of Europe. Her experience was that at least before 2004, the Estonian authorities neglected the CoE dimension as the membership in the EU and fulfilment of the membership criteria took priority. Her lobby work resulted however in an optional course on Human Development and human rights at the University in Tallinn. Barriers: lack of language. Interview with Anu Toots 1 June 2004.

Being an applicant country to the EU, Estonia received until May 2004 international support especially in the form of structural funding and also project money was made available (for example through the Estonian Integration Foundation). These resources were tangible in the activities of many NGOs and also at the Ministry of Education.[34] The UNDP and EU through PHARE, have been the main sources of finance for the work of the Integration Foundation whose main target (dictated by the funders) has been the 'Russian speakers'[35] After Estonia became a member, EU interest declined and many NGO have been criticizing that with membership, large parts of the funding disappeared.[36] Also in the ministries people complained about a lack of money.[37]

The Case Studies in Germany and Estonia

Germany

„Human rights [...] are still perceived as a domain of foreign policy and barely considered as a cross-sectional duty. The ombudsman for human rights of the German Parliament should therefore not be placed at the Ministry of Foreign Affairs but in all resorts of the Federal Chancellery of the Federal Republic of Germany".[38]

Among the six states, Armenia, Estonia, Finland, Slovakia and Spain, Germany was certainly not the easiest to analyse. The field of education in Germany is rather complicated due to the lack of federal competencies in the field of culture and education. Sixteen different states have their own approaches, laws and policies towards human rights education and the promotion of minority education. In 2004 we contacted the ministries of education and culture in all sixteen German states and asked each department who was responsible for the field of human rights education. The result was clear: there are different individuals responsible for the development of curricula, teaching materials, intercultural education, etc. but these individuals are not collaborating. This clearly shows that the article in the school laws paying attention to the respect of human rights should guide the whole education sector as a cross-sectional value does not work effectively in practice.[39]

A common feature among those key players interviewed for the purposes of our study was the dissatisfaction with the fragmented approach to human rights education. At the same time, there is a serious lack of understanding as to why education about and for minorities is necessary. In those states such as Saxony, Brandenburg, and

[34] For the smaller NGO without support by bigger organisations or state organs, this funding inaccessible: the applicants needed 20% of their own finances to be eligible for the EU funding. This is a problem for smaller organisations which do not enjoy state support such as the Roma organisations in Estonia.

[35] Matti Luik interviewed 28 May 2004.

[36] Interview with Aleksei Semjonov, LIHR, 1 June 2004.

[37] Interview with Katrin Rein, Ministry of Education, 30 March 2005.

[38] Forum Menschenrechte, Eine Halbzeitbilanz der Menschenrechtspolitik von Bundesregierung und Bundestag: Deutsche Menschenrechtspolitik: widersprüchlich und entwicklungsfähig, 21. October 2004,
http://forum-menschenrechte.de/cms/front_content.php?idcat=90&idart=206, translation RT.

[39] The interviews were conducted by Simone Holzwarth and the author in spring 2004.

Schleswig-Holstein where national minorities reside, the awareness level of authorities is higher; at least there are offices with special competences regarding minorities.[40] However, the activities in the area of general human rights education seldom if ever, meet with the activities in minority education. Human rights activists themselves simply do not recognize the special needs and circumstances of minorities. Economic, social and cultural rights in Germany are generally considered as rights which are violated only in the developing world.

As a multiethnic state with a large immigrant population (according to the 2005 census there are 15.3 million people with a migration background[41]) it is certainly understandable that many state and NGO activities have concentrated on the issues of asylum, rights of migrants and anti-racism. The national minorities have been generally considered as "normal" Germans and therefore it has been very difficult to frame the negative experiences by them as something that could constitute discrimination. Even when the minority activists are rather knowledgeable about minority rights, they seldom address these rights in the language of general human rights. The majority population, even in those states such as Saxony where national minorities are protected by specific laws, receives amazingly little information about minorities.

In 1980 the German Standing Conference of the Ministries of Culture (KMK) passed a recommendation on human rights education. In this document it was emphasised that it is not only the task of the state but particularly through actions of each individual in society to contribute to the realisation of human rights commitments. It continued that the school has to take decisive efforts to contribute to the corresponding personality formation of pupils and inter alia, to enhance the pupils' personality towards understanding and respecting of human rights.[42] The recommendation was updated 20 years later and thus became valid for the 'new' states of the former GDR. It is remarkable how little this resolution has been in the focus of educational activities.[43] This is not to say that it would not be important that human rights are now mentioned in the school laws and curricula in all German states. Often, however, they are either mentioned as underlying values or implicitly incorporated in themes such as basic rights or democracy education.[44] This is often seen in the German context as non-problematic because even public opinion proclaims that human rights are sufficiently protected by constitutional guarantees in Germany.[45]

Forum Human Rights is an umbrella organisation hosting 48 (as of January 2008) member organisations. It was founded in 1994 as a result of the Vienna World

---

[40] This became apparent in all interviews with authorities. It seemed to be easy to associate human rights with Roma but not with the Sorbian or Frisian minority (Interviews conducted by Toivanen 2003-2006).

[41] http://www.zuwanderung.de/1_statistik.html.

[42] Kultusministerkonferenz der Länder (KMK), Empfehlung der KMK zur Förderung der Menschenrechtsbildung in der Schule (resolution by the KMK on 4 December 1980, updated on 4 December 2002), Federal Ministry of research and Education, 11 January 2001, 15411 A-51303/30.

[43] As Sabine Hornberg points out, it is also much shorter and lacks any didactical proposals if compared with other resolutions of the KMK, see Hornberg in footnote17, p. 192.

[44] See here also Forum Menschenrechte, Standards der Menschenrechtsbildung in Schulen. Forum Menschenrechte, Berlin 2006, p. 21.

[45] Mihr, Anja / Rosemann, Nils, Bildungsziel: Menschenrechte. Standards und Perspektiven für Deutschland. Schwalbach/ts. 2004, p. 30.

Conference on Human Rights. It aims to coordinate joint efforts to improve human situations globally, Germany included.[46] Members range from religious organisations such as the Caritas, Ba'hai and evangelical organisations to German Amnesty International and the German UNESCO Commission to the German Institute for Human Rights. As Forum Menschenrechte debated in 2003, their future action plan, even some members of the Forum felt that human rights education is not a matter of urgency in Germany.

This attitude was also evident in a 2004 resolution of the Bavarian parliament where the parliament was requested to provide evidence[47] on how human rights education had been holistically implemented before the KMK recommendations in all subjects covering the entire education system.[48] The resolution contained as an attachment, a report by the Bavarian Ministry of Education. In this report the ministry meticulously showed how, in their opinion, human rights education naturally took place at all stages of education and particularly stressed that lessons concerning the constitution was a way of teaching human rights education.[49]

The statement by the Forum Menschenrechte cited in the beginning of this section seems fair. Human rights education in Germany lacks a systemic approach, the activities and initiatives towards human rights education so far have been possible because of enthusiastic and active teachers and NGO activists. School and after school establishments do not have the competencies to include human rights and that there is a dramatic deficiency in the human rights education of teachers and other educational staff.

Estonia

"We do not have any obstacles for human rights education in Estonia. The human rights education is a natural part of the curriculum."[50]

The Decade for Human Rights Education went unnoticed in Estonia. For example the head of the office for international affairs at the Ministry of Education said quite honestly that her office had only heard for the first time about the Decade when the end evaluation questionnaire from the United Nations office arrived.[51] The ministries responsible had more than enough work implementing European Union law reforms, the *acquis communautaire* with its 80,000 pages including the entire body of EU law requiring changes particularly in economic and administrative procedures. Since the ministries were overwhelmed with the reform work, the Jaan Tõnissen Institute and Legal Information Centre for Human Rights and some other NGOs jointly

[46] About us, http://forum-menschenrechte.de/cms/front_content.php?idart=225.

[47] The request was submitted by the MP Pfaffmann (SPD).

[48] Bayersicher Landtag, Förderung der menschenrechtserziehung in der Schule, Drucksache 15/810, 22 April 2004.

[49] Bayerisches Staatsministerium für Unterricht und Kultus, Bericht über die Förderung der Menschenrechtserziehung in der Schule, III-5S4400.20-6.51552, 2 August 2004.

[50] Answer by the Estonian Ministry of education on the United Nations questionnaire on the implementation of the United Nations Decade for Human rights education (1995-2004) (EUR/GOV/EST 2004).

[51] Interview with Katrin Rein, 30 March 2005.

made efforts from 1999 to 2002 to establish a human rights body called the Estonian Association for Human rights. Due to the lack of political and therefore financial support, this failed.[52]

The general development of human rights education in Estonia is described by Sulev Valdmaa in this volume. My effort here is to add a minority rights' perspective to his discussion. At the beginning of the second republic in 1991, when Estonia regained its independence, the efforts of the government concentrated around one question: '*How to make good citizens of the people originating from the former Soviet republics*?' These people made up one third of the population and turned out to pose a major challenge in the attempt to define 'Estonian'. The solutions offered by the Estonian political elite ranged from those who endeavoured to remove people who were not real Estonians (using very biological terminology) to moderates who postulated the notion of awarding citizenship to all those in 1991 living in Estonian territory. 'Moderate ethnicists' won the battle and ever since, the debate about rights in Estonia has been bipolarized around the two constructed "groups": Estonian and non-Estonians.

At the turn of the millennium, the name 'non-Estonian' was interpreted as having a pejorative meaning and the term 'Russian-speaker' became an apparently neutral name for the same "group". During the last few years, Estonian society has realized that Russians knew what they were expected to do but Estonians didn't.[53] Integration terminology was given from above; from international organisations, international experts and the Estonian government and it became important to begin to speak about a two-sided integration process which involved the Russian-speakers as subjects and not purely as objects. During our fieldwork visits, many interviewees stated that international organisations had negatively influenced the development of an Estonian human rights movement. The OSCE missions with Mr. van Stoel as the High Commissioner for National Minorities ruined, in the eyes of many Estonian politicians and activists, the whole concept of human rights for Estonia.[54] From the beginning of the 1990s when human rights rhetoric was used only by those furthering the rights of non-Estonians and those who were afraid of, or who acted cautiously towards Estonian nationalism, the concept had a bad, anti-patriotic flavour. This was also partly due to the fact that Moscow has constantly used the concept of human rights when it demanded more rights for former citizens of the Soviet Union in the Baltic area.

The Estonian case is very different to the German case. At the beginning of the 1990s the entire Estonian society underwent huge reforms and changes: all civil servants, judges, lawyers, teachers, ministerial workers etc., needed training for the new societal system. For example the Euro College at Tartu University, funded with European Union money, was actively involved in this training. The educators faced a situation where they realized that the civil servants knowledge of a modern democratic society was very limited.[55] One problem with minority rights was that the entire

---

[52] Interview with Jana Krimpe 23 February 2005.

[53] Interviews with Jana Krimpe 23 February 2005; Lauri Mälksoo 27 May 2005 and Vello Pettai 26 May 2005.

[54] This was discussed with Indrek Jääts, Estonian national Museum 28 February 2005.

[55] Interview with Michael Callagher 1 March 2005.

discourse was separated from human rights. As Estonians have tended to consider themselves as a minority, there has been difficulty in accepting that a group of people generally viewed as the "occupier" would need some additional protection.[56]

The policy of integration in Estonia was only adopted as a result of western pressure.[57] In 1997, the Estonian government established a minister without portfolio on ethnic affairs. In 1998, the government established a foundation to manage programmes concerned with ethnic integration. This Integration Foundation has been the main driver of governmental programmes aiming at integrating non-Estonians into Estonian society. The Integration Foundation was accused by the interviewees (NGO and minority representatives) of not having transparent funding schemes and independent researchers complained that the goals of the Foundation were unclear.[58]

The concentration on language issues in the integration policies has been easily supported by international money whereas socio-economic aspects or systemic discrimination have not been under the microscope of any integration instrument.[59] Some experts pointed out that the problems faced by so-called Russian speakers are not of a linguistic or cultural nature but are socio-economic which means that teaching in the Estonian language does not remove the problems.[60] At the same time, the integration and minority policies did not pay any attention towards the actual human rights law. As the director of the Legal Information Centre on Human Rights (LIHR), Aleksei Semjonov pointed out, Estonians used very little human rights based arguments and tended to regard them as propaganda. The Russian speakers use more human rights rhetoric but this does not imply that they know more about human rights.[61] This was verified in many interviews with Russian speakers: human rights are used – as with the Estonian speakers – as rhetoric without understanding the binding human rights conventions.

Whereas 'human rights' was considered to be an unsuitable concept, many activists therefore adopted the term 'civic education'. Two television campaigns by the Estonian Integration Foundation in 2001 and 2002 which addressed racism and discrimination in Estonia used the vocabulary of tolerance instead of bringing the topic into a human rights context.[62] The civic education in the 1990s had a completely reformed content when compared with Soviet style civic education. Human rights are currently a part of civic education taught by history teachers. There is one course in 2nd and 4th grade and then again two courses on civic education in grades 8 and 9.[63] In addition, civics is offered in upper secondary school. The contents are very practical and partly aimed at teaching students how to act properly as Estonian citizens. Hu-

---

56 See interviews e.g. with Sulev Valdmaa (25 May 2004) and Lauri Mälksoo (27 May 2004)

57 Interview with Raivo Vetik, Professor for Political Science and expert for the Integration foundation 22 March 2005.

58 For example sociologist Mikko Lagerspetz in an interview on 29 March 2005.

59 This was criticised by many interviewees such as Merle Haruoja and Vello Pettai (both interviewed 26 May, 2004). The director of the Integration Foundation, Mati Luik, however, defend the approach and said that a common language is according to his vision a 'Common value'.

60 This was criticised also by Jana Krimpe, Deputy Mayor's Adviser, Tallinn City Government, in an interview on 23 February 2005.

61 Interview with Aleksei Semjonov 1 June 2004.

62 Matti Luik interviewed 28 May 2004.

63 See Valdmaa in this publication.

man rights are nowadays part of the teaching materials but there are no mechanisms to control or investigate if and how teachers actually use them in classrooms. Those involved in the reforms confirmed that the constantly changing names and terminology in the subjects together with the regularly changing Minister of Education and administration staff has confused the efforts of consistent educational policies.[64] The ministry has also recruited graduates directly from university who tend not to stay due to the low salary. Establishing long term liaisons with the ministry has been especially challenging for the human rights activists and minority representatives. Maybe these changes also partly explain the difficulty of including human rights education or establishing a minority rights sensibility in educational programmes.

Similar to the German educational authorities, Estonian colleagues repeatedly said that they had human rights education in Estonia, and that 'they are implemented in our constitution and laws, so there is no need for a separate discussion on them'.[65] The National Examination Centre also expressed the concern that they cannot control who takes what in-service training courses as they are organised by private companies and NGOs such as JTI. Also of concern is the fact that Russian teachers have not learned Estonian despite the efforts of the Integration Foundation.[66]

Sustainability, Human Rights Education and Minorities - Germany

According to the German definition, Sorbs, Frisians, Danish and Roma/Sinti are the recognized national minorities.[67] National laws enshrine home territories for the three first mentioned minorities. The Sorbian minority is protected in both the constitutions of Brandenburg and Saxony (both former eastern Germany), and have a defined home territory in these states accordingly. The Frisian minority enjoys special protection in Schleswig-Holstein and also lives in Lower Saxony while the Danish minority has been protected by a bilateral agreement since 1955 in Schleswig-Holstein. The members of Roma and Sinti groups are spread throughout the entire country, but less so in the eastern part of the country. These four minorities have established a common forum, the German Minority Council, in which the Roma and Sinti are represented by the Central Council of German Roma and Sinti (Zentralrat der Roma und Sinti).[68] In July 2005 the Minority Council was awarded an office with a part-time secretary by the federal government of Germany.[69] The Minority Council has forcefully campaigned for an amendment to the German constitution which would add an

[64] Interview with Katrin Kello, National Curriculum Development Center, University of Tartu, on 16 March 2005; with Anu Toots at the Tallinn Pedagogic University, 1 June 2004 and with Maie Soll, Ministry of Education, 2 June 2004.
[65] Interview with Kello ibid.
[66] Interview with Mare Räis and Mare Oja at the National Examination Centre 13 March 2005.
[67] Declaration contained in a letter from the Permanent Representative of Germany, deposited on 10 September 1997, www.coe.int/T/E/Human_Rights/Minorities/ > declarations and reservations.
[68] The Sinti Alliance (another umbrella organisation) opposes this institution and has decided to stay outside the Council. The parliament has, however, made clear that the Sinti Allianz is also covered by the protective measures of the state.
[69] The office is located in Berlin and the position was taken by Thede Boysen, Frisian activist.

article ensuring national minorities in Germany cultural autonomy and political participation rights.[70]

The representatives of national minorities interviewed in Germany shared the opinion that the key to non-discrimination is the education of the majority. Only if the majority population understands the specific needs and the challenging issues of the national minorities, will they be able to recognize them.[71] The sustainability of a human rights approach is therefore dependent on the majority and its comprehension of what diversity means for a democratic society.

Since the early 20th century the Frisian minority (in Schleswig-Holstein and Lower Saxony) has been divided between those who see the Frisian as a cultural group in Germany and those who consider that the Frisian constitutes its own nation.[72] The nationally minded have fought for recognition as a national minority in Germany whereas other Frisian groups explicitly reject this concept.[73] This division in attitude and vision of the future is used by local authorities as an argument for not providing human rights education on the rights of minorities, not even in those regions where Frisians live. The Frisian activists explained the rejection of special protection with a fear of negative publicity and the activists repeatedly said that "*it is better to keep a low profile*" and not to "*provoke the German neighbours*".[74] This was further validated as we interviewed people working in the Schleswig-Holstein government and in the municipalities with Frisian inhabitants. They simply could not understand why one should take a human rights perspective regarding the case of the Frisian minority.[75]

Although the authorities easily argued against increased support for minorities, they, for example in Saxony and Brandenburg, stressed that Sorbian culture and language enriches Germany and should by all means be supported. Similarly, in 2006 the parliament of Schleswig Holstein unanimously adopted the motion to enshrine an article to protect and promote national minorities in the German constitution.[76]

The main domestic concerns in Germany have been racism and hate crimes. In 1995 the Bertelsmann Foundation initiated a programme called, "Education for Democracy and Tolerance". Together with the project partner CAP (Centre for Applied

---

[70] Südschlewischer Wählerbund, Minderheiten gehören ins Grundgesetz, Pressemitteilung Nr. 106/2006, Kiel, 15 September 2006, http://www.ltsh.de/presseticker/2006-09/15/17-07-22-5441/PI-RQrBqlRB-ssw.pdf,

[71] Interviews with Peter Amsler, Ba'hai Office 9 November 2004 in Berlin; Interview with Landesverband Sinti in Schleswig-Holstein 10 May 2006 in Kiel, Interview with Domowina organisation of the Sorbian Minority on 21 February 2006 in Bautzen.

[72] The former minded people are united in an organisation founded in 1902 and the nationally minded organized themselves in the 1930s Steensen, Thomas, 'Lieber tod als Skave? Die Nordfriesen und das Friesische 1933-1945', in: Robert Bohn / Uwe Danker / Jørgen Kühl (eds.) Zwischen Hoffnung, Anpassung und Bedrängnis. Minderheiten im deutsch-dänischen Grenzraum in der NS-Zeit, Bielefeld: Verlag für Regionalgeschichte, 2001, 113-123, here p. 117.

[73] Kühn, Jørgen, ‚Nationale Minderheiten im dänisch-deutschen Grenzland – Eine Einführung', in: Jørgen Kühn / Robert Bohn (eds.) Ein Europäisches Modell? Bielefeld: Verlag für Regionalgeschichte 2005, 9-58, here p. 18ff.

[74] Interview with the Northern Frisian Association on 9 May 2006 in Risum-Lindholm together with J-F Klein.

[75] Interviews with authorities in Schleswig-Holstein 8-10 May 2006.

[76] Op.cit. fn 70.

policy research in Munich) they launched a programme whose purpose was to create a consciously tolerant people who would combat racism and intolerance. Characteristically for Germany, the programme did not address human rights education explicitly.[77] It is also illustrative that when the international network Education for Democracy, Human Rights and Tolerance (formed as part of the above mentioned programme)[78] convened one of its meetings in 2000 in Bautzen, the "capital" of the Sorbian minority, this national minority was not included on the agenda.[79]

Different foundations have published booklets on human rights. The booklet by the Konrad Adenauer-Foundation provides a typical example.[80] The booklet mentions the 1993 Vienna Conference on Human Rights but not the Decade for Human Rights Education which started the following year. It introduced human rights in a commonly understandable language and with clear pictures and short stories. Although it's an excellent book on human rights and human rights work by the foundation, it does not address internal politics but covers stories on intercultural work and human rights problems in developing countries.

The Bund-Länder-Kommission in Germany launched a new programme "Learning & Living Democracy" in 1998. The goal of the programme was to foster democratic culture in German schools and to fight racism, prejudice and discrimination. The programme has a clear vision of why democracy is important but it does not mention human rights as a substantial element (only in connection with intercultural training), nor does it promote human rights education as a tool for fostering democracy.[81]

The Freudenberg Foundation is, in addition to Bertelsmann, one prominent foundation with several joint programmes in various parts of Germany. The foundation supports democracy and intercultural learning, anti-racism and integration projects and projects supporting asylum seekers, etc. It shows how foundations actually play a central role in fostering societal programmes in Germany. Human rights have a part in many of its projects but again as an underlying value and not as an explicit theme. The interviews with people working in projects funded by the Freudenberg Foundation revealed that they themselves did not know enough about human rights in order to include them in educational activities.[82]

Many projects in Germany addressed the Roma and especially the refugee Roma and their problems. However, we could not identify any human rights education projects for, or on the national minorities but it should be mentioned that the cur-

[77] Uhl, Kathrin / Seberich, Michael, ‚Toleranz lernen – Toleranz verstehen', In Tempora: Menschenrechte, Heft 9/2002, pp. 29-31.

[78] Homepage is found under http://www.tolerance-net.org.

[79] See the conference proceedings and summary http://www.tolerance-net.org/network/conferences/2000.html,

[80] Konrad Adenauer Stiftung, Menschenrechte im interkulturellen Dialog. Greven: Druckhaus Cramer, 1998.

[81] BLK Program, Wir wollen's wissen, – Demokratie Lernen & Leben, Berlin. The evaluation does, however, mention human rights a few times more and explicitly as elements of democratization, see Edelstein, Wolfgang / Frauser, Peter, http://www.blk-demokratie.de/fileadmin/public/dokumente/Expertise.pdf.

[82] More about the foundation: http://www.freudenbergstiftung.de. Interviews conducted by Toivanen and Mahler 2005-2006, eg. with RAA Berlin and Amadeu Antonio Foundation.

riculum in the schools of Saxony and Brandenburg foresees teaching the history and culture of Sorbs and some school materials paid attention to this demand. Still, this cannot qualify as conscious human rights education. The Federal Agency for Civic Education (Bundeszentrale für Politische Bildung) has published an impressive book on human rights documents and declarations[83] but also a smaller, but exemplary, booklet on the Sorbian minority, its history, interaction with German politics and culture and the current efforts to achieve minority rights. The Parliament of Schleswig-Holstein publishes reports on the situation of national minorities.[84] The challenge remains that there is no knowledge of how this material is used in the schools or free civic education sectors.[85]

Sustainability, Human Rights Education and Minorities - Estonia

During the years of the UN Decade for Human Rights Education minorities were very much at the centre of public debate and policy making in Estonia.[86] However this 'being at the centre' did not mean that there was a human rights effort to mainstream minority issues into Estonian politics. The so-called Russian speakers were the subject of several integration projects and the flow of money from international organisations (often through the Integration Foundation) and foreign governments, including the Russian Federation, was high towards this subject. Most of the programmes and projects were aimed at "helping" Russians to become Estonian.[87] Clearly speaking, these were less integration projects and more assimilation projects. The funding from the Union of Associations of Russian Compatriots in Estonia (redirected money from the Russian government[88]) was directed towards different cultural activities and support of Russian organisations but again no human rights education programmes were visible.

---

[83] Bundeszentrale für politische Bildung, Menschenrechte – Dokumente und Deklarationen, Bonn 2004 (4th edition).

[84] Der Präsident des Schlewig-Holsteinischen Landtages, Minderheitenbericht (1996-2000), Kiel 1999.

[85] Pech, Edmund/Scholze, Dietrich (eds.), Zwischen Zwang und Beistand. Deutsche Politik gegenüber den Sorben vom Wiener Kongress bis zur Gegenwart, Sonderausgabe der Sächsischen Landeszentrale für politische Bildung, Dresden/Bautzen 2003. the Also the Ministry of Interior has publiced materials on the national minorities, see Bundesministerium des Inneren, Nationale Minderheiten in Deutschland, Kölnische Verlagsdruckerei 2004.

[86] Brosig, Malte, 'Diffusing Fragmented Human Rights Standards: Minority Rights in Estonia', in: Malte Brosig (ed.) Human Rights in Europe? Op.cit fn 16.

[87] Lauristin, Marju / Heidmets, Mati, 'Introduction: The Russian Minority in Estonia as a Theoretical and Political Issue', in: Marju Lauristin / Mati Heidmets (eds.) The Challenge of the Russian Minority – Emerging Multiculötural Democracy in Estonia, Tartu: University Press 2002, 19-29.

[88] The special relationship between the government of the Russian Federation and its compatriots living in other states is underscored in many laws. It is also one of the main goals of foreign policy to defend the rights of compatriots residing in other states (Rossijskaja gazeta, 11.07.2000). One of the priorities lies in the support of language and culture maintenance of compatriots (Governmental Degree on the Main feature of the cultural co-operation of the Russian Federation with foreign countries, adopted by the president on 12 January 1995, № 22).

Russian speakers consist of a very diverse collection of people from Armenians to Uzbeks but they are generally treated as one people. They are seen to identify themselves basically with the Russian language as the lingua franca[89] Referring to them by one name seems questionable. It only makes sense when the aim is to discuss the rights of people who moved to Estonia in the Soviet era and today face specific challenges in a new Estonian speaking Estonia. Apparently another common feature is that they depend on Russian language media.[90]

In the interviews with around 20 different associations of "Russian speakers", one of our aims was to find out what kind of human rights activities would be necessary for true integration.[91] It became clear that the interviewees did not know much about international human rights law; they stressed that they did not want to be treated as a minority because being a minority would mean that help would always be needed from the majority. The shared view was that the organisations wanted resources to ensure a stable economic basis and to work independently strengthening non-Estonian cultural traditions and to support youth and the elderly.[92] Currently, many Russians are not willing to integrate because they see integration purely as assimilation. The Congress of NGO Russian complained that the government is dividing and ruling; the Estonian government applies a policy according to which "a perfect size of Russians would be 7% and they continue to repress until this number is reached".[93]

Most minority associations in Estonia are members of one of the two major umbrella organisations: The International Association of Nationalities in Estonia (Lüra) and the Organisation of Estonian Nationalities. They both shared the view that if the government needed some colourful culture events, Lüra was called in and when for example there were political leaders from foreign countries visiting Estonia, the Organisation of Estonia Nationalities was asked to send respective minority leaders to present their life in Estonia.[94] In that sense one umbrella organisation was considered by the government to be cultural and the other political. Many of the members of Lüra belong to the category of non-Estonians whereas the members of the latter tend to represent groups with patronage states such as Finns, Slovaks, Belarusians, etc.

In addition to the interviews and research on Russian speakers, we focussed on the Setu and the Roma. The Setu are clearly considered Estonian[95] while the Roma existence is basically ignored in the political sphere. The Setu are a small minority with approximately 5000 members. Their language is closely related to Estonian and has sometimes been called a south Estonian dialect. As a territorial minority they share history with Estonia and have been subjected to pejorative attitudes due to their

[89] This was also pointed out in several interviews, for example Mare Oja 31 May 2004.

[90] Interview with Raivo Vetik, Professor for Political Science and expert for the Integration Foundation 22 March 2005; this was also expressed in the interviews with Russian speakers associations and of course especially in Tallinn and Narva.

[91] We are most grateful for the instrumental help provided by our research assistant Maria Vogel.

[92] E.g., Interview with the Russian Congress in Tallinn 22 March 2005.

[93] Interview with the Russian Congress in Tallinn 22 March 2005.

[94] Interview with Lüra on 28 May 2004 and the Estonian Union of National Minorities 31 May 2004.

[95] Interview with Paul Hagu, 28 February 2005.

agrarian living style.[96] During the Soviet era the Setu were (and still today) treated as apolitical exhibition objects: "*It was always nice to show the Setu women singing in their traditional dresses.*"[97] A Setu Open Air Museum was built in 2000, partly financed by EU PHARE money.[98] For a minority such as the Setu, it is extremely important that the municipalities need them and there is even an economic interest to maintain Setu traditions as tourist interests. The cultural ministry and the Estonian Unesco committee are supporting the endeavours by Setu to become a living treasure of UNESCO[99] even though some Setu activists fear that this might lead to further musealization of the minority. The Setu institutions, the Setu Congress and the Board of Elderly are its decision making bodies. It seems that the Ministry of Culture is very much interested in working closely with them to find ways to maintain the Setu culture. Since 2003 there has been a ministerial programme supporting Setu culture with an annual budget of 3 million crones.[100] This money goes to Setu cultural activities, regional museums, language teaching, research and other purposes. A commission from the Ministry of Culture meets with Congress members biannually; this is due to high unemployment and bad public infrastructure in southern Estonia, a region which is in urgent need of government subsidies.[101] The media and school book analyses conducted for this research project provided evidence that the Setu were considered to be "our minority" by Estonians, which is somewhat archaic and apolitical.[102] The political demands by some Setu activists are dismissed in public debates as inappropriate.[103] We were also unable to find any project or programme taking a human rights education perspective on the issue of the Setu.

The Roma, in contrast to the Setu, are not recognized as an Estonian minority. Even human rights activists were openly racist towards the Roma which made us wonder how human rights education could be a problem solving tool in this kind of case. The number of Estonian Roma is estimated to be between 600 and 1500.[104] The Second Estonian Report to the Committee of the Framework Convention for the Protection of National Minorities assures that the Roma have taken part in the 'Round Table for National Minorities', led by the President, and are also otherwise very well integrated.[105] The European Commission against Racism and Intolerance (ECRI) also

---

[96] Hagu, Paul, Setukaisten identiteetin ongelmat, Viro-tietoutta 7/1994.
[97] Interview with Lõvi Laine, Setu Open Air Museum in Värska, 23 March 2005.
[98] Interview with Rein Järvilill, director of the municipality of Värska, 23 March 2005.
[99] Interview with Aare Hõrn, 23 March 2005.
[100] http://www.kul.ee/index.php?path=0x214x789.
[101] Interview with Anton Pärn, Ministry of Culture, 29 March 2005.
[102] This is apparent in the way the problems (2/3 of the home land on the Russian side of the border, etc) faced by Setu are addressed. In the school books we found Setu only in their traditional dresses, as folkloristic decorations. See the Estonian school books dealing with ethno-politics, Vernoka Kalmus, Ethno-Political Discourse in Estonian School Books, in: The Challenge of The Russian Minority op. cit. fn. 87.
[103] Interviews in Setumaa in Spring 2005.
[104] Toivanen, Reetta, ‚Unwissen, Vorurteile und andere "Gewohnheiten" – Notizen aus einer Feldforschung mit Roma in Estland', In: Reetta Toivanen / Michi Knecht (eds.) Europäische Roma – Roma in Europa, Berliner Blätter Heft 39/2006, 143-153.
[105] Second Report submitted by Estonia pursuant to Article 25, paragraph 1 of the Framework Convention for the Protection of National Minorities received on Thursday, July 15, 2004, ACFC/SF/II(2004)009. See under

mentioned the Roma in their second report on Estonia. There, it was emphasized that the problems of the Roma and other smaller minorities are often drowned out in a country like Estonia, where one large minority group dominates the discussion. 'The ECRI considers that it is most important to ensure that the differing needs and identities of these groups are addressed. At present, little seems to be known about the situation of some of these groups: for example, there seems to be a lack of information about Estonia's small Roma/Gypsy population.'[106]

The programme by the EU called EQUAL, designed for the improvement of employment and educational opportunities, financed by a Nordic cooperation project in order to empower the Roma. The main aim of the 'Dromedu-Project' was to improve the achievement of Roma children in schools. One of the project meetings took place in May 2003 in Tallinn and it could have provided the Estonian Roma with an excellent opportunity to have a two-sided discussion with representatives from the Estonian government. But, unfortunately the Minister for Ethnic Affairs, as well as all his substitutes, were unable to attend.[107] Furthermore, the negative and ignorant attitudes of participating Estonian authorities in the project were considered irritating by the foreign participants.[108]

The Estonian authorities have ignored the existence of Roma as best they could, but here the main aim of international pressure has become apparent. First, the European Commission against Racism and Intolerance, then the Advisory Committee of the Framework Convention on National Minorities and later different committees of the European Union pressured the Estonian government to show an improvement in the socio-political and especially educational situation of the Roma population. The Roma Education Committee was established as a consequence of this pressure at the Ministry of Education in September 2004. The Committee has, however, not been working properly and Roma people have not been included in sufficient numbers as full members of the committee. The Ministry paid no attention to results of the Dromedu Project but rather wanted to pursue their own Roma integration projects without considering consulting the Roma.[109]

There is a fundamental problem with project financing for NGOs who are not friendly with the government.[110] They tend not to get any support as the intergovern-

---

http://www.coe.int/T/e/human%5Frights/Minorities/2.%5FFRAMEWORK%5FCONVENTION%5F%28MONITORING%29/2._Monitoring_mechanism/3._State_Reports_and_UNMIK_Kosovo_Report/2._Second_cycle/PDF_2_SR_Estonia_eng.pdf,

[106] ECRI: Second report on Estonia adopted on 22 June 2001 and made public on 23 April 2002, Para. 61. Siehe unter http://www.coe.int/T/E/human_rights/Ecri/1-ECRI/2-Country-by-country_approach/Estonia/PDF_CBC2-Estonia.pdf,

[107] As well as this problem, it became apparent during the day that the attempts to enter into a productive dialogue made by the Roma-activists, mainly the chairperson of the Roma Association of Northern Estonian, Roman Lutt, met with little success.

[108] Memorandum of the International Drom-Edu project (EU-comenius), Meeting 15 – 18.05.2003 in Tallinn, see http://www.dromedu.org

[109] Diverse interviews with Roma people in Spring 2005 and with Roman Lutt 14 March 2005.

[110] See also Bauer, Wolfgang / Rainer, Karl, 'Möglichkeiten der Nutzung von EU-Förderprogrammen durch Minderheiten', Europa Ethnica, 1-2/2004, 21-28, who write that decisive for the successful application for EU grants by minorities remains the attitude of the majorities towards the minorities, here p. 28.

mental support is often based on finding a national official partner among the authorities.[111] For example, the UN association in Estonia received funding from the Ministry of Culture and national gambling society but only for 'Estonian topics' which means that to finance a project on the Roma, who despite hundreds years of settlement in the country, are not considered Estonian, falls outside the scope.[112] In Estonia the Integration Foundation is the main body distributing resources for cultural, integration and minority activities but in its decision making body there has been little, if any, minority representation.

Human Rights Education, Minority Participation and Sustainability

Generally it can be said that during the entire Decade, human rights education in Germany was viewed as a problem solving tool, applicable foremost in peace missions and development aid but also partly to domestic difficulties such as racism. Interest and awareness of human rights education is rising in Germany. The old "education after Auschwitz" with the never-again attitude does not suffice. The German Institute for Human Rights furthers teachers' in-service training and organises courses for social workers, teachers and activists and also for police force and prison personnel. The UN Decade was strongly promoted by the German UNESCO commission and the Decade gave tools to challenge the government and state institutions in an attempt to make human rights education a 'serious concern' among the authorities.[113] If there was a political will in Germany to educate the entire population on their rights and rights of others, there would be enough foundations, bigger NGOs and state institutions to implement this. Regarding minorities, it is fair to conclude that when it is about the culture and language of national minorities, it is easy to find acceptance among authorities (no serious body would dare say anything against them). But when the minority representatives ask for recognition and political participatory rights they are generally rejected.

Estonia has been much more open to diverse international campaigns which aim to promote diversity and multiculturalism without taking the human rights aspects into consideration.[114] In several official documents, Estonia has declared itself to be a multicultural society and has stressed as its foremost goal the realisation of equality between all citizens. At the same time, there have been, since the restoration of the republic, clear efforts to establish representative bodies, so-called roundtables for minorities. The first one was initiated by President Meri in 2003 as a presidential roundtable and local and regional variations followed. The question put forth by minority activists and scholars interested in these issues has been whether the roundtable has just been a forum to secure societal peace in turbulent times (these were

---

[111] This was something all umbrella organisations for minorities criticized heavily.

[112] Interview with Siim Saksing, the Chair of the Estonian United Nation Association in Tartu, 16 March 2005.

[113] Interview with the German Unesco Commission.

[114] Raivo Vetik has widely written on this theme both as an academic as well as policy adviser of the Government, see, e.g. Vetik, Raivo, 'Multicultural Democracy as a New Model of National Integration in Estonia', in: The Challenge of the Russian Minority, op. cit. fn.87, 55-62.

clearly the goals of the first roundtable) as some of the roundtables have been able to solve concrete day-to-day issues and created a feeling among some marginalized groups of being heard.

One of the most appalling research results concerns the minority participation in the externally funded human rights education projects. For example, when EU structural funds started positively affecting the *gitano* movements in Spain and many NGOs were founded in order to receive and coordinate the funds, basically no members of the Roma minority were involved in establishing and leading these initiatives. The official explanation was simply that *gitanos* were not considered to have the "proper qualification" to take these leading positions.[115] This tendency was also evident in other research countries: the members of the majority used (and this is not to deny the goodwill behind the initiatives) the external funds to "help" the members of minorities.[116] This certainly has tremendous influence on the focus and contents of the education projects. The Spanish section of Amnesty International which actively took part in promoting the Decade for Human Rights Education, was quite cautious in its efforts in the Basque country and considered the topic of the human rights of the Basques to be too much of a "hot potato" as nationalism and terrorism were too difficult to tackle. Similarly, in Estonia human rights NGOs have avoided the most problematic issues with Russian speakers and in Germany where the human rights education NGOs have avoided the topic of minorities as a whole. It appears to be very symptomatic of projects aiming at the empowerment of minorities that they forget to include the minorities in the planning phase of the programme (also often in the realisation). As Luptakova and Stern show in their contribution to this book, even in meetings and conferences addressing Roma and their educational or social needs, very few if any, Roma are invited.

In order to reach sustainability of human rights education programmes about and in collaboration with minorities, the contents of the projects have to be defined and coordinated concomitantly by the international community, representatives of states, minorities and civil society activists. The German example shows that a national focal point can play a central role in mainstreaming human rights education in different professional fields in the society. But even national coordination points for human rights education have to be sensitive to a minority perspective and pay extensive attention to the question of what an inclusive understanding of "who *we* are" means. Members of minorities and other marginalized sectors have to become integral partners in human rights education efforts if the state wants to live up to its promises to the international community and promote human rights based on a holistic approach to education.

115 I am here referring basically to the research conducted by our colleague Anja Mihr, see Mihr this publication.

116 See also Toivanen, ‚Unwissen, Vorurteile und andere "Gewohnheiten"', op. cit fn. 104.

IV Minorities and Human Rights Education

Human Rights Law as a Paradigm for the Protection and Advancement of Minority Education in Europe

Theodore S. Orlin

Introduction

As the twentieth century drew to a close a number of ambitious international instruments were drafted which stressed the importance of minority issues for the human rights agenda and established an attempt to protect minority interests and rights via the rule of law. The claims of the importance of pluralism found in the OSCE (CSCE) documents and efforts[1], the European Charter for Regional or Minority Languages, (1992)[2] the drafting and the ratification of the European Framework Convention for the Protection of National Minorities (1995)[3], the inclusion in the Convention of the Rights of the Child (1989)[4] of the protection of minority rights and linguistic education, seem to place minority rights as a newly found focus of human rights concerns. The recent attention international organisations, NGOs, both regional and global, place on minority issues, such as the protection of Roma rights, indigenous peoples and other targeted minorities and peoples, reinforced the impression that minority issues, long ignored, were at last to be given a high priority. With this attention there appeared to be a newly found commitment to the use of human rights law and policy that would attempt to redress the wrongs imposed on minorities for centuries. As these instruments are increasingly referred to as evidence of a growing respect toward minority rights, there are those who see this as a recent phenomenon reflecting the politics of a post cold war atmosphere; this may not be fundamental, but only a passing vogue in response to contemporary politics which could easily be discarded as the political landscape reflects new realities that may place less significance on the protection of minorities. With the concomitant resurgence of nationalistic agendas and claims for a revival of ethnocentric nationalistic policies, there is a threat that the demands of a pluralistic Europe and the protection of minorities may be increasingly threatened. The nascent and fragile legal protection now afforded by international legal instruments, at least de jure, if not de facto, must be seen as merely progressive

---

[1] The Conference on Security and Cooperation in Europe (CSCE) assumed IGO status when the Organization for the Security and Cooperation in Europe (OSCE) replaced the CSCE. See e.g. OSCE/CSCE documents: Document of the Copenhagen Meeting of the Conference on the Human Dimension of the CSCE, 1990, Paragraphs (33)-(40.7); Document of the CSCE Budapest Summit Meeting, 1994, paragraph 21.

[2] The Charter was open for signature on 5 November 1992 and entered into force on 1 March 1998. *ETS* No. 144.

[3] The Convention was opened for signature on 1 February 1995 and entered into force on 1 February 1998. *ETS* No. 157.

[4] The Convention was adopted by General Assembly Resolution 44/25, 20 November 1989. The CRC entered into force on 2 September 1990.

steps for the further development of legal protection and the creation of a more effective mechanism to make the often espoused rhetoric of minority protection a reality.

As often is the case we must look to educational efforts and policies as the principal means of ensuring that there is broad support for the protection of the human rights of minorities.[5]

If we are now to demonstrate that it is in the present and future interest of European national minorities to pursue its goal of quality minority education and minority protection using the principles enshrined in human rights instruments, rather than relying on nationalistic agendas and rhetoric; if we are to ensure that one of the principal goals of human rights education is the protection of minority rights, thus encouraging minorities to pursue the protection of their identity consistent with the human rights norms that European States have agreed to abide by as legal obligations, we must first explore the attempts of the past for their success and their failure to ensure the protection of minorities are founded on sound policies and principles. We must make clear, and be convincing, that despite the recent attention given to minority rights and human rights education, it is an issue that has concerned the international community for centuries and is truly worthy of our continued interest and protection.

For the human rights educator an interest in international law and its concerns for minority rights and minority education should be of particular significance. This chapter provides the human rights educator with an appreciation of the legitimacy the law provides for including in educational policy the necessity of human rights education to respect the rights of minorities. If we are to convince policy makers at the national, regional, and local levels of the importance of the inclusion of human rights education to protect the rights and interests of minorities then it is essential that we demonstrate that human rights is not just a question of good or ethical policy, but one mandated by legal principles that have also been recognized for some time and broadly accepted in Europe and elsewhere.

Human rights education directed to protect rights, including those of minorities and where appropriate "peoples", should not be seen as discretionary, but rather as a legal requirement. We should include human rights education on our educational agendas, not because we are enlightened, but because as global citizens we have an obligation to do so; as a matter of law and not based on the whim of policy or good intentions. There is a need to remind educators and governments who regulate education policy that the states they represent have made a legal commitment via the UN Charter and other international instruments to *"[...] to take joint and separate action...for the achievement of"* [...] *"the universal respect for, and observance of human rights and fundamental freedoms without respect as to race, sex, language and religion."*[6] Concretely, we must be mindful of the Universal Declaration of Human Rights' call that we "shall strive by teaching and education to promote respect for these rights and freedoms" and make it a critical component in our educational endeavours.[7]

[5] This argument is discussed in Claudia Mahler's contribution to this book.
[6] The Charter of the United Nations, signed June 1945, entered into force 24 October 1945.
[7] Universal Declaration of Human Rights, 10 December 1948, Resolution 217 (III).

When and where our governments and education policy makers ignore the legal imperatives of treaties and other sources of international law, our teaching should direct our students to question those policies. Our students must be convinced that the respect of others is central to their own respect and that international law makes minority rights an imperative we need to take seriously. The goal is that educational efforts demonstrating that legal mandates require respect for human rights and the rights of minorities will facilitate an atmosphere where the protection of human rights is integral to our political culture.

Early Legal Attempts to Provide Protection of Minority Interests in Education

"What is past is prologue." The Tempest, William Shakespeare

For the casual observer it may appear that the human rights issues of minorities were discovered only recently when they seemed to be placed near the apex of European concerns. One perception held is that only after a realization of the newer human rights instruments that now guide European policy, did Europe become concerned with minority issues and the need to provide the protection of human rights law for those who claim to be a minority or are perceived as a group subject to the abuse and discrimination of a majority.

A review of the history of international law reflects a different reality. To understand the development of recent attempts to protect minorities it is necessary to admit and consider that the very birth of the international system placed considerable attention towards minority rights. It could very well be argued that minority rights related to educational issues had been one of the central themes of international law from its very inception and it therefore can be seen from the very dawn of the international system as an essential and integral part of the human rights law agenda.

International legal scholars traditionally mark the beginning of the modern international system and the birth of modern international law with the completion of the Peace of Westphalia in 1648. The conclusion of the Treaty of Osnabruck between Sweden and the Holy Roman Empire along with the Treaty of Munster between France and the Empire (which officially ended the Thirty Years War) is seen as the point where the concept of sovereignty among European states became accepted as fundamental to the international system.[8]

What is often forgotten about the Peace of Westphalia is that as early as the seventeenth century, the Treaty of Osnabruck was a tangible confirmation that international law began to protect European minorities and educational interests of those minorities[9] Hence, we see that at the very birth of the modern international system, a confirmation that State sovereignty is not absolute and that the recognition of a States' power can be dependent on the State limiting its power conditioned on a commitment to protect the minorities which live under its sovereignty. The lesson is

[8] Janis, Mark W., An Introduction to International Law, Fourth Edition, New York: Aspen Publishers, 2003, p. *162*.
[9] See Ishay, Micheline R., The History of Human Rights- From Ancient Times to the Globalization Era, Berkeley and Los Angeles: University of California Press, 2004, *p. 78*.

not only clear, but poignant. This historical truth serves to remind us that minority protection, via treaty obligations, is neither new nor innovative.

The Development of Minority Protection as a Legal Obligation

"Nothing, I venture to say, is more likely to disturb the peace of the world than the treatment which might in certain circumstances be meted out to minorities." U.S. President Woodrow Wilson, 1919

The conclusion of World War I saw the recognition of a need for self-determination of European nationalities and the realization of sovereign entities for peoples who were once minorities in larger political entities like the Ottoman and Austro-Hungarian Empires. Concomitantly, the creation of new sovereign states, reflecting the demands of nationalistic majorities, created the need to recognize that these nationalistic states, must not abuse the religious, ethnic and linguistic minorities which became subject to the ethnic, religious and linguistic majorities, who now dominated the policies of their own nation states. The contemporary experiences of modern Europe continue to reflect the minority issues that were a concern in the early twentieth century and now must be dealt with. For human rights educators, the minority-treaty system which is associated with the League of Nations experience is not only illustrative of European minority history, but instructive as to the inherent problems associated with minority rights and demonstrates the need to seek more effective remedies to deal with the complexities of the issues than were tried in the past.

The Paris Conference resulted in treaties which created new States based on nationalist agendas and imposed legal conditions on both old and new States to protect minorities. Hence the establishment and international recognition of Austria, Hungary, Bulgaria, Turkey along with the newly recognized states of Czechoslovakia, Greece, Poland, Romania and Yugoslavia, were now required to protect the linguistic, religious and other issues that are traditionally the concern of European minorities. Similarly Albania, Lithuania, Estonia and Iraq made a unilateral declaration on their admission to the League of Nations vowing to protect minority rights. In addition, there were special provisions for the Åland Islands, Danzig, the Memel Territory and Upper Silesia.[10] Via these agreements, Europe began to see the legal institutionalization of minority protection. Earlier views that States were free to treat their subjects as they wished, immune from international pressure and concern, were challenged.

The attempts of the post World War effort was clearly a step in the direction of internationalizing the protection of minority rights not by "Great Powers" (as was the experience of the Treaty of Berlin), but by the community of states represented by the then new and emerging international organisation, the League of Nations. In responding to the failures of the nineteenth century it was argued:

"Experience has shown that this was in practice ineffective, and it was also open to the criticism that it might have given the Great Powers, either individually or in combination, a right to

[10] Op. cit., de Varennes, Fernand, Trifunovska, Snežana, at p. 5.

interfere in the internal constitution of the States affected could be used for political purposes. Under the new system, the guarantee is entrusted to the League of Nations."[11]

The system reconfirmed the necessity of conditioning independence and the exercise of sovereignty in international legal commitments to protect the rights and interests of minorities subject to the established governments.

Some Thoughts on United Nations Instruments

At the outset it must be remembered that the text of the Covenant of the League of Nations makes no mention of "human rights". If we rely on the early experience to demonstrate the need for minority protection, we must admit that human rights as a legal obligation does not exist until the drafting of the UN Charter.[12] It is for this reason that if human rights law is to be a paradigm for the protection and advancement of minority education in Europe, a brief discussion of UN instruments and mechanisms are necessary. As the early comments of the Chapter makes clear, human rights has become part of international law due to the nearly universal state acceptance of the Charter[13] and the other UN instruments which protect human rights. Furthermore, the commitment to education making human rights universal and to provide a "common standard" of understanding, found in the Universal Declaration, requires some discussion as to the nature and extent that UN treaty law protects minority rights and interests. If we are to succeed in bringing the human rights message to our students and to insist that our states support the interests and rights of minorities, we must explore where the UN instruments, mechanisms and practice work to protect minorities and where they fail.

The UDHR – The Wellspring of Human Rights Instruments

Whereas recognition of the inherent dignity and of equal and inalienable rights of all members of the human family is the foundation of freedom, justice and peace in the world [...] Whereas a common understanding of these rights and freedoms is of the greatest importance for the full realization of this pledge. Excerpts from the Preamble, UDHR (Dec. 10, 1948)

The Universal Declaration of Human Rights (UDHR), (1948), is unquestionably the wellspring of the more developed, more concrete and more descriptive human rights treaties that it inspired. The UDHR, although a recommendation of the General Assembly[14], which is not a legally binding instrument, was intended to be "a common

---

[11] Letter addressed by M. Clemenceau to M. Paderewski, June 24, 1919- Cited in Sohn, Louis B. and Buergenthal, Thomas, International Protection of Human Rights, New York: Bobbs-Merrill Company, 1973 at p. 216.

[12] Buergenthal, Thomas, Shelton, Dinah, Stewart, David, International Human Rights in a Nutshell, 3rd Edition,West Group 2002, St. Paul Mn., US at p. 7.

[13] The UN has 192 members as of November 2007.

[14] UDHR, 10 December 1948, General Assembly Resolution 217 (III).

standard of achievement for all peoples and all nations".[15] It was, and does add meaning to the Article 55 and 56 pledge of the Charter to, "*take joint and separate action [...] or the achievement [...]*" of "*universal respect for, and observance of human rights and fundamental freedoms for all without distinction as to race, sex, language, or religion.*"[16]

It is critical that we are mindful of the fact that the drafters of the Declaration stressed that the importance of education in its implementation, prior to its operative articles citing the rights and freedom: "*[...] every individual and every organ of society, keeping this Declaration constantly in mind, shall strive by teaching and education to promote respect for these rights and freedom [...]*"[17]

Yet, despite the above Article 55 reference to an equal application of rights, the UDHR does not actually use the term "minority rights" although its anti-discrimination clause(s) (Articles1,2,7) clearly provides protection for minority members.

According to the article 2, "*[e]veryone is entitled to all the rights and freedoms set forth in this Declaration without distinction of any kind, such as race, colour, sex, language, religion, political or other opinion, national or social origin, property, birth or other status [...]*". This article arguably provides minority protection by prohibiting the discrimination to the classes referred to, which easily can be seen to include religious, linguistic, racial and national minorities. Although Article 1, taken alone, can be seen as even more inclusive; "*All human being are born free and equal in dignity and rights [...]*" With the addition of Article 7, "*All are equal before the law and are entitled without discrimination to equal protection of the law. All are entitled to equal protection against any discrimination violation of the Declaration and any incitement to such discrimination [...]*", the UDHR clearly provides language barring discrimination which is directed at minorities.

"*National [...] origin*" as discussed by Johannes Morsink's work on the Origins, Drafting & Intent of the Universal Declaration[18], provides overwhelming argumentation that minorities are included as a protected classification; "national origin" was first proposed by Borisov, the Soviet expert, on the Sub-Commission [...] It links it to "race" and "colour" and strengthens the protection of the rights of members of ethnic and cultural groups."[19]

Furthermore the inclusion in Article 2 of "language", "race" and "colour" makes the discrimination bar inclusive of minorities;

"*All four items-[...] protect members of ethnic, cultural and linguistic minority groups from being discriminated against with respect to any of the rights in the Declaration. Such minority members cannot be kept from participating in the government of their countries (Article 21); they have just as much right to food, clothing, housing and medical care (Article 25); as members of majority groups; they have the right to work (Article 23) and cannot be barred from holding public office(Article 21(2)); they have the same right to freedom of movement within and between coun-*

[15] Some of the norms described by the UDHR are binding since they considered reflective of customary international law, e.g. the prohibition of slavery and the prohibition against torture.
[16] Article 55 and 56 ,The Charter of the United Nations, op.cit.
[17] UDHR, op.cit.
[18] Morsink, Johannis, The Universal Declaration of Human Rights: Origins, Drafting, and Intent, Philadelphia: University of Pennslyvannia Press, 1999.
[19] Id. at pp. 103-104.

tries (Articles 13 and 14); they also have the same right to nationality (Article 15 and the protection that comes with that status. More specifically, the right not to be discriminated against on the basis of language applies to 'all the rights and freedoms in this Declaration".

Significantly the UDHR makes no specific requirement to take positive steps to protect minorities, except arguably, for the right to education, *Article 26,* and specifically paragraph (3): "*Parents have a prior right to choose the kind of education that shall be given to their children.*" At the time of the drafting of the Declaration the Danish delegation presented to the Third Committee an amendment stating that members of minority groups had the right to "*establish their own schools and receive teaching in the language of their choice.*" Rene Cassin, the Nobel prize winner for his contribution to the UDHR stated in response to the suggestion, that Article 2 provided a secure basis to protect minorities without adding the additional alteration.[20] Nonetheless, we can argue that based on the considerable debate surrounding the right to education and the concerns for minorities, that the Declaration provides a basis to argue that there is an obligation to accommodate minority needs in educational policy.[21] Similarly the UDHR's Article 18 gives the right to minorities to use their own language in religious activities.

The lacuna of not including a minority protection article in the Declaration was not accidental nor without considerable controversy. John Humphries, as a member of the Secretariat and as a principal drafter of the early drafts of the UDHR, relying on suggestions of Lauterpact, was mindful of minority rights. In his report to the first session of the Commission when it created the Sub-Commission for the Prevention of Discrimination and the Protection of Minorities, he provided a definition for minorities: "*groups within a country that differ from the dominant group in their culture, religion or language and which usually desire to maintain and foster their culture, linguistic and religious identity.*" Importantly for future interpretation he noted that; "*protection of minorities include both protection from discrimination and protection against assimilation.*" Lauterpacht, quoted by Humphries, was very mindful of the then recent past; "the abandonment of the present {League of Nations'} system of protection of minorities, without an alternative and compensating international arrangement, would mean a disservice to the minorities, to the cause of international protection of human rights and international peace and progress."

Humphries placed a draft article before the delegates for consideration to specifically protect minorities, but ultimately even with considerable support (including Belgium, USSR, Lebanon, Yugoslavia, Poland and China) it failed to be included in the Declaration. The logic of Eleanor Roosevelt prevailed that "*provisions relating to rights of minorities had no place in a declaration of human right.*" The Indian delegate, Metha, argued that a minority clause was "*unnecessary because members of minority groups were protected as human beings by other articles of the Declaration.*[22]

While there is no clear or single "minority rights" article in the UDHR, ultimately the present Article 27 (paragraph 1) was approved; "*Everyone has the right to participate in the cultural life of the community, to enjoy the arts and to share in scientific advancement and its benefits.*"

---

[20] Id., citing (A/C.3/250) at p.105.
[21] Id., pp.263-269, Section 7.3
[22] Id., pp.269-280, Section 7.4.

Even in light of this criticism, the UDHR, despite its ambiguity and need for interpretation regarding the protection of minority interests, remains an important instrument for the promulgation of the human rights of members of minorities. The human rights educator should stress that the Declaration, with many of its protections is now seen as part of customary international law that makes its provisions universally applicable whether or not a state has ratified any of the later drafted human rights treaties which have more clearly pronounced protections for minorities.

The disputes surrounding the UDHR, its meaning and its application, fits well within the "paradigm" of human rights law in serving the interests of protecting minority rights and the minority interest in preserving its culture and language in the face of large majorities who may have nationalistic agendas. If the debates now surrounding minority rights issues can be focused within the framework of the Declaration, it will serve to sharpen the discussion and focus it on the meaning of human rights and its meaning for minority protection. By moving away from the acrimonious rhetoric of nationalistic politics and the intensity of ethnic and cultural protection and shifting it to a discussion of the meaning of rights found within Declaration, it has the advantage of moving the discussion to increased rationality and the reliance of normative standards that are widely respected as a common standard of the meaning of human rights. Accordingly, it can serve to strengthen the pursuit of more effective policies and mechanisms to better protect the legitimate interests of minorities.

CCPR - The Development of Legal Standards for Minority Protection and Peoples' Rights

If the Declaration is an instrument drafted as a recommendation to establish a "common standard", the treaties it spurred are legally binding and create clear legal obligations for those who ratified it. The International Covenant on Civil and Political Rights (1966), (CCPR).[23] is considered to be part of the International Bill of Rights.[24] Not only do we have legal language which is more precise, at times whose protective language is broader and at times narrower than the Declaration, we have the advantage of interpretation of the treaty via the review of periodic country reports and communications brought by individuals under the Optional Protocol[25], after they sought and exhausted their domestic remedies for alleged violations of human rights. This jurisprudence provides considerable examples to help understand the nature of how human rights law can describe the nature, extent and qualities of minority protection.

---

[23] General Assembly Resolution 2200 A (XXI), UN doc. A/6316 (1966), entered into force 23 March 1976.

[24] Orlin, Theodore S., Rosas, Allan, Scheinin, Martin, The Jurisprudence of Human Rights Law: A Comparative Interpretive Approach, Åbo/Turku: Institute for Human Rights- Åbo Akademi University, 2000.

[25] Optional Protocol to the International Covenant on Civil and Political Rights, 1966, entered into force 23 March 1976. There is a Second Optional Protocol to the ICCPR that aims at the abolition of the death penalty, General Assembly resolution 44/128, 15 December1989, entered into force 15 December 1989.

Demonstrative of the CCPR providing clearer and more pervasive protections for minorities is its Article 27, which compared with the Declaration's Article 27 (discussed above), reflects a different approach for minority protection, "In those States in which ethnic, religious or linguistic minorities exist, persons belonging to such minorities shall not be denied the right, in community with the other members of their group, to enjoy their own culture, to profess and practice their own religion, or to use their own language."

Thus we see the CCPR language goes further than the UDHR in providing a stronger and more positive State commitment to protect minority interests.[26] Yet, as has been made clear by legal commentators, CCPR Article 27's language is "cautious" and remains vague, requiring interpretation as to its meaning and breadth. [27] Unfortunately the scope of this chapter does not permit a full discussion of the interpretational approaches made by state parties in ratifying the Covenant, the Human Rights Committee, or other bodies in addressing the petitions and reports involving Article 27.

However, as illustrative of its value some discussion of its interpretation is useful. A critical example of the scope of interpretation problem is the inclusion of Article 1, common to both the CCPR and Covenant on Social, Economic and Cultural Rights (CSECR), which deals with "peoples' rights" and the "*right of self-determination*": "All peoples have the right of self-determination. By virtue of that right they freely determine their political status and freely pursue their economic, social and cultural development."

Clearly there is a critical legal distinction between whether a group views itself or is viewed as a either a "people" or a "minority". Since neither "minority" nor "people" is concretely defined, it presents interpretive problems in extending the protection of the CCPR and other human rights instruments that require a similar interpretation.[28] Nonetheless, it is of tremendous significance whether a group as a "people" may assert a right to self-determination proclaimed by (Article 1) or whether they claim the rights of a "minority" found in Article 27.[29]

This distinction takes on a significant importance as to how to treat the protection of "indigenous peoples", when they constitute a minority in a State and claim protection as a "minority".[30] Here, the General Comments of the UN Human Rights Committee (HRC)[31] and its case law provides insight as to the meaning of "peoples"

---

[26] Nowak, Manfred, op. cit. at p.481

[27] Id., at p. 485.

[28] Joseph, Schultz, Castan, op.cit. at p. 754.

[29] Id. Nowak asserts that "...the term "minority is extremely vague, is not defined by Art. 27... and is employed by governments in quite different manners", at p. 487. See also Benoît- Rohmer, Florence, The Minority Question in Europe, Germany: Council of Europe Publishing, 1996, p.14- In discussing Art. 27, OSCE and European instruments she stated: "*The difficulty of coming up with a general definition of the term "minority" accounts for the evasion of the problem by the international instruments, which simply confine themselves to identifying minorities by their ethnic, linguistic and religious characteristics*".

[30] Scheinin, Martin, The Right to Enjoy a Distinct Culture: Indigenous and Competing Uses of Land, in Orlin, Rosas, Scheinin, op.cit at pp, 160-161.

[31] General Comment 23 (paragraph 2): "*The Covenant draws a distinction between the right of self-determination and the rights protected under Article 27. The former is expressed to be a right*

and when they may assert "minority protection" as a numerically inferior group as an "ethnic" or "linguistic" minority under Article 27. Cases like *Lovelace v. Canada, Lubicon Lake Band v. Canada, and Kitok v. Sweden* [32] are illustrative of the fact that the HRC has used Article 27, as in the case of Sami rights, to protect the culture of an indigenous people as a minority threatened by the state's majority culture.

The HRC's case law provides the human rights educator with an opportunity to explain how human rights law deals with the competing interests that are often involved in disputes among minorities and the state parties who commit themselves to the obligation of the CCPR, but have economic and/or administrative interests which may be in conflict with the rights of minorities.

Although the CCPR offers no precise or fixed definition of what a "minority" is, the growing examples of minority protection gleaned from of the case law, the General Comments and the HRC's reporting process, serve to provide some meaning as to the nature of minority rights via a human rights law context. The experience permits an understanding that goes beyond the hypothetical and allows for a discussion of actual cases and controversies in the context of real, and not imagined circumstances. From the HRC's work and the state responses to their international commitments the understanding of minority rights has taken on a more concrete understanding. This is undoubtedly beneficial in pursuing the protection of minority interests. Now, consistent with the UDHR's urging that we must "*strive by teaching and education to promote respect for these rights and freedoms…*", it is incumbent on human rights educators, especially where their states have ratified the Covenant and its Optional Protocol, to bring the lessons of the CCPR to the classroom, to government officials and especially to the minorities and peoples who wish to assert their human rights in the face of challenges posed by majorities insensitive to their legitimate interests .

Further International Treaties Protecting Minorities

Before considering the most recent attempts via international law to protect minorities, it is valuable to consider the extent and limitation of these instruments which continue to provide legal standards for minority protection.

The Convention on Economic, Social and Cultural Rights (CESCR, 1966)[33], along with the UN Charter, UDHR, CCPR and its Optional Protocols, is considered part of the International Bill of Rights. In addition to its Article 1, protecting the "peoples" right to self-determination and its Article 2 (prohibiting discrimination), there are two other provisions which have special meaning for minority rights that are not included in the CCPR: Article 13 (1), which protects "the right of everyone to education."

---

belonging to peoples and is dealt with in a separate part (Part I) of the Covenant. Self-determination is not a right cognizable under the Optional Protocol. Article 27, on the other hand, relates to rights conferred on individuals as such and is included… "

[32] Id. Cited in Nowak at p. 494, HRC cases No. 24/1977, No. 167/1984, No. 197/1985.

[33] General Assembly Resolution 2200 A (XXI) of 16 December 1966, UN doc.A.6312, (entered into force 1976).

It must be noted that CESCR's Article 15 protects "the right of everyone (a) To take part in cultural right [...]; this may also provide a legal basis for the protection of minorities and Article 13 (3) which allows parents to choose for their children an alternative education to state sponsored education. A full discussion of the CESCR's and the UN Committee for Economic, Social and Cultural Rights work, including its General Comments, is well beyond the breadth of this work, but may prove to be a valuable source in the course of protecting minority rights and interests. [34]

The Convention on the Rights of the Child (CRC, 1989)[35] which has been widely ratified also provides within its articles which describe human rights for the purpose of "*improving the living conditions of children in every country [...]*"[36], provisions which are of particular interest to minorities, their cultures and their children in particular.

Consistent with the Covenants and other human rights instruments the CRC's Article 2 bars discrimination "to each child" on the basis of "race, colour, sex, language, religion, political or other opinion, national, ethnic or social origin, property, disability, birth or other status (paragraph 1). Furthermore, the article protects the child from discrimination on the basis of the parents' and family status.

Significantly, Articles 29's inclusion of educational issues "directed to the child", clearly provides language supportive of minority rights and education (Paragraph I. *(c)*.[37]). Furthermore, and perhaps more direct and expansive of minority rights is Article 30, largely built on CCPR Article 27 with modifications reflecting a later view of minority protection: "In those States in which ethnic, religious or linguistic minorities or persons of indigenous origin exist a child belonging to such a minority or who is indigenous shall not be denied the right, in community with the other members of his or her group, to enjoy his or her own culture, to profess and practice his or her own religion, or to use his or own language."[38]

Given its later date of creation the Committee on the Rights of the Child has a much more limited experience in interpreting the CRC's provisions than does that of the HRC. Furthermore, since there is only a reporting mechanism and there is no review of individual petitions as exists for the HRC via the Optional Protocol, the CRC is far from being as developed as that of the HRC. Nonetheless, the experience and commentary of the review of the CRC offers another critical source in the interpretation and application of minority interest through the focus of protecting the rights of the child.

The European Convention on Human Rights (ECHR, 1950)[39] (considered by most experts in human rights law as one of the most advanced regional systems of

---

[34] See: http://www.ohchr.org/english/bodies/cescr/

[35] General Assembly Resolution 44/25 of 20 November 1989, UN doc. A/44/49, (entered into force 2 Sept. 1990.)

[36] Preamble, CRC.

[37] See also Sia Åkermark in this publication,

[38] Emphasis added to show the variation in language – instead of use of "their" found in the CCPR, it is replaced in the CRC with "his or her"; included in addition to minority in the CRC is "indigenous origin".

[39] European Treaty Series No. 001 to 193 and the Council of Europe Treaty Series – The body of the ECHR was first signed on 4 November 1950 and entered into force on 3 Sept., 1950 and then modified by Protocols 1, 4, 6 and 7 as amended by Protocol No.11 (1998).

human rights protection) has no minority protection clause similar to the CRC (Article 30) or the CCPR (Article 27). The Convention "*does not contain any specific provision for the protection of minorities. The only article referring to national minorities is Article 14, which is, in fact a non-discrimination provision*".[40] Protection of minorities is found within its other substantive clauses which protect freedom of religion, the right of privacy, freedom of expression, etc. In order to argue discrimination, it is necessary that the individual complaint avers that the discrimination be consistent with the requirement that; "*The enjoyment of the rights and freedoms set forth in this Convention shall be secured without discrimination…*". Thus it is necessary to argue that as a member of a minority, discrimination has denied a right(s) found within the Articles of the Convention and/or its protocols. This has allowed for a multiple of cases directly impacting on the rights and freedom of a multitude of European minorities. Its jurisprudence is rich with examples and explanations of the extent and nature of minority protection and provides a wealth of legal discourse as to the nature of minority rights. Given the breadth of cases coming from those subjects to the jurisdiction of the Council of Europe's membership and given the binding quality of the Court's judgments it has significantly added to an understanding and judicial acceptance of minority rights not only for Europe, but for Courts, international and domestic, which mostly deal with similar issues within their own jurisdictions.

The work of the Court provides the human rights educator with a wealth of concrete examples as to the stresses of State interests as they come into conflict with rights of minorities. Unquestionably, following the case law of the ECHR is essential for the understanding of the legal issues surrounding the controversies which surround European minority issues.

More Recent Instruments to Protect Minority Rights

The intent of this chapter is to present the long and rich legal antecedents which have led to the development of human rights instruments that seemingly placed a new emphasis on the protection of minority rights via international human rights law.

The more recent instruments, (cited above), require a full and in depth review to understand their strengths and failings in protecting the rights of European minorities within a twenty-first century context. In this conclusion, suffice it to say, the drafting of these instruments reflects a political reality where minority issues have taken a new priority in our attempts to protect the rights of all Europeans. These instruments, like the earlier documents, provide guidance and insight as to the principles and norms that should direct the debate and pursuit for minority protection in this century. They also, like the human rights instruments which came before them, should be seen as part of an evolutionary process leading the way for the drafting of more comprehensive instruments and creating more effective mechanisms to protect minority interests via international human rights law.

---

[40] Trifunovska, Snežana, Protection of Linguistic Rights Within the Council of Europe in Minority Rights in Europe- European Minorities and Languages, The Hague: T.M.C. Asser Press, 2001, at p.147.

The Helsinki Accords and the Subsequent OSCE Documents

The Helsinki Accords[41] and subsequent OSCE documents including the Document of the Copenhagen Meeting from 1990, the Charter of Paris for a New Europe 1990, Document of the Moscow Meeting 1991, etc. were made towards the end of the Cold War, where democracy, pluralism and the rule of law became normative principles for all Europe.[42] These, legally non-binding but political undertakings have arguably established a governmental consensus for OSCE members for the protection of minorities. The Document of the Copenhagen Meeting (1990), often considered a "European Charter of Minorities"[43], reflects in its provisions an apparent political consensus, no doubt a great contribution in the development of minority rights, but must not be seen as the final step in the development of an effective process for the protection of minority interests and rights. Similarly, while the Charter of Paris in 1990 may have called for states to "foster the rich contribution of national minorities to the life of our societies," clearly minority issues remain a concern for the human rights advocate and educator.

Despite this effort, the emergence of a political climate which calls for nationalistic agendas on the part of majorities, continues to be a concern for minority protection, making the OSCE instruments still, if not more, relevant in the relationship among the OSCE member States. The OSCE, has evolved beyond the diplomatic conference of the CSCE into a working IGO, which includes a membership stretching from North America (USA, Canada) through Asia (Russia) and has cooperation from Japan and the Republic of Korea.[44] As an organisation it has been an important player for the creation of stability in a number of European crises, e.g. Bosnia and Herzegovina, Kosovo, Chechnya, etc., which have plagued Europe. The efforts of the OSCE High Commissioner on National Minorities has had some success in dealing with some of the many minority issues and conflicts which continue in parts of Europe, but by no means are the problems resolved to the satisfaction to the requirements of the documents. The OSCE principles expressed in its documents and the actions of it machinery increasingly needs to be brought to the attention of the educational and advocacy efforts concerned with minority issues.

---

[41] CSCE, Helsinki Final Act (1975), Principle VII of the "Declaration on Principles Guiding Relations between Participating States", - *"participating States on whose territory national minorities exist will respect the rights of persons belonging to such minorities to equality before the law, will afford them the full opportunity for the actual enjoyment of human rights and fundamental freedoms and will, in this manner, protect their legitimate interests in this sphere."*

[42] Buergenthal, Thomas, Shelton, Dinah, Stewart, David, International Human Rights in a Nutshell, St. Paul: West Group, Thomson, 2002 at pp.205-206- The CSCE was *"(C)onceived as a compromise instrument to bridge the ideological chasm that divided East from West in the 197O's the (Helsinki Final Act), ushered in a negotiating process that established a highly imaginative linkage between human rights and security concerns."*

[43] Benoit- Rohmer, Florence, Op.Cit. at p.25.

[44] Document of the OSCE Lisbon Summit, 1996, at paragraph 24.

Council of Europe

The European Charter for Regional or Minority Languages (1992) is an attempt, consistent with the European experience discussed earlier, to further protect and promote the use of these languages in private and public life. Its creative provisions allow parties to choose at minimum thirty five undertakings (from Part III, with certain requirements limiting the choice).[45] The Charter "provides for a dynamic process" and is not an end in itself.[46] It requires a reporting system which periodically provides an opportunity for the public and state parties to review the progress and respect among the ratifers as to the protection of minority and regional languages. The Charter to some extent reflects that the protection of regional and minority languages continues as a contentious concern. Hopefully its machinery will be more successful than earlier efforts as states are now required to report periodically their progress in protecting these languages.

Via its reporting system, overseen by its Committee of Experts (Article 17), we see a conscientious international effort to protect the languages which have been historically a central concern of European minorities. Once again the experience of the past and the complexities of the present have encouraged, via the rule of law expressed in a treaty, to protect a core element of minority culture; the traditional languages that have been challenged by majority cultures.

The Framework Convention for the Protection of National Minorities is the most recent attempt to protect minorities via an international legal commitment. It is an ambitious treaty that tries to protect minorities from majorities who reflect nationalism or perhaps an ethnic central view of their societies and states. It "*is the first legally binding multilateral document completing devoted to the protection of national minorities*." [47]

Like the Language Charter, it is open to non-members of the Council of Europe States (Article 27). The fact that the Convention doesn't have a common definition for a "minority" and that the European ratification allows for its ratifiers to self define the meaning of "minority", has become a source of criticism of the treaty. The ratification of the Convention is rife with reservations that self define which minorities are to be protected.[48] This very process is ample evidence to indicate the continued difficulty of coming to a single definition of the legal meaning of a minority. Yet this courageous effort to protect European minorities via an international agreement, should be seen as another and important step in the evolution of human rights law and the protection of minority interests and rights. What is important is that the effort continues. We must look to the past, to understand successes and failures to find more effective ways to protect minorities. What is significant is that we do this within the paradigm of human rights law and not the jingoistic rhetoric of nationalism or ethnocentrism. The debate and the discussions must be framed by the commitment to law and not just by the rhetoric of majority and minority politics.

---

[45] Article 2, (2).

[46] Trifunovska, Snežana,, op. cit. at p.150.

[47] Id. At p.151

[48] http://www.coe.int/T/E/Human_Rights/Minorities/.

Conclusion

The human rights educator serves as the communicator of human rights to those who seek the meaning and relevancy of human rights. It is critical that she or he is able to place minority rights high on the education agenda. While the breadth of human rights law is considerable, minority rights remains a central concern for the protection of the human rights of all Europeans.

Human rights lessons need to inform and acculturate our students with an appreciation of human rights for the protection of their rights and the rights of others, including minorities which have historically been targeted. Educators must provide evidence that the protection of minorities is central to the legal principles we must all abide by. Our teaching must include that the protection of minority interests are legitimized by law; that the need to respect other cultures, as we would like our own to be respected, is not a question of kindness, generosity or ethical correctness, but a matter of law demanded by our society expressed by state commitments. When and where our governments and education policy makers ignore the legal imperatives of treaties and other sources of international law our teaching should direct our students to question those policies. We need, through educational processes, to create a political culture that respects the human rights principles, especially the respect of the rights and interests of minorities that we have willingly accepted as a matter of our law. Our students must be convinced that the respect of others is critical for the respect of their own dignity and that international law, readily accepted by our states, makes minority rights an imperative we need to take seriously. The goal is that educational efforts demonstrating that legal mandates require respect for human rights and the rights of minorities, will facilitate an atmosphere where the protection of human rights is an integral part of our political culture. We must convert the rhetoric of international human rights law into a practical reality, where in our relationships with one another we practice the demands of human rights law to provide the dignity that the human right instruments and international treaties have so long attempted to protect. To accomplish such a goal requires a demonstration that international law demands the universal respect of all peoples including and, perhaps, especially minorities.

Human Rights Education and Roma in Slovakia

Inken Stern and Jana Luptáková

Introduction

The Slovak Republic is a multi-ethnic state with a high share of minorities. One of these minorities is the group of people of Roma origin who are recognized as a national minority. In the 2001 census 89,920 people considered themselves Roma.[1] The real figure is estimated to be much higher – between 380,000 and 520,000 people.[2] With this estimated representation of around 8 % of the total population, those with a Roma background form the second largest minority group in Slovakia (after the Hungarian minority) but at the same time, are the weakest part of Slovak civic society. Unfortunately there is a wide gap between Roma and non-Roma people in Slovak civil society. In general, we can say that the Roma are socially excluded mainly due to disadvantages in all important societal areas, for example in education, health, housing, social status, and duration of unemployment resulting in many Roma families suffering from long term poverty.[3]

The Slovak government refers to programmes which aim to change the problematic situation of the Roma community as an important part of its strategies.[4] Thus, legislative measures promoting desegregation and access to quality education do theoretically exist, but in practice, these measures have hardly any impact. Many Roma communities (were[5]) settled separately – without any infrastructure (like electricity, water, roads, telephone network etc.) – laying the foundations for segrega-

---

[1] Please visit the census-homepage: http://portal.statistics.sk/files/Sekcie/sek_600/Demografia/SODB/Tabulky/Tabulky_AJ_SODB/tab11.pdf (visited in January 2008).

[2] See Conception of Roma Children and Young People, Integrated Education, Including Secondary and University Education Development, Submission report by the Slovak Ministry of Education, approved by the SR Government Resolution no.498, dated 26 May 2004, p. 4f.; ERRC Report: Stigmata: Segregated Schooling of Roma in Central and Eastern Europe, a survey of patterns of segregated education of Roma in Bulgaria, the Czech Republic, Hungary, Romania, and Slovakia, 2005, http://www.errc.org/db/00/04/m00000004.pdf (visited in January 2008), p. 28; Human Development Report on Roma in Slovakia, prepared by Michal Vašečka, Bratislava: Institute for Public Affairs, 2002, p. 6; Dena Ringold / Mitchell A. Orenstein / Erika Wilkens, Roma in an expanding Europe, Breaking the poverty cycle; Washington D.C.: The Worldbank, 2005, p. 60f; Boris Vaňo, "The demographics of Roma children", in: Andrej Salner (ed.), Roma Children in the Slovak Education System, Bratislava, GSI, 2005, p. 32.

[3] Comments by the government of Slovakia to the concluding observations of the Human Rights Committee, adopted on 18 November 2004, doc.-no.: CCPR/CO/78/SVK/Add.1, dated 27 January 2005, para. 17; Conception of Roma Children and Young People, Slovak Ministry of Education, 2004, fn. 2, p. 2.

[4] For example in the fourth and fifth State Party Report to CERD by Slovakia, adopted 28 October 2004, doc.-no.: CERD/C/419/Add.2, dated 29 March 2004, paras. 66-121.

[5] The Czechoslovak state adopted policies towards an assimilation of the Roma as for example the law on the permanent settlement of nomadic and semi-nomadic people (No. 74) in 1958.

tion.[6] Nobody can be integrated into, and become an accepted part of society while living in a poor and segregated environment.[7] In view of the social and educational conditions, the law and legislative surroundings, it has to be admitted that the Roma people have hardly any chance of becoming members of the labour market.[8] This is a fact even though equality programmes and projects exist in Slovakia as the initiatives of the Teacher Club, (Roma) NGO's, the Ministry of Education, and some other agencies which are concerned with making conditions (equal opportunities) of the well-educated Roma better. Discrimination against the Roma is a widespread phenomenon and an increasing problem in Slovakia. Roma women and girls are battling multiple discrimination: as (young) Roma, as women, and as Roma women. This is why it is necessary to make sure that at least within human rights programmes the disadvantaged situation of Roma women is taken into account, especially in the field of education.[9]

The Slovak government's wish to preserve the present "achieved" standards does not help to change the situation between the Roma minority and the other parts of society. Active participation in societal processes can hardly be detected among the Roma and there is also a lack of sufficient discussion within society on "Roma issues" mainly due to a lack of interest – probably on both sides.

Even conferences, seminars, and workshops on topics like the elimination of racism or the support of human rights education in Slovakia and Europe are no guarantee for a room free from discrimination against the Roma. Discrimination in the form of discrediting of Roma language (for example by saying it is an unimportant dialect) has been experienced on several of such occasions. Furthermore, it is striking that at an international conference about the non-discriminative education of Roma children, only a few Roma people were present. Is that because the Roma community was not interested in this topic or rather because they were not invited or did not know about the event?

The Educational Situation in Slovakia and the Roma

The first topic of the National Action Plan of the Slovak Republic Regarding the Decade of Roma Inclusion 2005 – 2015[10] is education. This does not surprise since

---

[6] Klara Orgovanova, Roma in Slovakia; http://www.slovakia.org/society-roma.htm (visited in January 2008).

[7] Ringold / Orenstein / Wilkens, Roma in an expanding Europe, 2005, fn. 2, p. 67-71.

[8] Zuzana Šranková and Marcela Maslová, "Slovakia", in: Virginija Būdienė / Indra Dedze / Mercedes del Rosario (ed.), School Dropouts: Albania, Kazakhstan, Latvia, Mongolia, Slovakia, and Tajikistan; Budapest: Education Support Program (ESP) of the Open Society Institute; New York: OSI, 2007, p. 159-173, at 160.

[9] General Recommendation No. 27: Discrimination against Roma, adopted by the Committee for the Elimination of Racial Discrimination at the 57 session (2000), doc.-no.: Gen. Rec. No. 27, dated 16 August 2000, para. 22; concluding observations of the Committee on the Elimination of Racial Discrimination: Slovakia, adopted at the 65 session (2–20 August 2004), doc.-no.: CERD/C/65/CO/7, dated 10 December 2004, para. 6.

[10] National Action Plan of the Slovak Republic Regarding the Decade of Roma Inclusion 2005 – 2015, see please

the lack of education in the Roma communities is one of the main problems for the Roma. Slovakia is a country with nearly 900,000 children and young people in school.[11] The children of Roma origin make up more than 10 % of the children in Slovakia but the majority of them do not go to school, due amongst other reasons, to the high drop-out rates of Roma children.[12]

It seems that the higher the concentration of the Roma population, the lower the attained level of education is.[13] There are some regions – located in the south of central Slovakia and in eastern Slovakia – where many more Roma people have (been) settled for generations than in other parts of the country. Consequently, the share of the Roma children in these areas is traditionally higher and usually there still exist segregated classrooms and segregated schools.[14] This is due to the fact that many non-Roma parents prefer to enrol their children in schools with a low concentration of Roma children.

The Slovak government tries to use two principal ways to eliminate the segregation in the educational system. The first way is to use motivational measures such as giving financial grants to projects which aim at "instructing teachers how to educate Roma children, publishing textbooks, etc." The other way implies the usage of coercive means such as, for example "taking legal actions against school directors who are formally responsible for transferring children" into so called 'special schools' which were established for people with a (mental) disabilities. These decisions about transfers to 'special schools' should be subject to a thorough supervision by the national mechanisms[15] to prevent malpractice.[16]

In those cases where Roma children get the opportunity to participate in regular schooling, they are mainly students of elementary schools. Yet, often Roma children – in some regions even up to 80 %[17] – have to attend 'special schools'.[18] Sometimes it is the opinion of teachers or parents that such 'special schools' are able to

---

http://www.government.gov.sk/orgovanova/dokumenty/akcny_plan_eng.rtf.

[11] This data refers to the school year 2002/2003. See Analytical Report PHARE RAXEN_CC, Minority Education, RAXEN_CC National Focal Point Slovakia, People Against Racism, Report on National Strategies for Minority Schooling, EUMC, Vienna, 2004, Annex 2, Table 3-8, p. 26-28.

[12] General to that topic: Šranková and Maslová, "Slovakia", 2007, fn. 8, p. 159-173.

[13] Report on the Situation of Fundamental Rights in the Slovak Republic in 2005, submitted to the EU Network of Independent Experts on Fundamental Rights by Martin Buzinger on 15 December 2005, doc.-no.: CFR-CDF/SV/2005, http://cridho.cpdr.ucl.ac.be/documents/Download.Rep/Reports2005/NationalReport/CFRSlovak_Rep2005.pdf (visited in January 2008), p. 38.

[14] Vaňo, "The demographics of Roma children", 2005, fn. 2, p. 32.

[15] For Example: Order of the Ministry of Education no. 49/2004 Coll. which amends the Order of the Ministry of Education no. 212/1991 Coll. on special schools as amended.

[16] Racism and Xenophobia in the EU Member States- trends, developments and good practice, EUMC – Annual Report 2005, Part 2, p. 72f.

[17] Report on the Situation of Fundamental Rights in the Slovak Republic in 2005, CFR-CDF/SV/2005, fn. 13, p. 38; European Commission (ed.), The Situation of Roma in an Enlarged European Union; Luxemburg: Office for Official Publications of the European Communities, 2004, p. 18, para. 6.

[18] CERD, Slovakia, CERD/C/65/CO/7, 2004, fn. 9, para. 8; concluding observations of the Human Rights Committee: Slovakia, adopted at the 78 session, doc.-no.: CCPR/CO/78/SVK, dated 22 August 2003, para. 18.

take better care of the children referring to their special needs.[19] Sometimes this attendance is due to the social situation of Roma families since the next primary or secondary school is much further away than 'special schools' which often are very close to where the Roma reside. Usually the unsatisfactory results of psychological tests are named as the reason for such a decision. In reality most of these children do not suffer from a mental disability. In fact, the psychological tests do not take into account the fact that Roma children have a different cultural and social background.[20] Roma children, especially if having grown up in a segregated Roma settlement, "often come to school without pre-school education and sufficient knowledge of Slovak, lack basic hygiene and cultural and working skills, have limited concentration, patience and perseverance, and have underdeveloped fine motor coordination, different experience and knowledge of the world, and different interests and felt needs."[21] That is why a large number of Roma children typically are diagnosed with a mental disability and consequently placed in a 'special school'.[22]

There is a lack of effort to promote a better education for the Roma people. Neither the formal nor the non-formal education systems are sensitive towards the specific concerns of people with a Roma background. If they are allowed to take part in that system they are only recognized as learners and as a target group, and not as a group who can be learned from. But the general critical educational situation for the Roma cannot be solved or changed by the other groups in society alone. It has to be said that the Roma population also has a responsibility to take part in that process but has so far failed to fight hard enough for an equal stand in educational matters.

Contents of Education - Mother Tongue Language Education in Romani

Education in minority languages does take place in Slovakia but only for the Hungarian and Ukrainian minorities.[23] This means that there is no mother tongue language education for the Roma people even though it is guaranteed by the Slovak constitution[24] and the human right to be educated in their own mother tongue exists.[25]

The situation of the Romani language is specific insofar as there are different dialects which are known and used as the language of the Roma people. Most of the Roma who use Romani as their everyday language (approximately 60%)[26] live in the east of Slovakia. But the Roma language which was codified in 1971 in the Slovak

[19] Ringold / Orenstein / Wilkens, Roma in an expanding Europe, 2005, fn. 2, p. 83f.
[20] RAXEN-Report, EUMC, 2004, fn. 11, p. 17.
[21] Comments by the government of Slovakia to HRC, CCPR/CO/78/SVK/Add.1, 2005, fn. 3, para. 60.
[22] Ibid. Please see also the report on observation of human rights in the Slovak Republic for the year 2004, Slovak National Center for Human Rights, Bratislava 2005, p. 72ff.
[23] RAXEN-Report, EUMC, 2004, fn. 11, p. 13.
[24] See Art. 34 of the Slovak constitution, passed by the Slovak National Council on 1 September and signed on 3 September 1992, http://www.slovakia.org/sk-constitution.htm .
[25] See Art. 8 of the European Charter for Regional or Minority Languages, ETS. No. 148, http://conventions.coe.int/treaty/en/Treaties/Html/148.htm (visited in January 2008). Slovakia signed the treaty on 20 February 2001 and ratified it on 5 September 2001.
[26] RAXEN-Report, EUMC, 2004, fn. 11, Annex 4, graph 3, p. 31.

Republic was based on a dialect which was only used by a minority of Roma living in the west of the country. This codified dialect can hardly be understood by the majority of the Roma people. Therefore the usage of this codified language for educational purposes would be highly ineffective.[27]

The Roma do not show a huge interest in being educated in their mother tongue.[28] But even if they were interested they would not have the opportunity of an education in Romani. There have been attempts to re-codify the language. In 2002, a Romani grammar textbook was published which was based on the dialect which is spoken most. This grammar is supposed to become the basis for education in Romani.[29]

The instruction in Roma language, history and culture has gained in importance. Two schools in Košice – the Art High School and the Private Upper high school – provide some lessons in Romology including Roma language, history and culture. Both of them are participating in a verification test of basic pedagogical documents concerning the subject Romology. Hopefully, this orientation will be maintained when establishing new high schools and will lead to the introduction of Romology as a full and compulsory subject in basic schools in Slovakia. These developments should become one of the priorities for the Roma people as well as for the Slovak government which should ensure that the tendencies towards segregation are not restored or even fostered.

Insufficient Knowledge of Roma People – Target Group: "Majority"

The second problem is the insufficient knowledge of the Slovak "majority" population about Roma people, their history, culture, value orientation and social (non-) status. Information about Roma activists and famous people are not part of mainstream education or societal culture in Slovakia. Only a little knowledge exists about the fact that Roma people actually live in Slovakia and that there is Roma ethnicity and culture. That is more than before 1989, when civic society could not speak about Roma ethnicity, even though everybody was able to recognize and to distinguish between Roma and non-Roma people. This might be a challenge for Roma activists nowadays. It seems necessary to organize projects to strengthen civic and national awareness about Roma language, history, and culture.

[27] RAXEN-Report, EUMC, 2004, fn. 11, p. 13.

[28] RAXEN-Report, EUMC, 2004, fn. 11, Annex 4, Graph 5, p. 32.

[29] Second periodic report of Slovakia to the Committee on the Rights of the Child, adopted on 4 August 2006, doc.-no.: CRC/C/SVK/2, dated 21 September 2006, para. 93; RAXEN-Report, EUMC, 2004, fn. 11, p. 13.

Strengthening Self Responsibility for the Quality of Life – Target Group: "Roma"

The main structural problem of many Roma children not attending school at all or dropping-out early needs to be solved.[30] There are at least two reasons for Roma children not being successful in school which require the attention of the Roma themselves if change is to be achieved. First, Roma children are often unmotivated to become educated. Second, there is usually a lack of interest in the children's education, verging on discouragement on the part of their parents.[31] Although education is deep-rooted within the Roma family structure, participation in a formal public education system is not included. School as an institution with timetables, immobility and authority by one person is contrary to Roma societal processes. It seems as if parents fear that their children might lose their Roma identity by visiting such a strict formalized institution like school. Besides that, school has also been used to assimilate the Roma. Therefore, public education evokes a fear of getting colonialized on the one hand[32] and on the other it is recognized as a possibility for emancipation and empowerment.[33]

The Roma people are neither satisfied nor happy in their separated Roma settlements. That is why they need to learn how to use some structures of existing societies without losing their own culture and values to gain more quality of life. The only chance of reducing the drop-out rates of pupils with Roma origin, especially girls[34], is with the cooperation of Roma parents, associations and local communities.[35]

Teaching Methods

Teaching methods mainly reflect the values and expectations of the non-Roma population in Slovakia and that is why teachers usually fail to provide sufficient room for the development of the talents and capabilities of the Roma children.[36] Many things which ought to be learned or taught in school can be explained by using examples from everyday life. The school environments include some parts of children's family

[30] Concluding observations of the Committee on Economic, Social and Cultural Rights: Slovakia, adopted at the 29 session (11 – 29 November 2002), doc.-no.: E/C.12/1/Add.81, dated 19 December 2002, para. 18, 33.

[31] Report on observation of human rights in the Slovak Republic for the year 2004, fn. 22, p. 74; Human Development Report on Roma in Slovakia, 2002, fn. 2, p. 53; Ringold/ Orenstein/ Wilkens, Roma in an expanding Europe, 2005, fn. 2, p. 81f.

[32] Report and recommendations on the situation of Roma and Sinti in the OSCE area, OSCE High Commissioner on National Minorities, dated 10 March 2000, http://www.osce.org/documents/ hcnm/2000/03/241_en.pdf p. 68-70.

[33] Eva Sobotka, "Slovakia", in: Denied a future?, Vol. 2; London: Save the Children, 2001, p. 170-204, at 176.

[34] Roma girls often leave school after five or six years because they ought to become married, work at home or the parents fear any relationship involvement with a non-Roma boy. See the report and recommendations on the situation of Roma and Sinti in the OSCE area, 2000, fn. 32, p. 70f.

[35] CERD, Gen. Rec. No. 27, 2000, fn. 9, para. 17.

[36] RAXEN-Report, EUMC, 2004, fn. 11, p. 22.

ambit. Teachers consider family roots as a regular object, method and input of education. A big problem of this method is the use of stereotypes. The stereotype of a family in the classrooms of Slovak schools is typically not Roma. Similarly, Roma lifestyle or housing conditions would not be the examples that the teacher would refer to. The Roma family and language environments do not officially exist in educational processes. This is one of the main problems which could be easily solved. Selected experimental schools might try to include Roma structures into their lessons but they are exceptions, but fortunately, the number of these establishments may increase and this must be encouraged.

If teachers find out that their Roma pupils have difficulties following their lessons (maybe because they have difficulty understanding the Slovak language) it is up to the teacher to find an alternative or innovative way to teach the content of their lessons. Slovak teachers need to be given methodological guidelines which would encourage them to use all possible methods including the usage of Romani if necessary to solve problems.[37]

Further human rights education in schools should be evaluated with a focus on issues relating to racism and discrimination to ensure the application of effective teaching methods. This could guarantee that every school provides satisfactory teaching standards in this field. Furthermore, a review of all school books and other materials is necessary. Besides that, they need to be "in conformity with current best practice as regards the avoidance of stereotypes and prejudices,"[38] and they should include chapters about Roma history and culture.[39]

Structure

Roma children often perceive school as a complicated, unknown, and formal environment which does not take into account the multicultural attributes of Slovak society. Moreover, Slovak schools show resentment towards the Roma people.[40] Two further structural problems should be mentioned which result in the previously mentioned lack of motivation to go to school: Firstly, it is very important for Roma children to have persons in school they can identify with. Because there are usually no role models who could exemplify the value and the importance of education to Roma children through their own life, school personnel should be recruited from amongst members of Roma communities.[41] Secondly, the daily commuting distance between school and the pupils' homes is often several kilometres, so to counter this, a free school bus system would be very helpful.[42]

Teaching and education professionals usually do not have a Roma background. There are very few programmes encouraging Roma people to become teachers. If

---

[37] RAXEN-Report, EUMC, 2004, fn. 11, p. 22.

[38] Third report on Slovakia, adopted on 27 June 2003 by ECRI, doc.-no.: CRI (2004) 4, published on 27 January 2004, p. 13f., para. 42f.

[39] CERD, Gen. Rec. No. 27, 2000, fn. 9, para. 26.

[40] RAXEN-Report, EUMC, 2004, fn. 11, p. 22.

[41] CERD, Slovakia, CERD/C/65/CO/7, 2004, fn. 9, para. 18.

[42] RAXEN-Report, EUMC, 2004, fn. 11, p. 22.

they want to become a teacher of Romology however, there seems to be a chance of getting employment.[43] There are several skilled and educated Roma people who could be working especially with Roma pupils or teaching modules regarding Roma culture. Institutions are not willing to use that potential; rather they prefer to send non-Roma people to teach about Roma culture and history. This is a serious problem as it implies that a dramatically low number of teachers are skilled enough to teach Romology, or Roma language, culture and history. There are multicultural education programmes for teachers and assistants as a part of non-discriminative education, but these are not compulsory for pedagogical workers. The programmes are free or paid for from project funds. The participation of teachers is not promoted in general; their participation in these activities is rather dependent on their schools' decision. If teachers are not of Roma origin, they should be sufficiently prepared to cope with teaching in a multicultural class. This is unfortunately quite often not the case although most classes are composed of students with different cultural backgrounds.[44]

The children should also be sufficiently prepared to comprehend the teacher's instructions in the official language. This is a big structural problem since it seems as if some children (especially from isolated and segregated settlements) may be introduced to the Slovak language only on entering primary school.[45] This problem has been recognized and attempted to be solved by legislative measures which provide the establishment of preparatory classes to help children meet the standard school criteria. But this legislation is not obligatory so every school has to decide for itself if such classes are necessary and helpful. Many schools do not operate such classes and do not intend to start them in the future. If preparatory classes do exist then they usually belong to 'special schools', and attendance of these classes at 'special schools' frequently makes the Roma children continue their 'school career' there.[46]

Human Rights Education and the Roma

The Slovak Republic is party to international and European human rights treaties prohibiting racial discrimination and segregation and guarantees equal access to education for everyone. The Slovak constitution incorporates such treaty obligations and provides that they have precedence over contradicting domestic law. Furthermore, Article 33 and 34 of the Slovak constitution guarantees the rights of national minorities and ethnic groups among other things to develop their own culture and to receive education in their own language.[47] In order to comply with human rights treaty obli-

---

[43] In 2005 25 teachers with Roma background have been accredited by the Minister of Education to teach the Roma language and literature. They work in two schools in Košice, in one school in Zvolen and at the Gymnázium Juraja Hronca in Bratislava and should also educate teachers' assistants. See ENAR Shadow Report 2005, Racism in the Slovak Republic by Daniel Milo (People Against Racism), http://www.enar-eu.org/en/national/slovakia/
Slovakia_2005.pdf p. 15.

[44] Sobotka, "Slovakia", 2001, fn. 33, p. 170-204, at 174.

[45] Ringold / Orenstein / Wilkens, Roma in an expanding Europe, 2005, fn. 2, p. 80f.

[46] ERRC Report, Segregated Schooling of Roma, 2005, fn. 2, p. 39f.

[47] See for a detailed summary of anti-discrimination law in the Slovak Republic: Report on observation of human rights in the Slovak Republic for the year 2004, fn. 22, p. 59-74.

gations such as to "secure to everyone within their jurisdiction the rights and freedoms defined"[48], human rights education has been an effective tool to ensure that there will be a broad understanding of the state obligations, especially towards the people, and of the individual rights belonging to every human being.[49]

Human rights education describes lifelong learning about, for and by human rights and education for equality of human dignity. In general, it is directed at every age group by using formal, non-formal and informal educational activities. Moreover, various disciplines are touched on and many actors are involved which have to cooperate.[50] Human rights education aims at establishing a human rights culture by strengthening the respect for human rights for all and thus the promotion of a better life.[51]

In the Slovak context, formal human rights education means the possibility to educate children (including Roma children) in equal conditions, in a friendly space and respectful atmosphere, with the best that the school can offer.[52] Furthermore, this idea is connected with the hope that children will become adults by developing their own personality and the ability to recognize right and wrong in life. Human rights mean responsibility and possibility, limits and freedom, acceptance, tolerance and respect. All members of a society can, and have to learn that. Education needs to become inclusive whilst at the same time respecting diversity and cultural sensitivity, and ensuring everyone has access to it.[53]

In that sense, human rights education might be one way to eliminate discrimination of the Roma by deconstructing existing biases and racism.[54] This might become true if this deconstruction reveals the relationship of racism and intolerance to

---

[48] Art. 1 of the Convention for the Protection of Human Rights and Fundamental Freedoms of the Council of Europe; ETS No. 5; http://conventions.coe.int/Treaty/en/Treaties/Html/005.htm.

[49] Ligia Neacsu-Hendry / Ivan Turek / Jana Kviečinska / Kozara Kati / Theodore S. Orlin, "Implementing Human Rights Education in Three Transitional Democracies: Romania, Slovakia and Albania", in: George J. Andreopoulos / Richard Pierre Claude (ed.), Human Rights Education for the Twenty-First Century; Philadelphia: University of Pennsylvania Press, 1997, p. 484-516, at 485.

[50] Vedrana Spajic-Vrkaš, "Defining Human Rights Education", in: Adrienne Englert (ed.), Forum on Human Rights Education, Documentation, European Youth Centre Budapest, 7.-12. November 2000; Budapest: EYCB, Directorate of Youth and Sport, Council of Europe, 2001, p. 25-33, at 25.

[51] Janzsz Symonides, "The State Duty to promote Human Rights Education", in: Sia Anasthasia Spiliopoulou Åkermark (ed.), Human Rights Education, Achievements And Challenges; Åbo: Institute for human rights / The Finnish National Commission For UNESCO and UNESCO Turku, 1998, p. 11-30, at 11.

[52] Anette Faye Jacobsen, "Human rights education", in: Gudmundur Alfredsson / Jonas Grimheden / Bertram G. Ramcharan / Alfred de Zayas (ed.), International human rights monitoring mechanisms: essays in honour of Jakob Th. Möller; Den Haag et al.: Nijhoff, 2001, p. 285-292, at 286.

[53] Report on the right to education, submitted by the Special Rapporteur on the right to education, Vernor Muñoz Villalobos, doc.-no.: E/CN.4/2005/50, published on 17 December 2004, para. 99.

[54] Please see the contribution of Claudia Mahler to human rights education and national minorities in this book. Further Claudia Mahler/ Anja Mihr/ Reetta Toivanen, Do we need explicit Human Rights Education?, Comparing Human Rights Education with Civic, Intercultural, Diversity and Tolerance Education/ Summary of a Workshop with Prof. Katarina Tomasevski, held at the German Institute for Human Rights, January 12th 2005; http://www.uni-potsdam.de/humanrightsresearch/material/HREducation.pdf p. 1f., at 2.

the situation of minority groups living in Slovakia.[55] Human rights education is directed at everybody. The "majority" population as well as the "minority" population of Slovakia needs to be taught human rights. On the one hand, the "majority" population has to recognize that the Roma are part of Slovak society, have an interesting cultural background, and are a people that can also be learned from. This might lead to more friendly behaviour towards the Roma in general and it might decrease the rate of discriminatory crimes. On the other hand, human rights education will empower the Roma by informing them of their rights and how to defend them.

The cooperation between Roma and non-Roma persons can be an important element of (human rights) education projects. As some projects have shown, the best way to fight racism is to work together. In many cases, the Roma are seen as the target group only and that they have to be "educated" by non-Roma project teams and specialists (for all things). This is the usual situation which is not natural and it must not be tolerated. Some barriers between Roma and non-Roma people and organisations could be removed simply by a new arrangement of competences and by using abilities in a different way.

Even though human rights education should be provided in all schools at all levels,[56] today there is almost no human rights education in Slovakia. This is due to the insufficient knowledge of the existence of human rights education or even how to apply it as a method. "The material and the methods of teaching should focus on two important components: human rights education, and education reflecting the principles of multiculturalism."[57]

A National Plan for Human Rights Education (approved by the 2nd operational meeting of the Ministry of Education of 8 February 2005) for the time period of 2005-2014 has been drafted by the National Institute for Education (NIE) and the Ministry of Education of the Slovak Republic in cooperation with other directly governed organisations in the ministerial department of education and some NGO's. The national plan pays particular attention to the education of and about national minorities, namely to the Roma minority. It proposes the reform of the school system so that schools will become racism and discrimination free and that human rights education for children will be intensified. Furthermore, the plan contains teaching methods for primary schools. There is assistance also by the Effective Monitoring and Evaluation System of the Scope and Quality of Education in Human Rights which provides techniques and methodological tools for the educational process.[58]

Developments in Slovak Schools so far - Roma Teachers' Assistants

The horribly low educational attainment level of the Roma population results in an inability to participate actively in society or societal problem solving relating to the Roma communities' needs and potential. As a result, in 1996 Jana Luptáková, as the chairperson of the Roma women's club in Detva (Roma NGO), started to organise

[55] Third report on Slovakia, ECRI, CRI (2004) 4, 2003, fn. 38, p. 13, para. 42.
[56] CESCR, Slovakia, E/C.12/1/Add.81, 2002, fn. 30, para. 34.
[57] Report of Slovakia to CRC, CRC/C/SVK/2, 2006, fn. 29, para. 298.
[58] See ENAR Shadow Report 2005, fn. 43, p. 14.

some voluntary projects to promote the active participation of Roma people, mainly women, on improving the educational results of their children. At the beginning, only the organisation of clubs for the Roma children with (one of) their parents, mainly their mothers, needed to be arranged. Such a small local effort led to the assistance of children by adults with a Roma background at schools and at the free-time activity centre in the small town of Detva.

The principals of the local schools considered the initiative to be a helpful step in supporting the effective use of leisure, better school preparation and parents-school communication. This resulted in the cooperation between the Wide Open School Foundation and the Young Roma Association in Banská Bystrica. The outcome of this collaboration is the national project on Roma teachers' assistants. After 150 training sessions 237 people, almost all of whom were Roma parents, were employed in 27 regions in Slovakia from 2000 to 2003. The job of Roma assistants involves cooperation "with the teacher directly in the classroom and spending time with children during extra-curricular activities." Besides that, they are supposed to work with the family, mainly through visits.[59]

After continuing with the project, in 2004 the Slovak Ministry of Education accepted the model of assistance and even allocated the financial and administrative frame for it. Unfortunately, the authorities did not approve the term "Roma teacher's assistant" as a pedagogical profession and they preferred to omit the term "Roma" and to refer to "teacher's assistant". The initial project launched by Roma people now carries the simple name "teachers' assistants" and two-thirds of these assistants are of non-Roma origin. Why is it so important to create the position of a "teacher's assistant" which infers that it is neither filled by a Roma person nor that it is (also) specifically for Roma-children? Who benefits from it – Roma children or their parents? Or is it much more important to stop active participation of Roma people in the application of human rights in education?

Short-term Measures

Various short-term measures have made it possible for (Roma) teachers' assistants who have not yet graduated from university to work at elementary 'special schools', community centres, advisory centres or kindergartens until 2010. In some regions of Slovakia there are some short-term projects to employ doctors' assistants by Krajská asociácia rómskych iniciatív (KARI) and social and police assistants by the Ministry of Social and Internal Affairs. They actually have the power to change the attitude towards education and employment of Roma people, but even in these positions Roma people are substituted by non-Roma people. The importance of the original idea that Roma people in employment support other Roma people seems to have been forgotten even though it is evident that only such a practice might solve the problems both in education and employment.[60]

---

[59] RAXEN-Report, EUMC, 2004, fn. 11, p. 16.
[60] CERD, Gen. Rec. No. 27, 2000, fn. 9, paragraph. 23f.

In public, these short-term measures are only considered as supportive programmes.[61] Systematic steps to increase the Roma (non-)status are not present in Slovak civic society. Depending on the project, the salaries paid to those assistants barely reach the level of a minimal monthly salary.

J.J. Thurza in Detva

The basic school of J.J. Thurza in Detva (Slovakia) was established in 1979. It is a primary school from first to ninth grade, which means that the pupils are between 6 and 16 years old of which 8 % of students are of Roma origin. In the school year 2006/07 the school had 474 students, 33 teachers and 3 Roma assistants. Due to the amount of Roma children, the role of the Roma assistants is very important. In Slovakia the function of the Roma assistant has existed for many years.[62] The J.J. Thurza School in Detva has a lot of experience in working with the Roma assistants. The director of the school confirmed that there were 3 Roma teachers' assistants, one Roma working in the cafeteria of the school, two Roma helping in technical matters, and a Roma person working as a language teacher.

Furthermore, since the conditions required for children's activities and adults with a Roma background have been established, the school has opened up to the public. As a result, it has become noticeable that an atmosphere of acceptance between Roma and non-Roma people is possible, useful and good.

Indeed, the director has done a lot for the school and the Roma community through his decisions. But these experiences should be disseminated which would enable other Slovak schools to learn from them and even model themselves on the J.J. Thurza School. Besides this, it might be a good idea for the Slovak government to publish reports that give enough information on efforts made and steps taken to see these facts as a firm result. This example shows pretty clearly that the realization of human rights education measures depend mainly on individual schools and principals.

Secondary Education

Specific secondary education for Roma people in Slovakia means the possibility to study at the Gandhi School in Zvolen, at the Private Upper high school or the Art High School in Košice. But studying at these schools does not qualify a student to fulfil any profession according to the educational system. Most graduates have to continue in the education system and to study at a university to gain at least a bachelors degree. If they do as such, they can become specialists according to their specific area. They usually continue at the University in Prešov, Spišská nová Ves or Nitra, in the department of social work or the department of Roma culture.

---

[61] Conception of Roma Children and Young People, Slovak Ministry of Education, 2004, fn. 2, p. 16.

[62] Please see for further information under D.I.

Gandhi School in Zvolen

The Gandhi School, an 8-year boarding upper high school in Zvolen, is one example of programmes which encourage Roma children to study at a secondary school. The children at this school get food and boarding free of charge and they pay only part of their travel costs. They can stay as residents during the weekends, because it is a school with students from all over Slovakia. The pupils of this school are mostly from very poor Roma families. Some of them are non-Roma children of the same societal status. They are really disadvantaged children whose only chance to be educated at a high school exists at this establishment.

Private Upper High School in Košice

The Private Upper high school in Košice, which was established in 2003[63], offers its pupils an education in Romani.[64] As with the Gandhi School, it is also an 8-year boarding school with no fee for the dormitories and it does not cost anything to attend classes.[65]

Secondary Art High School in Košice

Since its establishment in 1992, the Secondary Art High School in Košice has focussed on the education of music, drama, dance, and acting of both Roma and non-Roma students. Besides state subsidies, the school secures its own financial resources from various foundations. According to the school's proclamation, it aims at the promotion of tolerance and equality. But it should be noted that most of the children enrolled in the school have a Roma background. Therefore, it remains largely a Roma school.[66] Although the school is directed at developing and teaching "Roma culture", the teaching language is usually Slovak and only some classes are held in Romani. The school provides an education lasting six years, and afterwards the graduates might find work in the Philharmonic Orchestra or at the Romani theatre "Romathan". Other possibilities include entering the teaching profession or studying at a university.[67]

---

[63] Milena Hübschmannová/ Jirí V. Neustupný, "'Terminological' Processes in North-Central Romani", in: Current issues in language planning 2004 (vol. 5) no. 2, p. 83-108, at 88.

[64] Roma Education Fund (ed.), Advancing Education of Roma in Slovakia, Country Assessment and the Roma Education Fund's Strategic Directions, 2007, p. 26.

[65] Kristína Magdolenová, "Jinxed, cursed or merely something else?", in: Roma press agency of 23 January 2007, http://www.rpa.sk/rpa.php?show=5617&target=print (visited in January 2008).

[66] In the school year 1998/99 the school had 109 students – all with a Roma background. In 2000 this number increased to 200 students of whom 95 per cent were Roma children.

[67] Sobotka, "Slovakia", 2001, fn. 33, p. 170-204, at 186.

Experimental Curriculum of Roma Language and History

The project "Curriculum of Roma language and history" was submitted to the Ministry of Education of Slovakia by the State Pedagogical Institute as a national project with financing from the European Social Fund of the Ministry of Labour, Social Affairs and Family of Slovakia. The Ministry of Labour, Social Affairs and Family is a direct body for the sectoral programme of human resources and the State Pedagogical Institute in Bratislava which is the final beneficiary of the national project's support. The project aims at offering help in the area of raising the Roma people's educational attainment level and increasing the chances of employment, improving the civic awareness of Roma people, and preparing conditions for specific social and pedagogical occupations, mainly for Roma people like: teachers' assistants, social workers, community organisers, state or public officials and NGO workers. Furthermore, it is supposed to implement knowledge about Roma culture, history and lifestyle as a part of multicultural and multiethnic education, realize the constitutional human rights of minorities such as education in their mother tongue and the elimination of the ethnic and social strain between the Roma minority and the rest of Slovak society. The following schools are involved in the project: Private Upper high school and the Art High School in Košice, the Gandhi School, Social Sciences Faculty and Roma Culture Department of the University of Nitra, and the University of Prešov.

Study Subject 'Romology' in the Curriculum of High Schools and Universities

The project of the State Pedagogical Institute – Study subject Romology in the curriculum of high schools and universities – can be considered a reasonable way to approach a positive change and progress in Roma human rights education. It is important to increase Roma peoples civic awareness, to strengthen personal responsibility for quality of life, to convey labour market principles and possibilities for non-educated and educated people, and to foster human rights education. Roma assistants, lecturers and teachers should become an equal part of one expert team. This initiative for Roma people has been launched because of the existence of an extremely low educational level, extremely high unemployment rate and the lack of adequate surroundings in education for Roma.

Perspectives

For Slovakia's non-Roma population, the only "positive" association in connection with the Roma is that of dancers, singers, musicians, and 'children of the wind'. This illustrates the usual problem of categorising and stereotyped thinking. But of course the Roma are individuals with different personalities, professional ambitions, needs, and societal opportunities, and as such, differ from each other.

Every Slovak school needs to approve, as a core objective, the elimination of the problems of Roma children in school but without the pressure of assimilation. The difficulty appears to be how to approach equal education and opportunities in the lives of the Roma minority without the loss of its specific cultural characteristics? It is the question of integration without assimilation, especially since stressing the latter has only resulted in increasing segregation.[68]

The first aim should be to improve and observe school access and the success of Roma children in general. Effective communication in the form of meetings between teachers and Roma children, moderated by skilled professionals can help to see and overcome barriers more effectively. These communication meetings should be monitored and evaluated by Roma and non-Roma people (parents, teachers, assistants, observers, advisors). This can help to establish suitable training programmes for all of the mentioned target groups. Furthermore, there needs to be a stimulation of local Roma individuals and communities to take initiatives and accept the responsibility for attaining better education for themselves and their children. Individual or group advice given to Roma by skilled Roma multipliers can be very effective to promote common activities and community development. They can learn to solve common problems and to share common help. All of this might lead to active participation of Roma people in society and also more active participation of Roma women.

Equal opportunities for all social groups – between women and men, Roma and non-Roma, the young and the old for example – should be an aspect of developing strategies to raise the Roma voice. Monitoring and evaluation of each step along the way will be supportive to the whole process of developing visions, adapting the strategies and identifying activities in which everyone has her or his role. The outcome will hopefully be the stimulation and contribution of Roma initiative, self-organisation, leadership, lobby and advocacy power and the establishment of networks and strategic alliances. Progressively this should lead to a framework of human rights education.

[68] The Human Development Report on Roma in Slovakia, 2002, fn. 2 provides more details on this topic on p. 61.

Is Human Rights Education a Means of Supporting Minorities?

Claudia Mahler

Introduction

This contribution attempts to work out if human rights education was a means of supporting national minorities during the Decade of Human Rights Education (1995-2004) and if human rights education can be seen as a tool to promote national minorities in general. For this effort the paper first tries to answer the question 'are minority rights human rights?' The second part follows the arguments which were found in recommendations by international monitoring bodies supporting human rights education and national minorities. The subsequent chapter will investigate where minority education can be found and what practical problems occur. Following that, it will be shown what content human rights education should have and why our chosen states should implement human rights education. The final section will discuss if there appears to be synergy between human rights education and the support of national minorities and consider why human rights education is not seen as a tool. I was able to include only a few examples from our survey and I am aware that there are many more valuable issues to be discussed.

Are Minority Rights a Part of Human Rights?

One starting point of our project was the research on the international legal framework which regulates the protection of national minorities and human rights education and their effects at the national level. We started to investigate which relevant United Nations treaties the chosen nation states have ratified and we came to the conclusion that all of our six states have more or less ratified the same international treaties, which was seen as a good basis for comparison. But as we have found out, the incorporation of these treaties is at very different levels. The same picture was drawn on the European regional level in the Council of Europe's Framework, the Organisation for Security and Co-operation in Europe (OSCE) and the European Union (EU), as a new component on the regional level. These findings were a good starting point to ascertain what kind of minority protection can be found at the compulsory and the soft law level.

When considering minority rights in public international law, we have to bear in mind that states created the law and these creators are the main subjects of public international law. The duty to protect and ensure the rights of groups and individuals were not the focus of creating international law. These target groups came to the centre of attention during the League of Nations era. This was at the time when the protection of minorities started at the multilateral/ universal level. But at the time of the League of Nations no framework for the protection of human rights was built to protect the rights of minorities. The bilateral/multilateral agreements had a political dimension to ensure the newly achieved freedoms between the nation states.[1]

After World War II the focus of the world community shifted to the protection of human rights to ensure friendly relations between the states. Minority rights were no major subject by establishing the United Nations (UN). The major task at the beginning of the UN was to create a human rights framework which had no special focus on minority rights.[2]

When we address minorities as a subject of rights we have to be aware that several different minority groups exist which belong to the so called vulnerable groups in the framework of guaranteed human rights. This article will only deal with national minorities as they were the target groups of our project and we had to make a decision to have a smaller focus in our research, even though migrants, the so called "New Minorities," would also be a very interesting target group beside others.[3]

The term 'national minority' is very often used in dialogues on human rights and discussions on the protection of human rights and minority rights. However, there exists no real definition on the term national minority in the framework of international law.[4] Many different approaches on how to characterize minorities can be discovered. The most popular description was penned in 1979 by Francesco Capotorti[5] which states:

"a group numerically inferior to the rest of the population of a state, in a non-dominant position, whose members -- being nationals of the state -- possess ethnic, religious, or linguistic characteristics different from those of the rest of the population and show, if only implicitly, a sense of solidarity, directed towards preventing their culture traditions, religion, or language."

Many similar descriptions can be found in the working definitions of several monitoring bodies of the UN or regional systems but many conventions e.g. the Framework Convention on National Minorities have no definition included due to the fact that the member States of the Council of Europe did not agree with the definition of the notion of national minorities.

Minority rights are special norms which protect national minorities in states. In the discourse, minority rights can be described as additional rights for certain groups. Some positions state that positive discrimination of minorities would put some groups in a more advanced societal position and cause the discrimination of members of the majority population which copes without any special support. These 'special' rights are not privileges but rather, seek to grant a person belonging to minority groups in diverse living situations the chance to reach the same living conditions as the major-

[1] Further details can be read in the contribution by Ted Orlin. Hilpold, Peter, UN Standard-Setting in the Field of Minority Rights, in: International Journal on Minority and Group Rights 14 , 2007, pp. 181-205.

[2] Klein, Eckart, Minderheitenschutz im Völkerrecht, in: Baadte/Rauscher (ed.), Minderheiten, Migration und Menschenrechte, Graz 1995, pp. 127-153, p .130f.

[3] Hilpold, Peter, Neue Minderheiten im Völkerrecht und im Europarecht, in: Archiv des Völkerrechts, 2004, pp. 80-110.

[4] See e.g., Capotorti, Francesco/Hofmann, Rainer, "Minorities", in: Bernhardt (ed.), Encyclopedia of Public International Law, Vol. 3, Amsterdam, Elsevier, 1997, pp. 410-420, at pp. 410-411.

[5] Capotorti, Francesco, Study on the Rights of Persons Belonging to Ethnic, Religious, and Linguistic Minorities, by Francesco Capotorti, Special Rapporteur of the Sub-commission on Prevention and Protection of Minorities, UN Doc. E/CN.4/Sub.2/283/Rev. 1, United Nations, New York 1979.

ity population.[6] This added protection through minority rights is necessary because the aim is to guarantee the minorities and majorities the same enjoyment of their human rights.

Two types of provision exist concerning the protection of minority rights: a special right of members of minority groups and the rights to non-discrimination. The protection of minority rights is incorporated in many international treaties. In principle it could be stated that the treaties deal with different areas of life, where members of minorities could be denied equal treatment, for example in the labour market, housing and education. Minorities have to find their place in society where they can function with their own culture without the fear of assimilation into the majority. To ensure this statement the international framework has developed several protection clauses for national minorities.

At the universal level the central specific clause is article 27 of the United Nations International Covenant of Civil and Political Rights (ICCPR).[7] Article 27 is broad in its scope and demands:

"In those States in which ethnic, religious or linguistic minorities exist, persons belonging to such minorities shall not be denied the right, in community with the other members of their group, to enjoy their own culture, to profess and practice their own religion, or to use their own language."

Another wide resolution for the protection and promotion for minority rights was declared in December 1992 and adopted by the UN-General Assembly. This resolution also sets international standards for the rights of national, ethnic, religious and linguistic minorities.[8]

At the European regional level there also exist specific treaties for the protection of minorities. The state parties to the Council of Europe's Convention on Human Rights and Fundamental Freedom never agreed on an additional protocol on minority rights. Instead of promoting a protocol to the convention, the Council of Europe developed the Charter on Regional and Minority Languages in 1992[9] and the Framework Convention on National Minorities in 1995.[10] The treaties of the Council of Europe set the standards which the member states have a duty to ensure and fulfil.[11]

Even though the European Union (EU) never focused on minority rights, the EU required the implementation of minority rights standards which were included in

---

[6] Strauß, Ekkehard., Protection of Minorities, in Volger (ed.) A Concise Encyclopedia of the United Nations, The Hague 2002, pp. 373-378, (at p. 375), the same view is expressed by Scheinin, Martin, Minority rights or added protection, in: Bergsmo (ed.), Human Rights and Criminal Justice for the downtrodden, Leiden/Boston 2003, p. 486-504, p. 487.

[7] International Covenant of Civil and Political Rights, GA. Res. 2200 A (XXI), of 16 December 1966, UN Doc. A/6316 (1967).

[8] Declaration on the Rights of Persons Belonging to National or Ethnic, Religious and Linguistic Minorities, GA. Res. 47/135 of 18 December 1992.

[9] European Charter for Regional and Minority Languages, ETS N. 148, of 5 November 1992, entry into force 1 March 1998.

[10] European Framework Convention for the Protection of National Minorities, ETS No. 157, of 1 February 1995 entry into force 1 February 1998.

[11] Weiß, Norman, Sind Minderheitenrechte Menschenrechte, in: Mahler/Weiß (ed.), Menschenrechtsschutz im Spiegel von Wissenschaft und Praxis, Berlin 2004, p. 292-320,

the political chapter of the Copenhagen Criteria for the new member states.[12] The new European Union member states had to ratify human rights and minority rights treaties to successfully accede.[13] In order to satisfy its international legal obligations to the above mentioned treaties, the protection of national minorities is not the state party's only duty as they have to also guarantee active support for the members of the national minorities.

International Pressure

International pressure from the international human rights regime and its International Governmental Organisations (IGO) such as the United Nations, the Council of Europe and the European Union together with the advocacy work of NGOs is a tool to request the implementation of minority rights and human rights education throughout Europe. International legal frameworks, treaties and recommendations from monitoring bodies with pressure from interest groups led to a higher sensitivity among decision makers to change and implement legal measures and human rights standards and to think of new ways of fulfilling their duties.[14] Although the pressure and methods of international organisations should not be overestimated, they play a crucial role in raising awareness among political decision makers.

As written in 1995, our research countries had ratified all significant international human rights treaties at the universal and regional level. These treaties are relevant in terms of the protection of minorities, the enhancing of human rights and by advising the countries how to realize human rights education. Throughout the UN Decade some of the UN treaty bodies and advisory bodies at the European level linked a number of recommendations and conclusions to aspects of human rights education and minority protection. For some countries these recommendations were to some extent a probable reason why the state authorities considered conducting human rights education programmes. Also, the attention of some NGOs was drawn to the field of human rights education and national minorities by the recommendations of the monitoring bodies.

Treaty Bodies Recommendations

In 1996 the Human Rights Committee[15] asked Germany to intensify education and training in the wider context of human rights education rather than programmes fo-

[12] Recently the protection of minorities was manifested in the Treaty of Lisbon amending the Treaty on European Union and the Treaty establishing the European Community, signed at Lisbon, 13 December 2007, 2007/C 306/01.

[13] Mahler, Claudia/Toivanen, Reetta, Nationale und ethnische Minderheiten im Prozess der Erweiterung der Europäischen Union, Europa Ethnica 1/2, 2004, pp. 16-20.

[14] Klein, Eckart, Menschenrechtsbildung aus Sicht des UN-Menschenrechtsausschusses, in: Mahler/Mihr, Menschenrechtsbildung, Wiesbaden 2004, p. 83-92.

[15] Human Rights Committee is the expert body of the UN Covenant on Civil and Political Rights, General Assembly resolution, 2200A(XXI) of 16 December 1966, entry into force 23 March 1976.

cusing on racism, anti Semitism and xenophobia for young people and police officer training. To achieve a broader approach the Committee insisted that the Federal and "Länder" governments introduce courses in human rights at school, colleges and universities and in police and defence academies with a view to strengthening the culture of human rights.[16]

After considering the situation of the Roma in Finland, the Human Rights Committee insisted on tolerance training for public authorities to overcome racist attitudes and to combat the actual discrimination against members of the Roma minority. These attitudes are evident in the area of housing, employment and services.[17]

In 1996, members of the CERD Committee[18] demanded that the Spanish government take effective educational measures against racism and xenophobia which greatly affected the Gitano community. In particular, the action was to tackle housing issues, access to education, childcare and the efforts being undertaken to lower the unemployment rate of Gitanos. The high dropout rate and high level of absence of Gitano children in primary schools was also a matter which was highlighted by the Committee.[19]

Regarding Finland particularly, and other countries in general, another issue which CERD mentioned was that media often presented immigrants and minorities, in particular the Roma, in a negative light. The Committee requested Finland's authorities to strengthen measures to promote tolerance and combat prejudices in the field of teaching, education, culture and information. To further this goal, Finland should introduce adequate protocols to make journalists and people working in the media sector more aware of racial discrimination.[20]

Other UN treaty bodies like the Committee of the Convention on the Elimination of All Forms of Discrimination against Women (CEDAW), the Committee of the Covenant on Economic Social and Cultural Rights (ICESCR) and the Committee of the Convention on the Rights of the Child (CRC) were also very active in raising Human Rights Education issues and the protection of national minorities. Some similarities in the recommendations of the UN treaty bodies have been noticed after looking at the conclusions of the countries under focus. All expert bodies promoted human rights education with the suggestion to implement human rights education programmes in the formal and non-formal education sector. All bodies requested that the states should train special groups and adopt positive actions to combat discrimination. The members of the monitoring bodies set different priorities but regardless of their specialisations some groups like youth, prison guards, law enforcement officers, journalists or civil servants appeared in many recommendations. By comparing the concluding observations it was evident that the weak minority groups such as the Gitanos, Sinti and Roma are very often discriminated against and therefore were in the

[16] CCPR Concluding Observations/Comments (CCPR/C/79/Add.73) 18 November 1996.
[17] CCPR Concluding Observations CCPR/C/79/Add.91) 8 April 1998.
[18] Committee of the International Convention on the Elimination of All Forms of Racial Discrimination General Assembly resolution 2106(XX) of 21 December 1965, entry into force 4 January 1969.
[19] CERD Suggestions and Recommendations and Concluding Observations (CERD/C/304/Add.95) 19 April 2000.
[20] CERD Concluding Observations/Comments (CERD/C/304/Add.7) 28 March 1996.

focus of recommendations of the treaty bodies. Consequently, the members of committees advise the state parties to fulfil the purpose of the treaties to enhance human rights awareness and to implement human rights standards with human rights education.

Other aspects of our surveys were the suggestion that the committees spread the content of the conventions in minority languages and another frequent remark was the implementation of human rights in general or human rights education in the curricula at the different school levels. Very similar recommendations were given by monitoring bodies at the European level.[21]

Minority Education

The requirements for minority education can be found at the international, regional and national level. For the most practical reasons I will start with the findings at the national level which are sometimes implemented because of the international or regional frameworks which try to incorporate education for minorities as a part of legislation at the national level. Minority education can be implemented because a long tradition exists of the minority present in the country and this is the reason why this area of education can be found in the countries legislation.[22] Many states, amongst others Germany and Finland, grant their national minorities special educational support in subjects like mother tongue teaching or have established nurseries in the minority language. But even if different national minorities exist in each Land (state), in a Federal state like Germany the special rights differ from Land to Land.[23] For example the Sorbs in Brandenburg are protected in the Constitution[24]:

1. *The Sorbian people are entitled to the protection, preservation and perpetuation of their national identity and of the area in which they originally settled. The Land, municipalities and associations of municipalities shall help to give effect to those rights and in particular to secure the cultural autonomy of the Sorbian people and their effective participation and politics.*
2. *The Land shall ensure that the Sorbs are able to achieve cultural autonomy transcending the borders of the Land.*
3. *The Sorbs have a right to the preservation and development of the Sorbian language and culture in public life and to their use in schools and day nurseries.*
4. *In areas where the Sorbs have settled, administrative documents shall also be drafted in Sorbian language. The colours of the Sorbian flag are blue, red and white.*

---

[21] For further details see the contribution of Sia Åkermark in this volume.

[22] See Mahler Claudia/ Weiß Norman, Der Einfluss der internationalen Menschenrechtsverträge auf die deutsche Bildungsrechtsordnung, Recht der Jugend und des Bildungswesens 4/2007, pp. 430-446.

[23] For further details see Weiß, Norman, The Protection of Minorities in a Federal State: The Case of Germany, in: Tarr / Williams / Marko (eds.), Federalism, Subnational Constitutions, and Minority Rights, Westport et al, Praeger 2004, pp. 73-87.

[24] Verfassung des Landes Brandenburg (Constitution of the Land Brandenburg) of 20 August 1992, Gesetz- und Verordnungsblatt für das Land Brandenburg, GVBl., Gazette of Brandenburg), 1992 I, p. 298.

5. *The means by which the Sorbs will be able to exercise their rights shall be laid down by a statute that will guarantee the participation of Sorbian representatives in maters concerning the Sorbs, in particular legislative debate.*[25]

Although the Sorbs have their rights granted at the constitutional level they face practical problems fostering their culture and language. During our research we were told by Sorbian representatives in Saxony that the whole system of bilingual education at the school level is at stake because of the lack of bilingual teachers and the very small number of students with a Sorbian background. To counteract the situation, the schools promoted their bilingual classes to include pupils with a German background.[26] Even though the legal national framework does guarantee national minorities their special education we had learned about very practical problems which portrayed more difficulties than expected.

In Finland for example, the Roma finish school mostly with very low educational achievement which is one major argument as to why they cannot find well paid jobs. The question why this situation has not changed in several years was not answered very easily. Some interviewees told me that they are of the opinion that one reason why this still occurs is that parts of the Roma population need to change their attitude toward education. If the family does not support their children to learn properly, the children have a very small chance of finding their way in school and of attending higher education because they get the idea that education is not as important as it is in the majority society.[27] Another example we came across in our survey was the announcement that the first Roma woman successfully completed her exams in teacher training college in 2004/5 which seemed an unusual acquisition especially in a country like Finland which is famous for its successful educational system.

A very negative example found in many human rights treaty reports is the high percentage of Roma children who go to special schools for very different reasons and it is reported that only a very small percentage are genuinely disabled. These children without any disability would need support in regular schools and should not attend these special schools because then they will have no chance of getting into higher education and of being an active participant in the working world.[28]

Some programmes for Roma assistance were started during the Decade with a special focus on bridging the gap between Roma students, their families and the school. However, the programme changed and the term 'Roma assistant' was changed into 'teacher assistant', a Roma background was deemed no longer a requirement and the special knowledge of the 'teacher assistant' particularly with Roma children was no longer seen as a special need and the attempt to bridge the gap between Roma families and school on how important education is for their children was excluded from the project aims.[29]

---

[25] Translation cited after Klein, Eckart, Traditional and New Minorities in Germany: Different Degrees of Protection, in: Scheinin/ Toivanen (ed.), Rethinking Non-Discrimination and Minority Rights,

[26] Several interviews in Bautzen with members of the Sorbs on the 20 and 21 February 2006.

[27] Interview with Finnish Roma on 19 September 2005.

[28] For further details on Roma in Slovakia see Article of Inken Stern and Jana Luptakova in this volume.

[29] Similar approaches can be found for example in Berlin, Germany.

When talking to people during our survey about what they regard as the key to fostering minority education, teachers were mentioned in the first instance. Teachers are seen as key players to integrate minorities or to provide knowledge on national minorities for the majority population. But I found only one or two examples where teachers could get special knowledge on national minorities or on human rights education. Almost no programme included national minorities which would be of special interest to the teacher even though they dealt with them very often and therefore should know about their background and include them as a target group during their special lessons on human rights education, which are also very rare.

We found special training on human rights education in two teacher training facilities in Finland[30] and as an additional subject in Slovakia at the Comenius University in the Ethics Unit for teacher education.[31] The special need to gain knowledge about national minorities can be found in training sessions for e.g. policemen, some administrative clerks and some brochures were found as an aid for people working in the health service.

Within the Finnish National Board of Education special units for the education of Roma have been established, which mostly deal with Roma language and history. The situation for the old Russians is very different because they are highly integrated or as some have said, 'assimilated' and they have no special section for their educational needs. Because of the high percentage of Russian speaking population there are Russian speaking schools and nurseries which have a bilingual approach.[32] A very high percentage of the Russian speaking population are 'new' Russians, who are migrants and therefore are not a part of the Russian national minority.[33]

Is Human Rights Education an Effective Tool?

Human Rights Education concerns learning and teaching respect about human rights, the knowledge of human rights and learning about the practice of human rights, which should be an accessible part of education for all members of society.[34] These ideas can be read in Article 26 of the Universal Declaration of Human Rights, which states its objective to *"[...] promote understanding, tolerance and friendship among all nations, racial or religious groups, and shall further the activities of the United Nations for the maintenance of peace [...]"* as education for human rights.[35] The con-

---

[30] Interviews with several Finnish experts on human rights and education in August 2004, August and September 2005.

[31] Interviews with students attending a training course on human rights education in Morhany and Prof. Erich Mistrik head of the department of Ethics and Civic education from Comenius University in Bratislava on 29 April 2004.

[32] Interview with experts of the Russian minority and members of the different Russian minorities in September 2005.

[33] Eg. Interview with Mikko Pummalainen on 11 August 2004 and other experts in September 2005.

[34] Marie, J.-B., Human Rights Education, a Fundamental Resource in the Prevention of Violations, in: Sicilianos (ed.), The Prevention of Human Rights Violations, The Hague et. al. 2001, pp. 269-276, p. 269.

[35] Art. 26 of the UDHR adopted and proclaimed by the UN General Assembly resolution 217 A (III) of 10 December 1948. http://www.unhchr.ch/udhr/lang/eng.htm. For background information

tent of Human Rights Education is knowledge transfer, awareness raising, skills-building and to establish a "culture" where human rights are understood, respected, and defended.[36]

Another function of human rights education is to provide information on human rights. People can only stand up for their rights and protect the rights of others if they are sure what human rights are and what the content of the documents is.

The next step is to find out where people can receive human rights education and learn the content. Human rights education can be developed in the formal, informal and non-formal educational sector.[37] And this is why we can find verifying content because of the different needs and context of the groups who are taught human rights education. One very important part is to improve ethnic relations in the states. The understanding of human rights, to live and provide education on human rights is the goal of human rights education, meaning to educate and learn for human rights in practice.

There are several links between the rights of education and human rights education. Without a minimum level of education many human rights can not be exercised. Therefore education is a precondition for the enjoyment of human rights.[38]

The classical formulation of what is meant by human rights education is the content of Article 26 of the UDHR[39], and the UDHR is the starting point for binding international human rights treaties. States parties to these universal instruments have undertaken legal obligations by ratifying international treaties or agreeing international declarations, to make human rights education available to all people living under the state jurisdiction. All member states have the duty to endorse legislation and to take other measures to fulfil its commitments on implementation of human rights education.

The main goal of human rights education is to effectively teach respect for, and knowledge of, human rights. In addition, human rights education strives to promote learning of human rights in practice, which should be an accessible part of the education for all members of society.[40] The idea of Human Rights Education which was a

---

see Richard Pierre Claude, The Right to Education and Human Rights Education, in: No. 2, SUR 2005, pp. 37-59, p.38ff.

[36] Human Security Network, Understanding Human Rights – Manual on Human Rights Education, Graz 2003, at p. 14-16. Shulamith Koenig emphasises especially the goal of evoking critical thinking among people, see ibid at p. 15.

[37] Cf. Mihr, Anja, Human Rights Education: Methods, Institutions, Culture and Evaluation, Discussion papers of the Otto-von-Guericke-Universität Magdeburg, Institut für Politikwissenschaft, Band 4, 2004, at p. 5. http://www.humanrightsresearch.de (visited January 2008) /material/Discussion-Paper-Band_4.pdf download at http://www.anjamihr.com. See also the interesting categorization by Lothar Müller which is based on empirical findings: "explicit HRE", "implicit HRE" and "education with human rights approach" (orig. Menschenrechtliche Erziehung), in: Müller, Lothar Menschenrechtserziehung an Schule und Hochschule, Arbeitsgemeinschaft Menschenrechte Universität Trier Occational Paper Nr. 6, 2002, at p.7-9.

[38] Nowak, Manfred, The Right to Education, in: Eide. et al (eds.), Economic, Social and Cultural Rights, 2nd ed., Dordrecht et al. Kluwer Law International, 2001, pp. 245-271.

[39] Universal Declaration of Human Rights, adopted and proclaimed by General Assembly Resolution 217 A(III) of 10 December 1948, at http://www. Un.org/Overview/rights.html.

[40] Marie, J.-B., Human Rights Education a Fundamental Resource in the prevention of Violations, in: Sicilianos (ed.), The Prevention of Human Rights Violations: Contribution on the Occasion of

milestone in the development of human rights education programmes was renewed in 1993 at the World Conference on Human Rights in Vienna when more than 150 states declared that states should *"[...] include human rights, humanitarian law, democracy and rule of law as subjects in the curricula of all learning institutions in formal and non formal settings."*[41] The Decade had the highly ambitious goal of promoting a human rights culture over ten years which was to be implemented in all societies.

To achieve these highly motivated plans the "International Plan of Action for the Decade" was developed to initiate the assessment of needs and the formulation of effective strategies. Throughout the Decade comprehensive, effective and sustainable educational programmes at the local, national, regional and universal levels were to become active and strengthened.[42] The UN High Commissioner for Human Rights was coordinating relevant UN education and public information programmes in the field of Human Rights and was responsible for the evaluation and supporting activities of the member states.[43] The Office of the High Commissioner for Human Rights published "Guidelines for National Plans of Action for Human Rights Education" and it was, in cooperation with UNESCO, the institution in charge of monitoring and following the progress of the UN Decade on Human Rights Education. In 1998, the UN High Commissioner for Human Rights, Mary Robinson, remarked that HRE was her highest priority. She stated, "This empowerment can also make a critical contribution to the prevention of human rights violations".[44]

The OHCHR and the UNESCO initiated a mid-term evaluation of the decade in 2000, which had no real results because most of the member states did not send their reports. Therefore the evaluation report represents only very basic information of the worldwide status of human rights education. The World Programme for Human Rights Education can be seen as a follow up for the Decade.[45] The first phase of the World Programme (2005-2007) focused on primary and secondary school systems and the implementation of human rights education. The definition of human rights education is almost the same as for the decade on human rights education.[46]

the Twentieth Anniversary of the Marangopoulos Foundation of for Human Rights (MFHR), Athens, The Hague, Sakkoulas, 2001, pp.269-276, at p.269.

[41] Vienna Declaration and Programme of Action, UN doc. A/CONF.157/23, Part II, para 79.

[42] Lehnhart, Volker, Pädagogik der Menschenrechte, Opladen 2003, pp. 89-95.

[43] General Assembly Resolution 48/141 of 20 December 1993.

[44] Mary Robinson Foreword, The United Nations Decade for Human Rights Education 1995-2004, Lessons for Life, 1998, iii. Geneva: United Nations Publication HR/PUB/DECADE/1998/1.

[45] The UN General Assembly adopted the revised Draft Plan of Action (A/59/525.Rev.1, 2 March 2005) in its resolution on the World Programme for Human Rights Education (53/312) on July 14, 2005.

[46] There can be found only one different sentence which says: d) The enabling of all persons to participate effectively in a free *and democratic* society *governed by the rule of law; e) The building of maintenance of peace; f) the promotion of people-centred sustainable development and social justice. (A/59/525/Rev.1, p. 3).*

What can be learned in the Countries of the Study?

There were some activities on human rights education during the decade in our six countries of research but most of them were not initiated by the decade as we learned from our interviews. Some of our chosen countries tried to develop an action plan e.g. Spain and Armenia, but most of them were stuck at the drafting process stage, e.g. Slovakia, or rethinking the idea of an action plan by the end of the decade e.g. Germany and Finland. Other states did not even try to fulfil their obligations and they were not active in drafting an action plan and had no desire to report the midterm evaluation. These are some findings which could be repeated for many other states which were part of the decade but not chosen countries for our survey. Some of our research countries reported on the midterm evaluation but their reported programmes were programmes which were initiated by NGOs or foundations e.g. Germany. It could be that part of these programmes were funded by the state but in many cases the state had no active part even though they agreed to be an active supporter by being a member of the decade and a party to the Vienna Declaration.

One similar finding was more or less discovered in all of our research countries: that there were no long lasting programmes established which could form a basis for human rights education and no long lasting programmes showing to the majority the value of living with national minorities.[47] We found special training for some groups such as policeman, people working in the health service, administrative clerks and additional teacher training but almost no programmes integrated in school teaching or for basic teacher training. Teacher training programmes appeared to be lacking in all countries and even though we were told from some administrative parties that all teachers teach human rights it could be that they refer to it by another name.[48] Many teachers in our research countries told us that some were very interested to integrate human rights teaching because of their own special interest but they lacked special training and did not want to deal with human rights due to a lack of knowledge. We were told that sometimes they would invite people from NGOs like Amnesty International who came to class and gave lectures.[49]

But one lesson in several years cannot be seen as human rights education in school. Another way to integrate human rights education in school are the 'Olympics on human rights' started several years ago and found e.g. in Slovakia. It is a very popular competition between students from different schools which is more or less an initiative from some individuals without much support from the government.[50]

We heard of some additional training for teachers Slovakia and in Finland. In Finland there is one very special programme for human rights education at the University of Oulu[51] and at the Slovak Comenius-University human rights education is

[47] For further details see the chapter of Reetta Toivanen in this volume.

[48] Interview with Birgit Kröner a German representative at the Berlin Government (Senatsverwaltung Bildung, Jugend und Sport) in December 2005.

[49] Several interviews with Finnish teachers in September 2005.

[50] Interview with Professor Kusy the initiator of the Human Rights Olympiad and first professor of the UNESCO human rights education chair at the Comenius University in Bratislava, 10.06.2005.

[51] After the Decade some new initiatives started to include human rights education in teacher training at other Finnish Universities.

included in ethics for teachers. Most of these courses in Slovakia seemed to be additional training and not part of the curriculum. However, national minorities could not be found in these special programmes. The different programmes did not deal with national minorities as a vulnerable group because the national minorities seem to have no major problems due to their very well established legal status. More often asylum seekers or migrants were seen as target groups and many materials include examples only from other parts of the world. Human rights are seen as an export which is very useful to help other Non-European states but most European states have in their own opinion, no real national problems and this is why there is no need for human rights education in the country. Even though we have had many discussions on security versus human rights due to the fight against terror, more or less all treaty bodies include in their reports recommendations to start human rights training for special groups and to include human rights in school curricula.

In Slovakia, Finland and Germany we found special training programmes for law enforcement officials, who need to have knowledge about the population as a whole. But most of this training was intercultural training which had a special focus on migrants and not on the national minorities. A different example was seen in Slovakia where the police underwent special training about the Roma because they very often dealt with the Roma in practice due to prejudice existing in police enforcement concerning this minority.[52]

One very important aspect is the dissemination of information about minorities showing the majority population that they exist in the country and telling who they are and what kind of life they live next door. The media has a key role in spreading information on which public opinion is built. We tried to get a broader picture by looking at how the print media describe national minorities in our research countries. The following paragraphs will show some findings from Slovakia.

Media analyses for example in Slovakia have shown how in particular the Roma population, the Ruthenians and Hungarians are discussed in Slovak newspapers.[53] In 2004, 115 articles in SME and 215 in Pravda could be found which dealt with the Slovak Roma population. According to official statistical data, the Roma population was 89,920 which is 1.7% of the total population of Slovakia,[54] but it is common knowledge that there are many more Roma living in Slovakia because they did not declare themselves as Roma for the census for various reasons.

The reporting about the three ethnic minorities, Roma, Hungarian and Ruthenians in Slovakia turned out to be very different. The Roma population received the most attention especially after the rioting in 2004 and was mostly mentioned in a

---

[52] Same prejudices were discovered in Finland.

[53] For this purpose we have analysed the reporting on these three minorities in two Slovak newspapers: The SME and the Pravda. Both papers have communist roots. The SME can be seen as a critical daily newspaper which became more neoconservative and sensationalistic during the Dzurinda administration. We were able to review the SME and the Pravda only for the year 2004 because the electronic archives contained too many hits for relevant articles for a very broad analysis how minorities are seen, described or which articles deal with which minority. In the whole period which could have been analysed via the electronic archives there were more than 500 articles found in the SME (1994-2004) and more than 950 hits for Pravda (1998-2004).

[54] Data from the Slovak Statistical Office available at http://www.statistics.sk/webdata/slov/scitanie/tab/zu.htm, visited January 2008.

negative way. This minority was very often associated with crime, looting, social deprivation and backwardness. The Roma, by far, got the most negative press, however a small section within the Roma were valued for their skills as musicians. Because the official figures appear to be far too low the percentage of Roma in the Slovak population is also discussed in the newspapers. These discussions can be seen in the following translated excerpts of articles:

"*The Statistical Office has in evidence as Roma only those persons who declared to be of Roma nationality in the last census. The applicable law does not allow having special statistics of the Roma inhabitants. That is why sociologists have to rely upon an evidence of Roma, which is secretly made by some deputies of the local self-administration.*" (Report of the sociologists: There are 320,000 Roma , Pravda. 01.10.2004)

"*The survey commission of the town of Martin published information, according to which out of 233 persons from Bambusky only 31 declared themselves as Roma, in spite of the fact that political representatives of the Roma encouraged them to do so.*" (The Roma from the settlement of Bambusky in Martin did not declare their nationality, SME, 15.6.2001)

Another point which seems to be mentioned very often is the growing number of Roma and the growing problematic Roma settlements.

"Shocking and for the public almost unknown are the facts of the report of the Commission for Health and social matters of the National Assembly of the Slovak Republic, about the social situation of the citizens. It includes remarkable important facts about the Roma. For SME Edith Bauer, deputy for the National Assembly of the Slovak Republic said that the facts show that the number of inhabitants of Roma settlements increases from 14,988 in 1988 for 123,034 the past year, There are now 238 more Roma settlements, and there are an increased number of settlements without running portable water and public lighting. "Only 20% of the Roma declared themselves as Hungarians, the rest declared themselves as Slovaks. In spite of that the SMK pays an especially great attention to the Roma" Edith Bauer said. (For SMK there are also four Roma election candidates, SME 22.09.1998).

Synergy between Human Rights Education and National Minorities

As many of the chosen examples showed most programmes were initiated to deal with the promotion of minorities or human rights education, there seemed to be no human rights education programmes which had chosen national minorities as a special target group.

Today, most people are specialised in their own field of knowledge. The same happens with members of minorities, or people with a minority background who know their minority rights and the special conventions for the protection of minorities. They are fully aware of how to implement their rights in the state they live and most of them further the teaching and learning in their own minority language. As it was argued before minority rights are a very prominent part of human rights and one would assume the field of human rights should be also very well known by minority representatives. Therefore these people should be very interested in human rights education and should be a main source for us to learn where, and in which ways human rights education programmes are implemented and taught. After some interviews it became apparent that those specialists were not aware of their human rights even though minority rights belong within the framework of human rights. It seemed strange that the minority leaders or representatives seemed not very interested in human rights education and it showed us that even in this context the concept of human rights education was not known and that human rights seemed too abstract to be seen as a very useful tool for argumentation and to get more support for their own projects. On one hand the Council of Europe with its Conventions and monitoring bodies were well known and seen as a tool to gain more rights for minorities. But on the other hand the framework of the United Nations human rights system was not so important and it was only mentioned that they were aware of the system and that they were working with the Council of Europe's advisory bodies but had never been contacted and asked to provide data for example for reports to the UN. These answers illustrated how important human rights education would be to show that the broader concept of human rights would have included many useful arguments and tools to further develop their role in society.

Conclusion

Our study highlighted that minorities face similar problems in states like Slovakia and Finland, even though Finland, has a very good record in implementing human rights and educational programmes and has initiated many different programmes to support their Roma population. Nevertheless, it would be a positive improvement to include concerned minorities in the drafting and preparation of new programmes to match the needs of the group. Some Finnish programmes failed because the Finnish authorities did not include Roma when conceptualizing the goals and content of new projects. Slovakia, which also developed several supportive initiatives for their Roma minority, faced similar problems. However, in each country the Roma minority have a very different status not from the legal standpoint but from the practical situation and face de facto discrimination. Many Roma children attend special schools and therefore do not have the same opportunity as children of the majority population. Human rights education could be a tool to show the valuable diversity of the different groups living together in one state. The majority should gain knowledge on the needs and cultural background of the national minorities who live in their neighbourhood. And the national minorities should see themselves as part of the human rights framework which should be a means to all people regardless if they are members of the majority or minority population.

One very interesting observation during our survey was that different minority groups regardless of their legal status have similar problems at the practical level. Interviews in Finland showed that Swedish speakers have many practical problems when using Swedish even though Swedish is an official language in Finland, granted by the Finnish constitution. This is surprising because constitutional guarantees have a much stronger protection than minority rights can provide. But the Swedish speakers said that they often have difficulties in using their granted rights because for example when a Swedish speaking doctor or judge is not available then they cannot use their own language which makes it more difficult to express themselves correctly.[55] This issue highlights perfectly that the majority needs to accept differences and with it, not only allow the use of minority languages, but the need to furnish an environ-

[55] Interviews with several members of the Finland Swedes in Turku/Abo in September 2005.

ment in which the language can be used. This shows that the best laws are useless if the acceptance of the majority is prerequisite to the laws′ successful implementation. In this sense, human rights education would be a valuable tool for the fostering of an environment of acceptance. Human Rights Education is vital to the spreading of information about minorities and their special needs, including teaching the importance of recognizing differences to change the practical living conditions, even though the protection given by law seems to be perfect.

These are very exceptional observations and more significant issues are to be discussed concerning concrete examples in future analyses. The major conclusion from our project and this paper is that human rights education would be a perfect tool to support national minorities.

List of Authors

Elena Ippoliti, Human Rights Officer in the Methodology, Education and Training Unit of the Office of the United Nations High Commissioner for Human Rights, Geneva.

Theresa Khorozyan, Project Coordinator for UNDP-Baseline study on Human Rights Education in Armenia and Senior Programme Manager for *Counterpart International*, Civic Advocacy Support Programme, Yerevan.

Carolyn Kissane, Ph.D., Clinical Associate Professor of Global Affairs, NYU Center for Global Affairs, New York.

Jana Luptáková, School and Executive Director of the School Plus network of NGOs promoting Roma education in south and central eastern Europe, Slovakia.

Claudia Mahler, Dr.iur, Senior Researcher, Human Rights Centre, University of Potsdam.

Paul Martin, Professor, Former Executive Director of the Centre for the Study of Human Rights, Columbia University New York.

Anja Mihr, Dr. Phil, Director, European Master Degree in Human Rights and Democratisation, European Inter-University Centre for Human Rights and Democratisation, Venice.

Theodore S. Orlin, Clark Professor of Human Rights Scholarship and Advocacy, Utica College, Utica New York, USA; President, International Human Rights Education Consortium, (IHREC).

Audrey Osler, Professor and founding director of the interdisciplinary Centre for Citizenship and Human Rights Education and Professor at the University of Leeds.

Sia Spiliopoulou Åkermark, Dr.iur, Director of the Åland Islands Peace Institute, member of the Advisory Committee on the Framework Convention on National Minorities of the Council of Europe.

Inken Stern, Doctoral Candidate, Faculty of Law, Department of Public Law and Gender Studies, Humboldt University Berlin and Research Assistant at the Human Rights Centre, University of Potsdam.

Reetta Toivanen, Dr. Phil., Senior Researcher, Centre for Research on Ethnic Relations and Nationalism and Centre of Excellence in Global Governance Research, University of Helsinki.

Sulev Valdmaa, Director of the Civic Education Centre, Jaan Tõnisson Institute, Tallinn.